Entrepreneurship - Contemporary Issues

Edited by Mladen Turuk

Published in London, United Kingdom

IntechOpen

Supporting open minds since 2005

Entrepreneurship - Contemporary Issues
http://dx.doi.org/10.5772/intechopen.87345
Edited by Mladen Turuk

Contributors
William Martin, Moha A. Abdullah, Md. Siddique E. Azam, Ribin Seo, Mohammad Rezaur Razzak, Suaad Jassem, Knut Ingar Westeren, Christina Whidya Utami, Hendro Susanto, Herring Shava, Emanuele Rossi, Simone Boccaletti, Alexander Tabares, Tales Andreassi, Maurizio La Rocca, Francesco Fasano, Tiziana La Rocca, Veronica Marozzo, Veronica Chiodo, Irene Bengo, Valentina Tosi, Felipe Baeta

First published in London, United Kingdom, 2021 by IntechOpen
IntechOpen is the global imprint of INTECHOPEN LIMITED, registered in England and Wales, registration number: 11086078, 5 Princes Gate Court, London, SW7 2QJ, United Kingdom
Printed in Croatia

British Library Cataloguing-in-Publication Data
A catalogue record for this book is available from the British Library

Additional hard and PDF copies can be obtained from orders@intechopen.com

Entrepreneurship - Contemporary Issues
Edited by Mladen Turuk
p. cm.
Print ISBN 978-1-83880-999-7
Online ISBN 978-1-83881-003-0
eBook (PDF) ISBN 978-1-83881-004-7

For EU product safety concerns:
IN TECH d.o.o., Prolaz Marije Krucifikse Kozulić 3, 51000 Rijeka, Croatia, info@intechopen.com or visit our website at intechopen.com.

Meet the editor

Mladen Turuk, Ph.D., is currently an Assistant Professor at the University of Zagreb, Croatia. He earned his postgraduate specialist degree in Strategic Entreprencurship in 2009 and his Ph.D. in Business Economics in 2016. He has authored or co-authored over 20 scientific papers, has acted as a reviewer, and has been engaged as a visiting professor at Macquarie University of Sydney, Shanghai University of International Business and Economics, and the University of Johannesburg. He has participated in several domestic and international projects. In addition to his academic career, he has more than ten years of experience in the industrial sector and is active in civil society organizations. He is the Editor-in-Chief of the International Journal of Contemporary Business and Entrepreneurship and the President of The Entrepreneurship Club.

Contents

Preface

Entrepreneurship plays an important role in the development of economies and is a vital source of change in all aspects of society. Throughout history, successful entrepreneurs have created great businesses and contributed to economic and social development, created jobs, increased productivity, and contributed to a higher quality of life. This book attempts to address a number of contemporary entrepreneurship issues critical for understanding entrepreneurship and business creation.

While this book empowers academics interested in entrepreneurial research, it is not only for them. Any student who reads this book will learn about the entrepreneurial process, the role of entrepreneurship in the economy, and its contemporary issues. This book also encourages would-be entrepreneurs to start and grow their new ventures.

The book consists of 12 chapters systematically organized into 4 sections: "Entrepreneurial Strategy", "Entrepreneurial Education and Opportunities", "Entrepreneurial Finance" and "Entrepreneurial Dynamics, and Innovation". What follows is a brief synopsis of what each chapter entails.

Chapter 1 explains how strategic alliances act as a platform to implement collaborative entrepreneurship while exposing a range of challenges. The objective of the chapter is to explore how to deal with the potential coordination issues that can make an alliance vulnerable and its returns diminished through a preliminary integrative approach to the interface between collaborative entrepreneurship and strategic alliances. The chapter contributes to a better understanding of how firms can enact collaborative entrepreneurship productively to gain greater benefit from the alliance configuration for collaborative advantage.

Business harvesting strategies are examined in Chapter 2. Entity harvesting is as equally important as setting up a new entrepreneurial venture and this chapter explores this issue. During the harvesting process, the entrepreneur recovers value through the sale of an entrepreneurial entity or its assets. Having spent several years building and adding value to the business, the entrepreneur must design an entity harvesting strategy that would provide maximum returns on the investment of time, effort, and money. Several reasons may compel the entrepreneur to harvest the business and this chapter provides some of these reasons based on extant literature and primary data collected from small and medium-sized entity (SME) owners in Sub-Saharan Africa. Further, the chapter outlines various entity harvesting strategies preferred by SME owners in Sub-Saharan Africa and circumstances in which they deem appropriate to apply such.

The entrepreneurial marketing behavior of start-up and scale-up companies and their dominant dimensions are the focus of Chapter 3. The results of the study suggest that there is no difference in entrepreneurial marketing behavior between start-up companies and scale-up companies. Value creation networking is shown to be the most dominant dimension for start-up companies in terms of its impact on entrepreneurial marketing behavior. As for scale-up companies, the most dominant dimension is the closeness to market dimension in its impact on entrepreneurial marketing behavior.

Chapter 4 is a comprehensive review of existing approaches for impact measurement and management implemented by socially oriented ventures (both not-for-profit organizations and for-profit businesses) focusing on methodological, governance, and operational barriers and enabling factors of the practices. The chapter drafts a framework that helps any venture to structure a process and methodology to measure its blended performance. The research not only contributes to the scant literature on impact entrepreneurship, but impact ventures might offer a compelling laboratory to disentangle the obstacles posed by the combined achievement of financial and social objectives and how organizations might address these challenges.

Chapter 5 examines the role of prior knowledge in the process of recognizing entrepreneurial opportunities. Recognizing opportunities has often been raised as a crucial aspect of the entrepreneurial process. The ability to identify, analyze, and develop entrepreneurial opportunities is what differentiates entrepreneurs from non-entrepreneurs. The chapter highlights the relevance of understanding the variables that have an influence on the process of recognizing opportunities.

Entrepreneurial behavior oriented to the pursuit of international opportunities is introduced in Chapter 6. The chapter aims to depict antecedents, mechanisms, and outcomes of such entrepreneurial behavior. The chapter makes four contributions. First, it outlines antecedents at three levels (individual, firm, environmental) as driving aspects that lead to the international opportunity-related behavior. Second, it reveals the mechanism by which different actors discover, enact, evaluate, and exploit international opportunities. Third, it describes the outcomes of this opportunity process. Fourth, it suggests establishing a conceptual basis on the topic.

In recent times scholars of the Islamic economy have introduced a new term, 'Halal entrepreneurship' or 'Halalpreneurship' to define and differentiate entrepreneurs in the Halal industry from the conventional entrepreneurs. Its concept and business opportunities are explained in Chapter 7. The chapter aims to achieve two main objectives. Firstly, to provide a comprehensive overview of Halalpreneurship by identifying its salient features that differentiate them from entrepreneurs. Secondly, to explore the business opportunities in different sectors of the global halal industry for the Halalpreneurs to tap.

Chapter 8 joins the stream of research investigating the relationship between local financial development, economic growth, and entrepreneurship. Relevant contributions highlighted that the probability of an individual to start a new business is higher when he/she moves from the least financially developed region to the most financially developed one. The chapter aims to further deepen the role of local financial development on entrepreneurship and on research spin-offs.

The financial policy of corporate bond issuers in the new Italian junior bond market specifically dedicated to unlisted firms and SME's is analyzed in Chapter 9. The aim of the chapter is to assess the extent to which SME's financial choices regarding non-equity external funding can become a key factor in facing real and financial shocks like those triggered by the current Covid-19 pandemic.

Chapter 10 provides a selective review of the literature and a narrative analysis that illuminates insight to inform academics and practitioners regarding the intersection of age and entrepreneurship. These insights are first built upon a conceptual foundation grounded in a developmental perspective and then organized into opportunities and challenges facing entrepreneurs at various ages along the developmental continuum.

Innovation processes in aquaculture are presented in Chapter 11. The chapter provides a theoretical background and an empirical analysis by comparing companies in Chile and Norway, and is focused on how innovations take place in different stages of the production process and how these are built into the production and managerial system.

Chapter 12 examines contemporary entrepreneurial opportunities, such as vertical indoor farming driven by advanced technologies. In order to mitigate the possibilities of food shortages in densely populated cities, initiatives need to be undertaken to foster the growth of large-scale entrepreneurship by individuals that can venture into this field on a smaller scale and with less capital outlay.

This book tries to facilitate a fundamental rethinking of entrepreneurial activity and how it is manifested. It addresses a critical shortcoming in much of the research, education, and economic development work that deals with entrepreneurship. Instead of the general theories of entrepreneurship, the book lays a foundation for developing theories of different kinds of entrepreneurial ventures. As the reader navigates these pages, he or she should hopefully broaden their entrepreneurial landscape and identify critical factors that drive contemporary entrepreneurship.

This book is the result of respected international authors collaborating from 10 countries. I gratefully acknowledge and thank all the authors for their valuable contributions.

Mladen Turuk
Faculty of Economics and Business,
University of Zagreb,
Zagreb, Croatia

Section 1

Entrepreneurial Strategy

Chapter 1

Collaborative Entrepreneurship for Continuous Innovation: A Strategic Alliance Perspective

Ribin Seo

Abstract

Strategic alliances act as a platform to implement collaborative entrepreneurship while exposing a range of challenges. By capitalizing on entrepreneurial opportunities for continuous innovation, alliance partners can promote the productive utilization of resource-pooling systems and facilitate innovation processes for value co-creation. Simultaneously, the heterogeneity of partners in terms of different motivations and interests interferes with the advancement of collaborative entrepreneurship for resource exchange and orchestration. The objective of this paper is thus to explore how to deal with the potential coordination issues that can make an alliance vulnerable and its returns diminished through a preliminary integrative approach to the interface between collaborative entrepreneurship and strategic alliances. From this approach, three elements that can contribute to leverage values of collaborative entrepreneurship for continuous innovation are identified: social capital, entrepreneurial orientation, and interorganizational learning. Based on the discussion about the functions of each element in the context of alliance partners' dynamic interactions, a model of analysis on collaborative entrepreneurship for continuous innovation is proposed. Hence, this chapter contributes to a better understanding of how firms can enact collaborative entrepreneurship productively to gain greater benefit from the alliance configuration for collaborative advantage.

Keywords: collaborative entrepreneurship, strategic alliances, continuous innovation, social capital, entrepreneurial orientation, interorganizational learning

1. Introduction

In the current complex and turbulent business environment, continuous innovation has been viewed as an important strategy for gaining sustainable competitive advantage and the capacity to consistently carry on innovative initiatives as a necessary condition for the long-term growth of firms [1]. The continuing need for strategic response to changes in environments forces a firm to innovate constantly, but continuous innovation is one of the most challenging tasks for firms [2]. Accordingly, research interest in how ventures could be innovative on a continuously efficient basis has emerged, and scholars provide a rational explanation that one of the answers is linked with the firms' capability to configure and manage strategic alliances [3, 4].

As a collective process where two or more parties work with each other to achieve mutual and private benefits, strategic alliances enable firms to be entrepreneurial in capitalizing on new opportunities through continuous innovation [2]. Alliance firms find it easy to identify and explore opportunities with partners who possess complementary resources and capacities, thus having an advantage over those who are not able to do so [5]. As noted by Antoncic [6], firms can enact entrepreneurial behavior to be innovative, proactive, and risk-taking with a capacity for constant innovation when configuring collaborative partnerships across organizational boundaries. As such, strategic alliances are gaining the attention of research on entrepreneurship, as represented by the concept of collaborative entrepreneurship.

Collaborative entrepreneurship addresses a firm's managerial process to collaborate outside the organization for collaborative advantage [1]. Research on entrepreneurship emphasizes the potential role of firms' collaborations with external parties in an entrepreneurial process from opportunity discovery to value creation [4, 7–9]. In this process, collaborative entrepreneurship involves a group of firms with a common strategy to facilitate innovation processes through the construction of collaborative partnerships [10]. The alliance configuration can be motivated by a firm's entrepreneurial intention to leverage resource complementarity and economies of scales, gain low costs of new market entry, build new capabilities by learning, manage risks by sharing, and, ultimately, create economic value [7]. By capitalizing on entrepreneurial opportunities to co-develop innovations in continuous ways, firms enacting collaborative entrepreneurship can promote the productive utilization of the resource-pooling system for value co-creation.

While interfirm collaboration performs as a strategic platform for collaborative advantage, it also exposes a range of challenges [11]. The heterogeneity of partners with different motivations and interests interferes with the advancement of common grounds for resource exchange and orchestration. Potential coordination issues, including opportunism to manipulate alliances, conflicts between sharing and protecting knowledge, and high transaction and monitoring costs, can make a partnership vulnerable and its returns diminished [12, 13]. As such, failing to manage these challenges discourages the productive dissemination, assimilation, and incorporation of network-available assets that are complementary to continuous innovations.

The performance-creating mechanisms underlying collaborative entrepreneurship remain a "black box" in the literature and are an interesting research topic [4]. The knowledge gap is not as much about whether ventures benefit from enacting collaborative entrepreneurship in their partnerships but rather about how and why its potential performance implications occur. Specifying potential elements to enhance a process of collaborative entrepreneurship will contribute to developing existing theories of strategic alliance as well as practical approaches that need to be fine-grained for better collaborative advantage. To fill this caveat, this book chapter examines the elements that would form and affect that collaborative entrepreneurial process by integrating theoretical models and philosophical principles.

Considering that the success of collaboration depends heavily on a firm's entrepreneurial ability to manage the relationship with its counterpart(s) possessing complementary knowledge-based resources needed for continuous innovation [14], we draw upon the theories of social capital, entrepreneurial orientation, and interorganizational learning. The basic assumptions for this theoretical perspective are that (a) social capital at the alliance level may serve as a strategic asset that sparks partners' decisions to get more entrepreneurially involved in the value-co-creation process [15], (b) entrepreneurial orientation may address the strategic intention of alliance firms to transform network-available resources into a source of collaborative advantage [7, 9], and (c) interorganizational learning may elucidate a systematic combination of the partners' collective learning initiatives [16, 17].

The main contribution of this book chapter is to establish an interface among the research constructs in the process of collaborative entrepreneurship which becomes an important research area in the strategic management literature. Examining the potential contributions of each of the proposed elements to continuous innovation will improve an understanding of how firms can leverage the value of collaborative entrepreneurship in sustaining competitive advantage. Therefore, the remainder of this paper is organized as follows: Section 2 explores some characteristics of collaborative entrepreneurship and strategic alliances. Section 3 offers the concept and dimensions of each element that affects collaborative entrepreneurship. The paper concludes by proposing a conceptual model for future analysis, which explains how the alliance configuration can be a form of productive collaborative entrepreneurship for continuous innovation.

2. Collaborative entrepreneurship and strategic alliances

2.1 Collaborative entrepreneurship

2.1.1 Entrepreneurship for alliance configuration

Entrepreneurship addresses the managerial process by which individuals—either on their own or inside organizations—pursue new business opportunities without regard to resources they currently control [17]. According to Stevenson and Jarillo [17], a key feature of entrepreneurship is a focus on achieving exceptional growth, which is a goal that motivates firms to take risks and become innovative and proactive. To achieve growth, entrepreneurial firms—in Miller's [18] explication, those being innovative, proactive, and risk-taking simultaneously—aggressively pursue opportunities in their environment. Teng [19] evinces that entrepreneurship is about the relentless pursuit of entrepreneurial opportunities that indicates the situations in which new market offerings, resources, and operational methods can be introduced in novel ways. The ongoing pursuit of opportunities is not only a fundamental objective of entrepreneurship, but also an approach in entrepreneurship [19]. As such, entrepreneurship can be identified by a firm's activities to recognize and realize new opportunities for economic value creation.

In the process of entrepreneurship, a strategic alliance is perceived as a valuable fertilizer for entrepreneurial firms to better explore and exploit new opportunities [20]. Firms with high entrepreneurial orientation tend to constantly scan their environment to identify new opportunities to improve their competitive positions [21]. As part of their environment-scanning and opportunity-pursuing activities, entrepreneurial firms look for external sources in greater depth, which advances innovation development for performance [7, 9]. Being more open to new ideas and resilient from risks, they are willing to use new approaches to transfer internal innovation to external parties in profitable ways and overcome some barriers in integrating complementary knowledge bases among alliances [8]. Kreiser [8] attests that within interfirm partnerships, non-entrepreneurial firms may not be sufficiently motivated to make necessary investments and commit resources to make partnerships configure and succeed.

This notion leads to a rational question: Is the creation of a strategic alliance as a body of organizations with different functions an entrepreneurial behavior to pursue an opportunity? While personal independence or self-fulfillment is one of the most important reasons why people would prefer to be self-employed, their entrepreneurship does not occur without interactions with environments [19, 22]. Under certain conditions, the firm's collaboration with external parties can be more efficient to leverage potential returns than pursuing the opportunity alone [4]. Ribeiro-Soriano and Urbano [1] explain that entrepreneurship is a collective phenomenon that is as much the outcome of a joint effort as an individual endeavor. Covin et al. [22] observe that to interact with environments, entrepreneurs tend to seek alternative ways to pursue the opportunity by configuring collaborative networks or consortia rather than exploiting an opportunity alone.

2.1.2 Collaborative entrepreneurship by alliances

The establishment of strategic alliances is regarded as a way of putting entrepreneurial activities to promote the productive utilization of its resource- pooling system into practice. Behind alliances, there is the objective of attaining or sharing valuable resources when these cannot be obtained through market exchanges or fusions or acquisitions. Montoro-Sánchez et al. [23] show that entrepreneurial firms use strategic alliances as a way of filling gaps in their resources. For firms to exploit new opportunities, they need to obtain resources beyond those they already possess and control, and for that reason, they are often subject to greater risk. Teng [19] explains that strategic alliances emerge when firms in vulnerable strategic positions need new resources, or, when strong, very well-positioned firms capitalize on their resources to create entrepreneurial opportunities for cooperation. Collaborative entrepreneurship involves developing a firm's strategy which allows continuous innovation in its entrepreneurial process to exploit new opportunities for value co-creation [2, 4, 6].

These selective reviews lead to a rational explanation that the alliance configuration is particularly involved with the phenomenon of collaborative entrepreneurship which produces new market offerings by utilizing and combining knowledge-based resources that each partner possesses. Alliances allow integration of fundamental strategic resources and other businesses so that increasingly entrepreneurial firms manage to reach their objectives [24]. This resource-pooling system for value co-creation is one of the contributive elements to collaborative entrepreneurship [14]. Gupta and Govindarajan [25] state that collaborative entrepreneurship is predicated on the creation of economic value arising out of jointly created original ideas that emerge from sharing knowledge-based resources. Accordingly, the entrepreneurial motives of alliance configuration include leveraging resource complementarity and economies of scales, gaining low costs of new market entry, learning capabilities, and managing risks by sharing [7].

The rationale for explaining the concept of collaborative entrepreneurship is that entrepreneurial firms show a strong tendency to proactively seek and form potential partnerships that are complementary to the productive exploitation of new opportunities [8]. According to Franco and Haase [4], collaborative entrepreneurship is adopted by various firms to remain competitive, allowing growth. Thus, the firm's objectives must include increased flexibility, innovation, collaborator initiative, and risk acceptance. Ribeiro-Soriano and Urbano [1] identify collaborative entrepreneurship by a firm's ability to collaborate outside the organization, arguing that collaboration enables a firm to entrepreneurially explore and exploit new opportunities for collaborative advantages. During the co-creation of new resources and competences for continuous innovation, enacting the entrepreneurial behavior of individual alliance partners is needed for productive entrepreneurship in collaboration. Strategic alliances can thus provide a fertile ground that enables alliance partners' entrepreneurial interactions, which are contextualized by an institutionalized system of their social exchange, toward continuous innovation.

2.2 Strategic alliances

Strategic alliances refer to "a process in which autonomous actors interact through formal and informal negotiation, jointly creating rules and structures governing their relationships and ways to act or decide on the issues that brought them together" [26], p. 23. It occurs when a group of autonomous stakeholders in a domain engages in an interactive process to act or decide on issues related to that domain, using shared rules, norms, and structures [9]. Teng [19] explains that strategic alliances are interfirm cooperative arrangements that allow firms to temporarily seek resources from others. To ascertain a unit of analysis, we define strategic alliances as interdependent partnerships adopted by two or more organizations to commit resources conjointly under common objectives. In line with Franco and Haase [4], we consider all formats of alliances, including contractual agreements and temporal partnerships, both with and without shared risks and rewards, minority equity positions, and shared equity ownerships.

To address the phenomenon of alliance configuration in practice, research has adopted multidisciplinary theoretical perspectives to study the alliances' managerial implications. First, network-based research analyzes the interactional structure of social contexts where partners' collaborative process takes place [8, 9]. This line of research addresses how to efficiently form and maintain the collaborative networks of alliance partners. Second, strategic-based research addresses sources of collaborative advantage achieved through alliances [4, 7]. This stream highlights the importance of the orchestration between alliance environment and internal resources/capabilities. Last, knowledge-based research regards alliances as a path for knowledge sharing and learning among partners [11, 16]. This line emphasizes the expansion and creation of knowledge bases in alliances, which occur through learning mechanisms.

Along with the development of such theoretical perspectives, a large body of research focuses on investigating factors that affect the effectiveness of alliance configuration. Thomson and Perry [26] argue that the success of alliances is a matter of the choice of appropriate partners, the accumulation of relational capital, and the management of partnerships. According to Meier et al. [13], the performance mechanism of interfirm alliances relies heavily on trust, mutual commitments, and dedicated support of key actors, which help reduce transaction costs. The collaborative behavior of each actor can be influenced by the organizational and individual experience of alliances [4]. Particularly, organizational culture connected with personal attitudes toward the external environment can determine the quality and quantity of alliance activity. Research also reports some barriers that impede the development of effective alliances. For instance, Lisowska [27] points out some barriers for successful alliances, such as the lack of funding for collaborative projects, knowledge about cooperation, propensity for cooperation, innovativeness, willingness to change, qualified employees, and the inability to visualize the goals and benefits of collaborations.

The notion that firms can receive clear benefits (bright side) from strategic alliances is not novel, but scholars only pay attention to the potential disadvantage (dark side) of the partnership. The discussion of the bright and dark sides of strategic alliances in this section highlights that firms often find it challenging to achieve collaborative advantage from engagement in partnerships for continuous innovation. Thus, how to create and capture the value of strategic alliances remains an important practical matter for alliance firms.

2.2.1 The bright side of strategic alliances

The alliance configuration helps to expand a firm's knowledge base and accelerate its innovation process by exchanging and mobilizing complementary knowledge-based resources across partners [8]. As a result, pooling knowledge in the partnership allows small firms to overcome the liability of smallness by increasing rents from the interaction activities [26]. By sharing costs and risks of continuous innovation with external parties, alliance firms can capitalize on new opportunities for value creation in more efficient ways than doing alone [28]. These benefits of strategic alliances can be summarized as follows.

- *Resource sharing*. Some alliances are designed for sharing knowledge-based resources for better innovation performance. By building a common resource pool that each partner possesses, their resource base can be more expanded than by investing in internal resource development [26].

- *Competence sharing*. Strategic alliances frequently need the engagement of specialized labor who has tacit knowledge needed for the achievement of common goals [29]. Recruiting such experts is challenging for a firm that suffers from resource constraints. Collaborative partnerships enable the acquisition and assimilation of unique competences of its counterparts.

- *Cost/Risk sharing*. An innovative initiative is typically costly, requiring huge resource commitments [12]. It also involves risks of failure, derived from the uncertainty about its outcomes. Sharing the costs and risks with partners contributes to the managerial stability of alliance firms [28].

- *Reward sharing*. Depending on the nature of partnerships, alliance partners have joint ownership of collective outputs developed jointly [26]. In this case, they share a percentage of alliance partners receive a percentage of profits generated through the commercialization of collective outputs [5].

- *Idea co-creation*. Engagement in strategic alliances is a source of creativity and innovation. Intellectual interactions of alliance partners with heterogeneous resources often result in the cross-fertilization of original ideas that are effective in solving current business issues [24].

- *Decreased time-to-market*. The resource-pooling system in an alliance helps a firm produce innovative outcome faster than they could alone [30]. This allows the firm to introduce product/service (s) to a market and stay ahead of the competition.

- *Access to new markets*. Some alliances become a pathway to enter new markets or access new customers. Alliance configuration often provides an entrepreneurial opportunity to experiment and commercialize product/service(s) in new markets [12].

Research emphasizing the bright side of strategic alliances offers a rationale behind the benefits that firms can gain from their alliance participation. Given this basis, the mainstream of research advocates positive contributions of the firms' engagement in strategic alliances with external parties to their competitive advantage and innovation [1]. However, the next section about some barriers to successful alliances indicates that achieving the collaborative advantage is challenging due to potential issues in the network of relationships among alliance partners.

2.2.2 The dark side of strategic alliances

The heterogeneity of collaborating partners with different motivations and interests interferes with the advancement of common grounds for resource exchange and orchestration. Multiparty-involved collaboration creates significant barriers to success, including higher coordination costs, communication barriers, a lack of shared understanding, and disagreements over invention and innovation strategy [29]. Along this vein, scholars explain several factors that make collaborative partnerships vulnerable. For instance, working together for a joint project with different stakeholders adds difficulty to controlling the innovation process [7, 12]. The more partners involved in the joint project, the more complex the exchange of knowledge and information [29]. In addition, the coordination of partners' collaborative behaviors for resource exchange becomes a source of the increase in transaction costs [31]. The following are the potential disadvantages of strategic alliances, which may lead to diminishing returns of collective actions.

- *Opportunistic behavior*. While maximizing the effectiveness of resource exchange in an alliance requires behavioral transparency [32], opportunism to manipulate the partnership for one's interests and not for mutual benefits can increase the transaction costs in resource exchange [28].

- *The tension between sharing and protection*. The potential leakage of knowledge in a partnership dilutes one's source of competitive advantage [12]. For this reason, although the success of strategic alliances is based on the mutual effort to fertilize resource exchange, partners are reluctant to share specific knowledge-based resources with their counterparts [33].

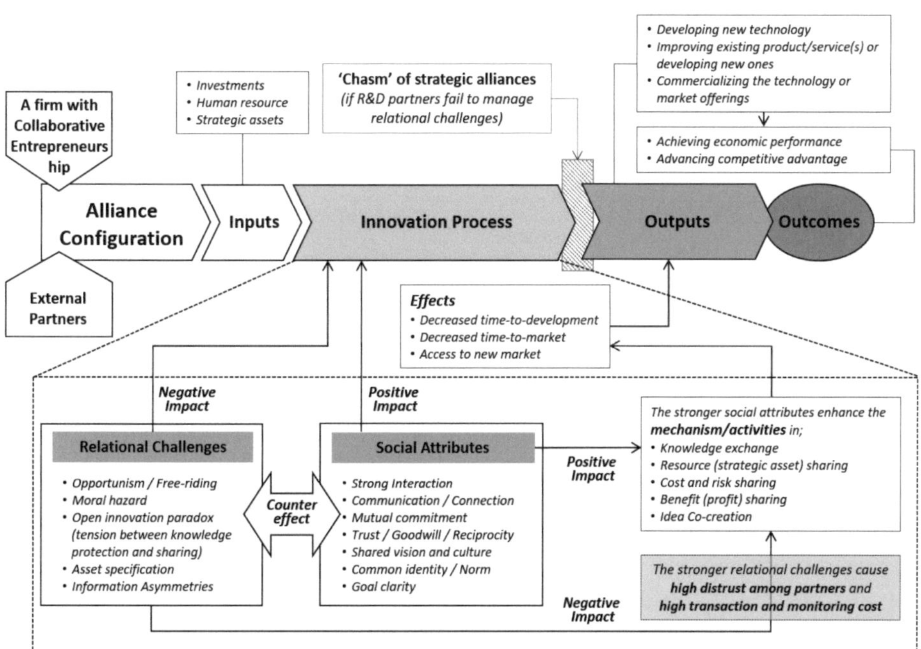

Figure 1.
Collaborative entrepreneurial process of strategic alliances.

- *Lack of mutual trust*. Distrust among alliance partners prevents gaining potential benefits from collaborative entrepreneurship [13]. If partners fail to build trustful relationships in an alliance, they experience communication breakdown, vague role/responsibility set-up, and due diligence based on faulty assumptions in the partnership as well as higher transaction costs than expected [31].

We call these unfavorable conditions to collaborative entrepreneurship the "chasm" of strategic alliances. The chasm built by failing to reduce the negative impact of these disadvantages hinders alliance partners from taking advantage of their partnership. Under this circumstance, alliance partners tend to depreciate their interdependency and safeguard themselves to protect knowledge, resulting in alliance inefficiency. **Figure 1** illustrates the collaborative entrepreneurship process of strategic alliances, discussed above.

3. Collaborative entrepreneurship for continuous innovation

In today's globally competitive business environment, firms are forced to productively implement continuous innovation and thus seek an opportunity for collaboration entrepreneurship for collaborative advantage. The configuration of strategic alliances with various potential benefits is one of the effective strategies for firms to address the challenging demands of overcoming the insufficient internal resources and the restricted competence base [34]. For alliance firms at a crossroads between the bright and dark sides of alliances, however, how to create and capture the value of collaborative partnerships while resolving the dark side remains an important matter for the firms' continuous innovation. For the "how" question, we suggest several intrafirm-level and interfirm-level factors that can determine the level of collaborative entrepreneurship in strategic alliances. As this requires adopting the theoretical lenses addressing specific constructs at the multilevel of alliances, we draw upon the longstanding theories of social capital (SC), entrepreneurial orientation (EO), and interorganizational learning (IOL). In the following sections, we explain the definition, dimensions, and roles of each construct in the context of collaborative entrepreneurship and strategic alliances.

3.1 Linking social capital to collaborative entrepreneurship

As delineated earlier, interfirm partnerships for value co-creation are sensitive to partners' relational characteristics contextualizing the common platform in which they interoperate [35]. As such, the relational characteristics of strategic alliances become a critical unit of analysis in explaining learning-related outcomes associated with collaborative advantage [36].

Accordingly, extant research emphasizes the relational traits featuring the contexts where collaborative entrepreneurship is used, evincing that trustfulness among partners is crucial for learning effectiveness [13]. While the benefits of trust-based relationships are acknowledged, trustfulness is only one of the various relational traits characterizing social exchanges in the consortia; others include network ties/configuration/stability and shared goals/value that can contextualize the collective learning mechanism [37]. The extent of collective entrepreneurship is determined by the partners' interactive and conjoint routines based on these relational traits [38]. However, considering one-dimensional traits in isolation provides a narrow perspective on the multifaceted mechanism; a single approach to incorporate the traits can provide a better viewpoint of the institutionalized social contexts underlying alliance partners' interactions for resource exchange.

The SC theory takes advantage of its comprehensive description of the different traits characterizing the idiosyncratic nature of collaborative entrepreneurship at the alliance level. Referring to "the sum of actual and potential resources embedded within, available through, and derived from the networks of relationships possessed by individuals or social units" [39], p. 243, SC encompasses three dimensions: structural, relational, and cognitive capitals [37–40]. According to Inkpen and Tsang [37], structural capital refers to the strength and stability of consortium members and facilitates knowledge flow across organizational boundaries; relational capital, represented by trust and reciprocity, contributes to repressing the risk of relational issues and conflicts; and cognitive capital, defined as shared vision and value, conveys a sense of identity and homogeneity among members and coordinates individual actions as a unique entity to achieve common goals.

One of the dominant arguments in the literature is that high-quality SC can create network-level conditions favorable for collaborative interactions across heterogeneous organizations [41]. The degree of SC embedded in a network affects participants' decisions on whether to engage actively in collective action with counterparts (structural capital), interact faithfully in responding to a shared understanding of counterparts' interests (relational capital), and work within collaborative institutions inside the network to achieve common goals (cognitive capital) [15, 42]. Pinheiro et al. [41] explain that the accumulation of SC in an alliance can serve as an assimilated fertilizer that spurs partners to productively exchange and generate knowledge assets by producing collaborative orchestrations.

This notion allows a postulation that the system of conjoint research activities based on high SC can create an institutionalized social platform that enables alliance partners to exploit innovation opportunities for value co-creation; this is because the network-based asset helps them transform firm-specific resources into collaborative advantages [37, 40]. The structural capital of networks between organizational units enhances their network-related ability to recognize fine-grained opportunities for the refinement of existing resources and the creation of new resources through experimentation [15].

SC also determines the socio-institutional background that enables partners to expand a spectrum of resource pools for joint problem-solving and risk-sharing [41]. Partnerships embedding higher relational and cognitive capitals can also provide partners with perceived safety to actively interact with each other with a strong mutual belief toward shared goals [43]. Under such circumstances, alliance partners will enrich the information being shared because the development of normative reciprocity and trust within networks changes the nature of information exchanged. Such an exchange based on the high-quality SC is geared toward collective performance as alliance partners commit to joint problem-solving.

We thus propose that SC embedded in strategic alliances, represented by structural, relational, and cognitive capitals, can be a source of collaborative advantage that incentivizes alliance partners to commit to common goals toward continuous innovation. This proposition is theoretically supported by the resource-based view, suggesting that possessing firm-specific resources allows firms to outperform competitors by doing things differently. When strategic alliances entail higher SC that makes the partnerships distinct from others, the partner will conceive it as an interfirm-specific resource to be exploited for performance improvement. Contrarily, alliances with lower SC will suffer from coordination issues that disrupt the productive dissemination and incorporation of network-available resources, thus limiting the partners' performance potential.

3.2 Linking entrepreneurial orientation to collaborative entrepreneurship

EO, by far the most popular construct in entrepreneurship literature, is defined as a firm's strategic posture to simultaneously exhibit innovativeness, proactiveness, and risk-taking [44] and represents the firm's priority in identifying and exploiting entrepreneurial opportunities [45]. Its first dimension, innovativeness, is the tendency to support new ideas and experiments to introduce new products and processes. Proactiveness is the propensity to seize market opportunities and develop a first-initiative preference ahead of competitors. Risk-taking is the willingness to accept high risk by venturing into the unknown with strong commitments. As a combination of these dimensions, EO has been theorized to contribute to firm growth and facilitate innovation [21, 45].

The literature accepts that EO plays a significant role in affecting a firm's strategic behaviors and managerial beliefs, emphasizing the proactive deployment of diverse innovation types with uncertainty. Within this wave, research explicating mechanisms underlying the EO's performance implication urges more studies to explore the relationships in diverse contexts, which are contingent upon contextual conditions that firms encounter [22, 44]. In the contexts of strategic alliances, higher EO can promote firms' participation in alliances to translate dynamic and complex resource-exchanging interactions among partners into higher competitive positions in markets.

The resource-based view posits that not all resources translate into competitive advantage; the novel, competitive resources make a real difference for innovation to occur in alliances [5]. This will not be a major concern for alliance firms with high EO, as they focus on breaking through old routines and procedures to make a difference [8]. EO embedded in an organization can address the managerial process of alliance firms to capture the nucleus of heterogeneous resources and convert competitive resources for collaborative advantage [9]. Li et al. [9] document that the higher the EO of alliance firms, the more they commit to their dynamic interactions for resource mobilization and utilization with counterparts for the success of the alliance.

The dimensions of EO, including innovativeness, proactiveness, and risk-taking, can help alliance firms generate greater competitiveness. Specifically, partners must face challenges in combining knowledge-based assets, which are rooted deeply in individual organizations. Innovative alliance firms can be motivated to address such challenges in novel ways with continuous experiments for problem-solving [45]. Second, strong proactiveness may help alliance firms create a first-mover advantage through an early collaborative response to market needs and trends, thereby enhancing the market appeal of collective outputs [46]. Finally, the success of alliances requires all partners to commit to alliance-relevant activities for competitive development with high uncertainty. Risk-taking alliance firms are willing to deal with the risks involved in interorganizational activities by making a strong commitment to and a valuable investment in their alliance projects [7].

The extent to which alliances produce competitive collective outputs is a critical determinant of alliance performance. Entrepreneurial firms' engagement in strategic alliances can contribute to the joint development of collective outputs that will promote their competitive position in industries. Li et al. [9] explain that EO remains an enabler for alliance firms to identify productive routines to manage dynamic resource-integrating activities and develop superior resource-managing capability through entrepreneurial processes. Shu et al. [47] find the positive impact of EO on knowledge spillover in alliances, suggesting that it helps discriminate valuable resources contributing to the achievement of common goals. Thus, EO can motivate alliance firms to contribute inputs to the partnerships for the cogeneration of competitive outputs [8]. In contrast, firms with low EO may be unable to exploit the output-cogenerating opportunities due to high concerns about protecting their valuable resources from the appropriation for their interests [19]. Thus, we can postulate that the EO of alliance firms potentially determines the extent to which they gain the mutual benefits of strategic alliances.

Few studies elaborate on the SC–EO interface, arguing that firms take advantage of the value of SC which drives them to engage entrepreneurially in external networks. For instance, Wu et al. [43] found that the SC/EO degrees simultaneously determine a firm's intention and ability to seek and utilize external complementary resources. Stam et al. [20] stress that both SC and EO affect new ventures' performance, contingent on their network positions. According to Gedajlovic et al. [48], as SC can be logically both an antecedent and a consequence of entrepreneurship, the relationship between SC and EO needs to be situated within a temporal context, here, strategic alliances. Thereupon, high-quality SC among alliance partners will promote their dynamic entrepreneurial collaboration to (1) solve technical problems and commercial issues in innovative ways, (2) proactively identify and embed market needs in their joint projects, and (3) tolerate risks of their resource commitment to the project.

3.3 Linking interorganizational learning to collaborative entrepreneurship

As an avenue for sustaining innovativeness and competitiveness, IOL becomes one of the key mechanisms to refine existing knowledge and generate new knowledge, expressing the purpose of partnership formations [16]. IOL refers to the network-based learning process that involves knowledge exploitation and exploration between or among different organizations in the presence of high interdependency [32]. Its outcomes should either be enhanced capabilities for adapting environmental changes or strategic decisions for radical and/or incremental changes in an existing knowledge base for competitive advantage [49].

Despite no unified IOL dimensionality, scholars have conceived IOL's two distinctive forms, which are exploitation and exploration, since March's [49] seminal research [35, 50, 51]. Exploitation involves the utilization and refinement of existing knowledge to strengthen the excellence of present operations, whereas exploration is the search for new knowledge, the use of unfamiliar knowledge, and the creation of products with unknown demand. IOL supports alliance partners' common refinement and utilization of existing knowledge available in their network—exploitation—and their joint discovery and generation of new knowledge that can be a future source of collaborative advantage—exploration [51].

Along this vein, Westerlund and Rajala [50] argue that distinguishing exploration in seeking effectiveness of new knowledge development from exploitation in seeking efficiency of existing knowledge bases captures better the IOL process because the two learning forms produce different results. In this vein, exploitative learning and exploratory learning can be drawn as IOL practices. According to March [49], p. 71, exploratory learning entails "search, variation, risk-taking, experimentation, play, flexibility, discovery," whereas exploitative learning involves "refinement, choice, production, efficiency, selection, implementation, execution." Holmqvist [35] asserts that exploitative learning refers to refining and deepening existing knowledge to improve current technical value, whereas exploratory learning refers to the pursuit of new knowledge that leads to more variations in original technical value.

Research recognizes the value of collective learning to achieve common goals, ensuring that expanding a knowledge base by learning at the consortium level is essential for collaborative advantage [30, 35]. A primary purpose of the alliance configuration is the advancement of a co-innovation process to develop novel, competitive outputs by exchanging and combining the complementary knowledge-based assets of each partner [7, 13]. Using a common learning platform improves the process, supporting alliance partners' conjoint routines to refine and using current knowledge bases to improve technical value (exploitative learning) and to create new knowledge that leads to more variations in original technical value (exploratory learning) [50].

The potential contribution of explorative and exploratory learning at the alliance level to continuous innovation deserves further scrutiny in the context of strategic alliances. The enjoyment of collaborative advantage requires partners to transform their existing knowledge with high asset specificity into exchangeable and understandable forms of resources. For this, they should access, assimilate, and apply existing and complementary knowledge, introducing fine-grained opportunities to fill the mutual knowledge gaps and initiate the best innovation practices. This process is based on exploitative learning, which improves the accessibility, veracity, and availability of heterogeneous knowledge and expands an existing knowledge base in the network [52]. For a consortium to remain effective for innovation, collaborators need to move the focus of their learning from exploitation to exploration to co-create new knowledge. This exploratory learning process supports the multiplication of knowledge throughout the network and the ongoing innovations of market offerings. Consequently, the original knowledge base becomes a source of collaborative advantage that motivates partners to engage actively in the alliances and provide resource commitments for better collective outputs [33, 52].

We thus propose that IOL, represented by exploitative and exploratory learning, enables alliance firms to benefit from their alliances in terms of better advantage in innovation. For exploitative learning, existing knowledge and its further utilization will conduce to the development of a common knowledge base within an alliance. This base not only provides partners with chances to improve their operational routines by adapting others' best practices or know-how, but also allows companies to promote fine-tuned capabilities for continuous innovation. Refining and using the network-available existing knowledge by exploitative learning cannot be solely responsible for alliance results. To transform a collaborative partnership into a source of collaborative advantage, exploratory learning is necessary to codevelop new technical knowledge that helps partner firms to be capable of competing against others and cope with the changing environment. The new knowledge will be better reconciled with the alliance firms' innovation strategies than the counterparts' knowledge gained by exploitative learning.

4. Concluding remarks

In today's highly uncertain and rapidly changing environment, strategic alliances can provide a common ground that enables alliance firms' exploitation in seeking the efficiency of existing resource bases and their exploration in seeking the effectiveness of new resources and competencies. Despite the increasing research interest in strategic alliances, value-co-creating mechanisms underlying the alliance partners' dynamic interactions were a missing link. Given the basis that collaborative entrepreneurship involves motivating firms to configure strategic alliances in their entrepreneurial processes to exploit new opportunities for continuous innovation [2, 10], this paper explores the potential roles of SC, EO, and IOL that may contribute to the success of strategic alliances.

First, research posits that the collaborative advantage depends on the social context of partner interactions at the alliance level, focusing on relational traits such as trustfulness, mutual commitment, common vision, or shared value [13, 37]. The literature advocates these traits' potential contribution to the enhancement of interactions across organizations, which cannot be a spontaneous phenomenon in the presence of high interdependency and heterogeneity, representing the idiosyncratic nature of strategic alliances [39]. SC can offer the holistic view of the multiple traits that institutionalize the alliance partners' conjoint routines toward common goals by encompassing various traits—such as network ties/stability, trustfulness, and shared value/vision—in three dimensions: structural, relational, and cognitive capitals [40]. SC involves regulating and relieving physical/mental relational issues and leveraging entrepreneurial initiatives of actors in a partnership [36, 48].

Second, we introduce the alliance firms' entrepreneurial orientation (EO) as one of the possible explanations that contextualize the success of continuous innovation through collaborations. Referring to a firm's strategic posture to be innovative, proactive, and risk-taking for value creation [44], EO becomes an important element for firm growth [45], while the EO–performance relationship is contingent on specific contexts which firms encounter [21]. According to Jiang et al. [7], the system of conjoint research activities renders an idiosyncratic context in which partners entrepreneurially substantialize the economic values of network-available assets. In this instance, SC at the network level may serve as a strategic asset that sparks partners' decisions to get more entrepreneurially involved in the value-co-creation process, and their EO may address the strategic intention to transform the network-embedded asset into a source of collaborative advantage.

Lastly, research deliberates the importance of adopting IOL elucidating a systematic combination of alliance partners' collective learning initiatives [16]. IOL addresses the network-based learning practices that involve mutual exploitation and exploration of knowledge in the presence of high interdependency and heterogeneity [32, 35, 50] which underscore the idiosyncratic nature of collaborative entrepreneurship toward continuous innovation [14, 17]. The literature advocates the IOL's potential contribution to the knowledge mobilization over organizations,

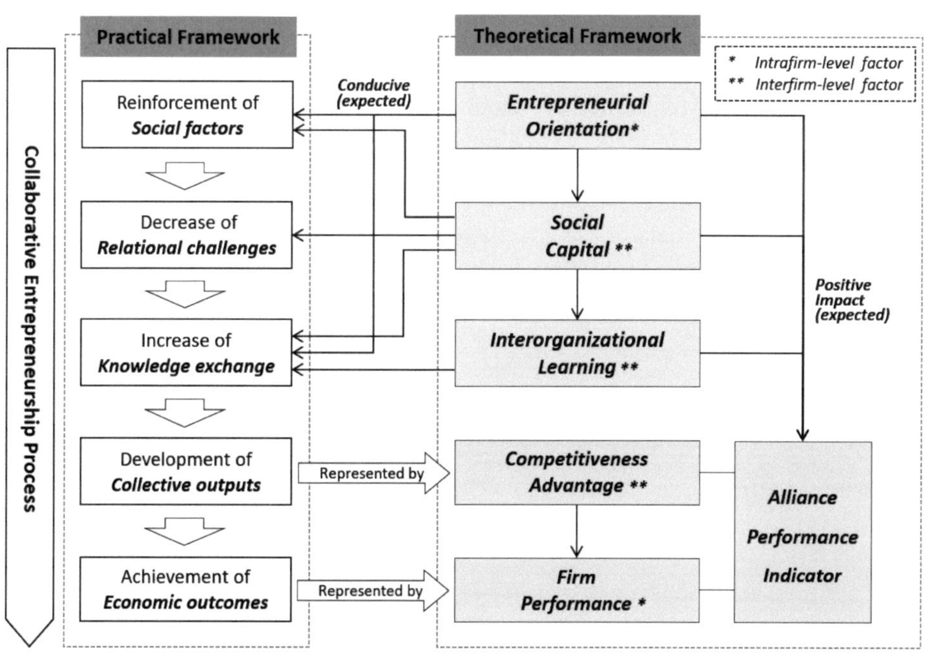

Figure 2.
Proposed model of analysis on collaborative entrepreneurship.

which is presumed as a critical success factor of strategic partnerships but cannot be a spontaneous phenomenon of the alliance configuration [11, 50].

By shedding new light on the managerial implications of SC, EO, and IOL in the context of interfirm collaborations, the present paper contributes to advancing the understanding of the interface between collaborative entrepreneurship and strategic alliances. According to the theoretical framework developed, we suggest a model of analysis on collaborative entrepreneurship for the potential effects of SC, EO, and IOL on alliance performance (see **Figure 2**). The prescriptive value of the model lies in supporting entrepreneurs and entrepreneurship scholars to understand strategic decisions leading to successful alliances. Empirical verification, in particular adopting a holistic perspective, is almost absent from the literature. Hence, what remains is the empirical testing of the approach and the investigation of the quantitative impact of defined variables. In terms of guidelines for future research, this topic should be addressed by collecting information for expanding the model presented here.

This paper is subject to several limitations that can be addressed in future research. First, given the linear linkages among the phenomenon for the model conciseness, it is important to acknowledge that each construct has its unique impact on the optimal conditions for continuous innovation. For instance, a firm's over-embeddedness in the networks of strong ties can provide liability, instead of benefit, which inhibits from sensing emerging innovation opportunities and realizing potential growth [53]. Thereby, the potential performance implications of high SC in an alliance could level off or remain negative beyond a certain threshold. Future research can adopt this view in explaining more deeply the performance-creating mechanism of strategic alliances.

For an empirical study to test our model, measuring the levels of SC and IOL in the interorganizational context, which can be affected by partners' motivations and expectations toward an alliance, may differ from that of their counterparts. Single respondent's perception of an alliance may generate more than the usual amount of random error in measuring the research constructs. Future research could avoid this single-respondent bias by collecting dyadic or even polyadic data from all partners in an alliance.

Lastly, potential endogeneity problems stemming from an implicit recursive model in our theoretical framework should be considered. While we introduce a strategic alliance as a platform of collaborative entrepreneurship for continuous innovation, our conceptual framework still prevents the elaboration of causal inferences regarding the chain of effects. Due to the potential for endogeneity, we interpret the model of analysis as correlational relationships rather than causal relationships. Avenues for future research are to pay explicit attention to the dynamics of the interface of SC, EO, and IOL and clarity the directions of their causality with continuous innovation.

Author details

Ribin Seo
Pohang University of Science and Technology, Pohang, Republic of Korea

*Address all correspondence to: ribinseo@postech.ac.kr

References

[1] Ribeiro-Soriano D, Urbano D. Overview of collaborative entrepreneurship: an integrated approach between business decisions and negotiation. Group Decision and Negotiation. 2009;18:419-430. DOI: 10.1007/s10726-008-9134-x

[2] Miles R, Miles G, Snow C. Collaborative entrepreneurship: a business model for continuous innovation. Organizational Dynamics. 2006;35:1-11. DOI: 10.1016/j.orgdyn.2005.12.004

[3] Anderson BS, Kreiser PM, Kuratko DF, Hornsby JS, Eshima Y. Reconceptualizing entrepreneurial orientation. Strategic Management Journal. 2014;36:1579-1596. DOI: 10.1002/smj.2298

[4] Franco M, Haase H. Firm resources and entrepreneurial orientation as determinants for collaborative entrepreneurship. Management Decision. 2013;51:680-696. DOI: 10.1108/00251741311309724

[5] Dyer JH, Singh H. The relational view: Cooperative strategy and sources of interorganizational competitive advantage. Academy of Management. 1998;23:660-679. DOI: 10.5465/amr.1998.1255632

[6] Antoncic B. Intrapreneurship: A comparative structural equation modeling study. Industrial Management & Data Systems. 2007;107:309-325. DOI: 10.1108/02635570710734244

[7] Jiang X, Yang Y, Pei YL, Wang G. Entrepreneurial orientation, strategic alliances, and firm performance: inside the black box. Long Range Planning. 2016;49:103-116. DOI: 10.1016/j.lrp.2014.09.003

[8] Kreiser PM. Entrepreneurial orientation and organizational learning: The impact of network range and network closure. Entrepreneurship Theory and Practice. 2011;35:1025-1050. DOI: 10.1111/j.1540-6520.2011.00449.x

[9] Li L, Jiang F, Pei Y, Jiang N. Entrepreneurial orientation and strategic alliance success: The contingency role of relational factors. Journal of Business Research. 2017;72:46-56. DOI: 10.1016/j.jbusres.2016.11.011

[10] Miles R, Miles G, Snow C. Collaborative Entrepreneurship: How Communities of Networked Firms Use Continuous Innovation to Create Economic Wealth. Stanford: Stanford University Press; 2005. 144 p. DOI: 10.1177/0170840606066420

[11] Seo R. Interorganizational learning for R&D consortium performance: A social capital perspective. Journal of Knowledge Management. 2020;24:395-414. DOI: doi.org/10.1108/jkm-06-2019-0265

[12] Bogers M. The open innovation paradox: Knowledge sharing and protection in R&D collaborations. European Journal of Innovation Management. 2011;14:93-117. DOI: 10.1108/14601061111104715

[13] Meier M, Lütkewitte M, Mellewigt T, Decker C. How managers can build trust in strategic alliances: A meta-analysis on the central trust-building mechanisms. Journal of Business Economics. 2016;86: 229-257. DOI: 10.1007/s11573-015-0777-1

[14] Rocha H, Miles R. A model of collaborative entrepreneurship for a more humanistic management. Journal of Business Ethics. 2009;88:445-462. DOI: 10.1007/s10551-009-0127-8

[15] Maurer I, Bartsch V, Ebers M. The value of intra-organizational social

capital: How it fosters knowledge transfer, innovation performance, and growth. Organization Studies. 2011;32:157-185. DOI: 10.1177/0170840610394301

[16] Rajala A. Examining the effects of interorganizational learning on performance: A meta-analysis. Journal of Business & Industrial Marketing. 2018;33:574-584. DOI: 10.1108/jbim-08-2017-0205

[17] Stevenson HH, Jarillo JC. A paradigm of entrepreneurship: Entrepreneurial management. In: Cuervo Á, Ribeiro D, Roig S, editors. Entrepreneurship: Concepts, Theory and Perspective. Berlin: Springer Berlin Heidelberg; 2007. p. 155-170. DOI: 10.1007/978-3-540-48543-8_7

[18] Miller D. The correlates of entrepreneurship in three types of firms. Management Science. 1983;29:770-791. DOI: 10.1287/mnsc.29.7.770

[19] Teng BS. Corporate entrepreneurship activities through strategic alliances: A resource-based approach toward competitive advantage. Journal of Management Studies. 2007;44:119-142. DOI: 10.1111/j.1467-6486.2006.00645.x

[20] Stam W, Arzlanian S, Elfring T. Social capital of entrepreneurs and small firm performance: A meta-analysis of contextual and methodological moderators. Journal of Business Venturing. 2014;29:152-173. DOI: 10.1016/j.jbusvent.2013.01.002

[21] Lumpkin GT, Dess GG. Clarifying the entrepreneurial orientation construct and linking it to performance. Academy of Management Review. 1996;21:135-172. DOI: 10.5465/amr.1996.9602161568

[22] Covin JG, Green KM, Slevin DP. Strategic process effects on the entrepreneurial orientation–sales growth rate relationship. Entrepreneurship Theory and Practice. 2006;30:57-81. DOI: 10.1111/j.1540-6520.2006.00110.x

[23] Montoro-Sánchez A, Ortiz-de-Urbina-Criado A, Romero-Martínez AM. The decision to use alliances as corporate entrepreneurship: The role of resources and skills. Group Decision Negotiation. 2009;18:431-448. DOI: 10.1007/s10726-008-9135-9

[24] Alvarez SA, Ireland RD, Reuer JJ. Editorial: Entrepreneurship and strategic alliances. Journal of Business Venturing. 2006;21:401-404. DOI: 10.1016/j.jbusvent.2005.03.001

[25] Gupta AK, Govindarajan V. Knowledge flows within multinational corporations. Strategic Management Journal. 2000;21:481-510. DOI: 10.1002/(SICI)1097-0266(200004)21:4<473::AID-SMJ84>3.0.CO;2-I

[26] Thomson AM, Perry JL. Collaboration processes: Inside the black box. Public Administration Review. 2006;66:20-32. DOI: 10.1111/j.1540-6210.2006.00663.x.

[27] Lisowska R. The potential of business environment institutions and the support for the development of small and medium-sized enterprises. Entrepreneurial Business and Economics Review. 2016;4:85-101. DOI: 10.15678/EBER.2016.040307.

[28] Czarnitzki D, Ebersberger B, Fier A. The relationship between R&D collaboration, subsidies and R&D performance: Empirical evidence from Finland and Germany. Journal of Applied Economics. 2007;22:1347-1366. DOI: 10.1002/jae.992

[29] Pippel G. The impact of R&D collaboration networks on the performance of firms: a meta-analysis of the evidence. International Journal of

Networking and Virtual Organizations. 2013;12:352-373. DOI: 10.1504/ijnvo.2013.057282

[30] Lin C, Wu YJ, Chang CC, Wang W, Lee CY. The alliance innovation performance of R&D alliances: The absorptive capacity perspective. Technovation. 2012;32:282-292. DOI: 10.1016/j.technovation.2012.01.004

[31] Tripsas M, Schrader S, Sobrero M. Discouraging opportunistic behavior in collaborative R&D: A new role for government. Research Policy. 1995;24:367-389. DOI: 10.1016/0048-7333(93)00771-K

[32] Fredrich V, Bouncken RB, Kraus S. The race is on: Configurations of absorptive capacity, interdependence and slack resources for interorganizational learning in coopetition alliances. Journal of Business Research. 2019;101:862-868. DOI: 10.1016/j.jbusres.2018.11.038

[33] Frishammar J, Ericsson K, Patel PC. The dark side of knowledge transfer: Exploring knowledge leakage in joint R&D projects. Technovation. 2015;41-42:75-88. DOI: 10.1016/j.technovation.2015.01.001

[34] Parida V, Westerberg M, Frishammar J. Inbound open innovation activities in high-tech SMEs: The impact on innovation performance. Journal of Small Business Management. 2012;50:283-309. DOI: 10.1111/j.1540-627X.2012.00354.x

[35] Holmqvist M. A dynamic model of intra-and interorganizational learning. Organization Studies. 2003;24:95-123. DOI: 10.1177/0170840603024001684

[36] Dyer JH, Hatch NW. Relation-specific capabilities and barriers to knowledge transfers: Creating advantage through network relationships. Strategic Management Journal. 2006;27:701-719. DOI: 10.1002/smj.543

[37] Inkpen AC, Tsang EWK. Social capital, networks, and knowledge transfer. Academy of Management. 2005;30:146-165. DOI: 10.5465/amr.2005.15281445

[38] Liao J, Welsch H. Roles of social capital in venture creation: Key dimensions and research implications. Journal of Small Business Management. 2005;43:345-362. DOI: 10.1111/j.1540-627X.2005.00141.x

[39] Nahapiet J, Ghoshal S. Social capital, intellectual capital, and the organizational advantage. Academy of Management Review. 1998;23:242-266. DOI: 10.5465/amr.1998.533225

[40] Adler PS, Kwon SW. Social capital: Prospects for a new concept. Academy of Management Review. 2002;27:17-40. DOI: 10.5465/amr.2002.5922314

[41] Pinheiro ML, Serôdio P, Pinho JC, Lucas C. The role of social capital towards resource sharing in collaborative R&D projects: Evidences from the 7th Framework Programme. International Journal of Project Management. 2016;34:1519-1536. DOI: 10.1016/j.ijproman.2016.07.006

[42] Rauch A, Rosenbusch N, Unger J, Frese M. The effectiveness of cohesive and diversified networks: A meta-analysis. Journal of Business Research. 2016;69:554-568. DOI: 10.1016/j.jbusres.2015.05.011

[43] Wu WY, Chang ML, Chen CW. Promoting innovation through the accumulation of intellectual capital, social capital, and entrepreneurial orientation. R&D Management. 2008;38:265-277. DOI: 10.1111/1467-9914.00120-i1

[44] Covin JG, Wales WJ. Crafting high-Impact entrepreneurial

orientation research: Some suggested guidelines. Entrepreneurship Theory and Practice. 2019;43:3-18. DOI: 10.1177/1042258718773181

[45] Rauch A, Wiklund J, Lumpkin GT, Frese M. Entrepreneurial orientation and business performance: An assessment of past research and suggestions for the future. Entrepreneurship Theory and Practice. 2009;33:761-787. DOI: 10.1111/j.1540-6520.2009.00308.x

[46] Wiklund J, Shepherd D. Knowledge-based resources, entrepreneurial orientation, and the performance of small and medium-sized businesses. Strategic Management Journal. 2003;24:1307-1314. DOI: 10.1002/smj.360

[47] Shu C, Liu C, Gao S, Shanley M. The knowledge spillover theory of entrepreneurship in alliances. Entrepreneurship Theory and Practice. 2014;38:913-940. DOI: 10.1111/etap.12024

[48] Gedajlovic E. Honig B, Moore CB, Payne GT, Wright M. Social capital and entrepreneurship: A schema and research agenda. Entrepreneurship Theory and Practice. 2013;37:455-478.

[49] March JG. Exploration and exploitation in organizational learning. Organization Science. 1991;2:71-87. DOI: 10.1287/orsc.2.1.71

[50] Westerlund M, Rajala R. Learning and innovation in inter-organizational network collaboration. Journal of Business & Industrial Marketing. 2010;25:435-442. DOI: 10.1108/08858621011066026

[51] Wang CH, Hsu LC. Building exploration and exploitation in the high-tech industry: The role of relationship learning. Technological Forecasting and Social Change. 2014;81:331-340. DOI: 10.1016/j.techfore.2013.04.008

[52] Kim YC, Lu JW, Rhee M. Learning from age difference: Interorganizational learning and survival in Japanese foreign subsidiaries. Journal of International Business Studies. 2012;43:719-745. DOI: 10.1057/jibs.2012.19

[53] Gargiulo M, Benassi M. The dark side of social capital. In: Leenders RTAJ, Gabbay SM, editors. Corporate Social Capital and Liability. Boston: Springer; 1999, p. 282-322. DOI: 10.1007/978-1-4615-5027-3_17

Chapter 2

Business Harvesting Strategies for Entrepreneurs

Herring Shava

Abstract

Entrepreneurship plays a pivotal role in our societies, such as employment creation. This is a key to addressing income inequalities leading to poverty reduction and economic growth. As a result of this critical role, the campaign is on establishing more entrepreneurial entities, and there is very little concern regarding harvesting an entrepreneurial entity. Entity harvesting is equally important as setting up a new entrepreneurial venture and this chapter explores this issue. During the harvesting process, the entrepreneur recovers value through the sale of an entrepreneurial entity or its assets. Having spent several years building and adding value to the business, the entrepreneur must design an entity harvesting strategy that would provide maximum returns on the investment of time, effort and money. Several reasons may compel the entrepreneur to harvest the business and this chapter provides some of these reasons based on extant literature and primary data collected from small- and medium-sized entity (SME) owners in Sub-Saharan Africa. Further, the chapter outlines various entity harvesting strategies preferred by SME owners in Sub-Saharan Africa and circumstances at which they deem appropriate to apply such.

Keywords: harvesting, entrepreneur, buyouts, mergers, outright sale

1. Introduction

The start-up process of a new entrepreneurial venture and until such time the entrepreneur decides to exit the business is a contentious issue. On the one hand, the entrepreneur is found working on a business plan intending to start an entrepreneurial venture. On the other hand, the entrepreneur is also found crafting a long-term business harvesting strategy. As contradicting as this may sound, this gives the entrepreneur a clear entrepreneurship roadmap which in many circumstances will be adjusted as the business owner responds to macro- and micro-environmental changes. Having a harvesting strategy upfront is critical for guiding the entity owner towards achieving the business mission. A business harvesting strategy could be characterised as the path to the finishing point at which the entrepreneur is expected to celebrate the sacrifices made, that is, effort, time and money. It is at that finishing point where the entrepreneur recovers the value-added into the business by selling either the firm in its entirety or partly in the form of assets. When this is done, the entrepreneur can start a new entrepreneurial venture or retire completely from the entrepreneurship career.

The significant contribution of entrepreneurship in our societies cannot be underestimated, especially on employment creation [1]. This is a key to addressing income inequalities leading to poverty reduction and economic growth [2]. As a result of this critical role, the campaign is mainly on establishing more entrepreneurial entities, and there is very little concern about harvesting an entrepreneurial entity [3]. There is very little empirical evidence on this subject from an African perspective [4]. However, it is important to note that entity harvesting is equally important as setting up a new entrepreneurial venture [5]. Resultantly, this chapter contributes to this gap in the literature by exploring this subject matter relying on primary data from SMEs in Sub-Saharan countries (Botswana, Eswatini, South Africa and Zimbabwe). The goal of this chapter is to explore the preferred entity harvesting options of SME owners in Sub-Saharan Africa and to determine why they prefer such options.

The next section will define business harvesting, followed by reasons for harvesting and a discussion on harvesting strategies available to entrepreneurs. The methodology used to gather primary data is explained, and a discussion of the findings is made. The chapter further outlines the implications of investigating small- and medium-sized entities (SME) harvesting practices, areas for further research.

2. Business harvesting

After entity start-up, the entrepreneur invests time, effort and money with the intent of growing the business. The entrepreneur invests time, effort and money to make money from the firm in the future. Through such entrepreneurial efforts, the entity accumulates value and ends up attracting competition. In such instances, the business could be vulnerable to hostile takeovers, and harvesting the business provides the entrepreneur with maximum returns on the investment made. By definition, business harvesting is a systematic practice by which the entrepreneur recovers value gained by the entity through the selling of individual assets or the entire firm as a whole. Various reasons compel the entrepreneur to harvest the entity and the section to follow outlines some of them.

2.1 Reasons for harvesting

Factors beyond the control of the owner or entity management could influence the mentioned entity players to consider harvesting [6]. Macro-environmental factors such as the global pandemic similar to Covid-19 have seen most entrepreneurs harvesting their entities as most entities could not operate under the global lockdown, which has extended for at least 3 months in some countries. Owing to the global lockdown, supply chain networks have been severely affected. Firms that rely on imported raw materials have suffered the most as movement of non-essential goods are currently suspended globally. Some factors leading to business harvest include the untimely death of the entrepreneur, serious ill health, or poor mental health. Unrest in the labour market or loss of key expertise may force the entrepreneur to harvest the business. Generally, harvesting reasons are unique to each entrepreneurial entity [5].

Micro-environmental factors speak to reasons for harvesting the entity which the entrepreneur has significant control over. The first example relates to the goal of the entrepreneur [7]. Some entrepreneurs start an entity and work hard to grow the firm so that it becomes very attractive to competition and later sell the entity for a substantial profit. The second example for wanting to harvest the entity could be that the entrepreneur falls in the category of serial entrepreneurs [8]. These are individuals who start entrepreneurial entities but after running the entity for a given period, they develop other lucrative business ideas and sell the existing firm to raise the needed capital for the new entrepreneurial venture.

Succession is another micro-environmental reason for harvesting the existing entity and it is common in family business [7]. Under succession, the family business owner steps down and pass entity ownership to the next family member. When the family business is carefully run, through succession, the firm will pass from generation to generation and this may continue over many decades. Further, the entrepreneur may start a new entity hoping that this would afford him free space and more time to himself but only to find out later that business demands are far much greater than envisaged. Traditionally, the entrepreneur still has to balance both home and business demands. Unfortunately, the inability to find a middle point between these competing issues may drive the entrepreneur to the point of harvesting the business. However, not all entrepreneurs fail to balance home and business demands. Some entrepreneurs are good at what they do such that the entrepreneurial entity they have built can outlive their physical and mental strength. When this happens, entrepreneurs often choose retirement as they no longer have the physical and mental strength to keep up with both business and home demands. Resultantly, they recover the value added in the business in the form of cash which in this case could be equated to a retirement package.

Choosing between available business harvesting options may not be that easy for the entrepreneur. Each harvesting option has its advantages and disadvantages. Therefore, the entrepreneur must diligently make the difficult decision to pick the one that would yield maximum returns in line with sacrifices made in building the entity. The next section looks at harvesting strategies that an entrepreneur can exercise.

2.2 Business harvesting options

Several harvesting options exist and these range from buyouts, mergers, outright sale, employee share ownership scheme and an initial public offering. The paragraphs to follow elaborate on the mentioned harvesting strategies.

2.2.1 Buyouts

Buyouts or an outright sale of entity results in the establishment of a new independent entity owned and controlled by managers and sometimes by a private equity entity. Buyouts are generally in five types:

- Leveraged buyout (LBO). LBO happens when a large portion of a publicly quoted entity is sold to a private equity firm. During the sale process, the private equity firm gains a larger number of shares.

- Management buyout (MBO). In an MBO scenario, the current management of the entity raises funds to buy out the entity owner. In instances where the firm decides to divest in a subsidiary, the current management takes control of a significant amount of equity. As much as the management remains in control of the larger share of the voting equity, to ensure continued smooth flow of operations, that is, firm relations with customers, creditors and suppliers, the previous owner may retain ownership of an equity stake in the firm. This practice is common in family-owned businesses where a small number of managers take control of a portion of equity.

  MBO can be extended to other managers or employees and at that point, it then becomes a management employee buyout (MEBO). In many instances, employees are factored in the equation because of the key expertise they possess. This is common where branches of the entity are geographically dispersed, and it becomes an issue of common sense to involve the branch manager in the MEBO to facilitate easy management control. From a business perspective, the success of the branch becomes of interest to the manager owing to stake ownership. MBO or MEBO is advantageous to the owner as it offers a quick exit. The big disadvantage is that the management may not possess similar entrepreneurial traits to those of the departing owner, leading to the downfall of the newly established business.

- A management buy-in (MBI). External managers are granted the opportunity to buy equity in the firm. Often the challenge here is that the newcomers have no extensive knowledge of the existing business particularly regarding how it operates. In rare cases, newcomers may be from the same sector as the existing business and therefore come with valuable insights concerning technology, knowledge on the competition, and how to grow the business leading to its success.

  A more advantageous scenario is a hybrid buy-in/management buyout (BIMBO), and this is where a portion if inside managers and a portion of outsiders both acquire a stake in the firm. This is advantageous in the sense that existing managers have profound knowledge on the operations of the firm, meaning there will be little disruptions. More importantly, the incoming managers bring valuable operational insights towards growing the existing business which may have been missing all along.

- Investor-led buyout (ILBO). The entire entity or part thereof is purchased by a privately owned equity firm. Depending on the circumstances or the state of the acquired firm, new management can be brought to run the affairs of the newly acquired entity. This is normally done to safeguard the investments made, especially when the acquired firm is in a precarious position. Conversely, when the newly acquired firm's affairs are in order, existing management is likely to be retained, or a mix of new management and existing management may be the one responsible for the acquired firm. Unfortunately, in an ILBO, existing managers occupying specific office positions in the firm are normally not given the option to purchase stocks.

- Leveraged build-up (LBU). When the goal of a private equity firm is to generate profits from a buyout or buy-in investment, they practice leveraged build-up. This is where the newly acquired entity, as a result of buyout or buy-in, is used as an investment platform, where a series of acquisitions are continuously added to it, forming a large corporate group. This move brings with it the ability to lure skilled and experienced managers, who can exponentially grow the entity through further acquisitions.

2.2.2 Business mergers

Merging a business is a process where the smaller entity is absorbed, often by a larger entity mostly to provide an extra muscle on the weaknesses of the small entity and to maximise on its strengths. The outcome of a merger is a large and very competitive entity. The entrepreneur who intends to harvest the entity through merging with another firm focuses more on the price, structure and terms of the proposed deal. Where mergers occur, special attention is also given to issues about organisational culture, the coming together of different personnel into a single entity, and the coming together of different products under one firm. Other issues that need to be addressed are the fears of employees regarding downsizing or retrenchment that may be necessary to ensure the viability and success of the new entity. More important, operational and marketing issues need further attention considering that products and services may have become so diverse as a result of the merger. Management has to decide as to which products and services they will discontinue or continue offering based on each product/service's cash inflow strength. Research and development initiatives and manufacturing methods are some of the issues that will require special attention. More importantly, the entity has to decide with regards to supply chain partners they would want to continue to be in business with. When supply chain partners have been decided, that also influences the distribution channels they will adopt to ensure a hustle-free logistics management process.

2.2.3 Outright sale

The entrepreneur who opts for an outright sale of his firm as the harvesting option sells the entire business to any person who is willing to pay for the asking price. The buyer could be a supplier interested in forward integration, or the customer who is interested in backward integration. Sometimes the buyer is completely a neutral player from another sector whose intentions are to spread and diversify the risk. Often, entrepreneurs shy away from selling the business to the competitor as this entails disclosing or providing access to trade secrets, which could backfire if the deal fails to materialise.

2.2.4 Employee share ownership scheme (ESOS)

Various governments, particularly in developing countries, have been advocating for employee share ownership schemes as a means of maximising productivity and also as a means of fighting the inequality gaps as far as wealth distribution is concerned. In Africa, it is no secret that the majority of the wealth is controlled by a minority who are predominantly white. From the Africans' point of view, this is gross injustice as they feel they are not benefiting from what is rightfully theirs (riches of Africa). To address this challenge, most African countries have crafted and legalised the employee share ownership scheme [9]. By definition, the employee share ownership scheme is a legalised route by which the employer can transfer some or all of the shares to employees who in turn assume ownership of the shares received [10]. By the end of the deal, employees develop a vested interest in the entity's well-being and become motivated to participate strongly in the growth of the entity to realise as much wealth as they can. Through the ESOS, the entrepreneur harvesting the entity receives cash at different intervals on his way out. The advantage is that the management continues to run the entity at the same time benefiting from the scheme. The disadvantage is that this could also result in the loss of the entrepreneurial drive in the entity. Often, the ESOS is best suited for large corporations given the complications surrounding the structuring and mapping of the finances involved.

2.2.5 Initial public offering (IPO)

The entrepreneur who chooses initial public offering as a harvesting option enlist the entity on a public stock exchange and have its shares publicly traded [11]. As attractive as this is, the downside is that the entrepreneur now must account to several shareholders on issues related to entity growth and many other key issues shareholders may be interested in [12]. In other words, this could add more administrative issues to the entrepreneur that he/she may have not anticipated before choosing this harvesting option.

3. Methodology

This research is exploratory and predominantly quantitative. However, open-ended questions were incorporated to solicit further insights concerning the subject in question. A self-administered questionnaire was designed from extant literature on the subject of entity harvesting. Qualitative data gathered from open-ended questions provided rich insights as to the SME owner's preferred method of harvesting and motivations to harvest the business. A sample of 612 SMEs was approached in Botswana, Eswatini, South Africa and Zimbabwe (Sub-Saharan Africa). Opportunistic convenience sampling was carried out. In the absence of a trusted sampling frame, field workers approached SME owners who were willing to participate in this research. Field workers explained the goal of the research and participants' rights with regards to research that is the right to terminate participation without questions asked, right not to answer questions that infringe on their privacy, anonymity and truthful presentation of their views. Having explained at length issues related to the rights of the participants, their consent was sought and obtained. Descriptive statistics were performed to make the meaning of quantitative data. Similarly, qualitative data obtained were grouped into themes and each theme was observed and monitored in terms of recurrence. Thus, the frequency distribution of each theme was established to determine how popular that theme was among SME owners.

4. Findings

The results presented in this section provide a detailed background of the business owner and the SME. These cover issues related to the age of the business, location of the business, industry or sector in which the business is operating, the ownership structure of the business, the business development stage and sales revenue growth. Further, this section presents findings concerning harvesting practices preferred by small businesses in Sub-Saharan Africa.

4.1 Demographic distribution of SMEs

Data on the year of business establishment for the SMEs were gathered. The findings revealed that 40% of SMEs were between 5 and 10 years old whilst the other 40% were between 10 and 20 years old and 20% of the SMEs were established more than 20 years ago. Therefore, all the SMEs were in business for a considerable amount of time. This implies that the SME owners in question are fairly experienced business players. The findings with regards to the location of the SMEs reveal that that 20% of the SMEs were based in Gaberone, Botswana, 25% of the SMEs were based in Harare, Zimbabwe, 40% were based in Johannesburg, South Africa, and 15% of the SMEs were located in Mbabane, Eswatini. Data with regards to sector distribution of the SMEs revealed that 40% were in manufacturing, while mining, tourism, transport and logistics and retail sector were each represented by 15%, respectively. Data further revealed that 60% of the SMEs were registered as private companies, while partnerships and sole traders were both represented by 20%, respectively. The chapter further reveals that all SME owners who participated in this research are multiple business owners with 60% having total control and ownership of three operational SMEs, while 20% owned four operational SMEs and a further 20% being owners of two operational SMEs.

SME owners were further asked to identify the stage at which they thought their businesses occupied in the business life cycle (the SME at which they were found during fieldwork, that is, ignoring other SMEs they owned). The findings reveal that SMEs were at varying stages of the business life cycle with 20% being at the growth stage, while 40% were at the maturity stage and a further 40% already at their decline stage. A country analysis showing sales revenue growth in the past 12 months shows that SMEs in Botswana realised a more satisfactory movement (44%) followed by SMEs in Eswatini (42%) and SMEs in South Africa represented by 40%. Only 12% of SMEs in Zimbabwe registered satisfactory movement in sales revenue. This could be a reflector of the ongoing economic crisis that has affected the Zimbabwean economy for over a decade. As shown in **Table 1**, Zimbabwean SMEs further leads on the declining sales revenue option as 34% of SMEs registered a decline in sales revenue and 54% registering non-satisfactory movement in sales revenue in the past 12 months.

4.2 SMEs preferred harvesting options

SMEs were given a list of entity harvesting options and were asked to rank in order of preference to identify the harvesting option they would consider when the time of harvest has come. Findings are summarised in **Table 2**. They reveal that the majority of SMEs in Sub-Saharan Africa preferred the outright sale harvesting option, M = 4.6, SD = 0.89, followed by the management buy-in harvesting option, M = 4.4, SD = 0.89, mergers, M = 3.8, SD = 1.3, investor-led buyout, M = 3.6, SD = 1.67 and leveraged build-ups with M = 3.4, SD = 1.51 concluded the top five preferred SMEs entity harvesting options.

4.2.1 Justification for choosing the outright sale entity harvesting option

SME owners who identified outright sale as their preferred entity harvesting method cited unavailability of an heir to take over the business, desire to pursue other interest, business reaching its peak performance level, retirement reasons,

Country	Sales revenue movement in the past 12 months	%
Botswana	Satisfactory movement	44
	Non-satisfactory movement	36
	A decline in sales revenue	20
Eswatini	Satisfactory movement	42
	Non-satisfactory movement	28
	A decline in sales revenue	30
South Africa	Satisfactory movement	40
	Non-satisfactory movement	40
	A decline in sales revenue	20
Zimbabwe	Satisfactory movement	12
	Non-satisfactory movement	54
	A decline in sales revenue	34

Table 1.
SMEs sales revenue growth by country.

Harvesting option	Mean score	Standard deviation
Outright sale	4.6	0.89
Management buy-in (MBI)	4.4	0.89
Mergers	3.8	1.30
Investor led buyout (ILBO)	3.6	1.67
Leveraged build-ups	3.4	1.51
Management buyout (MBO)	3.0	1.41
Employ share ownership scheme (ESOS)	2.8	1.30

Table 2.
SMEs preferred entity harvesting options in Sub-Saharan Africa.

Justification	Frequency (%)
Absence of an heir	33
Desire to pursue other interests	22
Business performance reached peak level	18
Retirement plan	12
Uncertain business environment	9
Failure of a business turnaround strategy	6

Table 3.
Reasons behind choosing the outright sale harvesting option.

uncertain business environment and unavailability of a working turnaround business strategy as factors that would drive them to consider an outright sale of the entity. **Table 3** provides descriptive statistics summarising the observed frequencies of the mentioned reasons.

The paragraphs to follow further expand on the findings outlined in **Table 3**.

- Absence of an heir. In the absence of an immediate family member to take over the business, SME owners pointed out that it is rather wise for them to cash in on their businesses and enjoy the fruits thereof than to leave the business to a distant relative who never contributed towards the well-being of the entity.

- Business performance is at peak. Other SME owners pointed out that they would consider an outright sale harvesting option when the entrepreneurial entity has reached its all high-performance mark. This move is advantageous considering that this is the point where the business will be very attractive to competition and other individuals or organisation interested in a takeover. Given this situation, the entrepreneur has more bargaining power and is more likely to receive a significant amount better than the firm's asking price.

- Desire to pursue other interests. The desire to pursue other interests in this research was found to be triggered by the failure of the current enterprise to bring forth the anticipated results. Although some SME owners are genuinely interested in pursuing other business avenues, SME owners pointed out that they would rather cash in on the business especially once signs and symptoms of decline are noticed. They argued that rarely does it pay to continue investing time, effort and money once the business has started showing negative signs of performance.

Conversely, not all SMEs were of the view that they would harvest the entity through outright sale when it is poorly performing. The findings also revealed that most entrepreneurs preferred harvesting their ventures on discovering new and exciting opportunities, which they viewed as more profitable than the existing one. In support, some respondents also argued that where an entrepreneur comes up with a more lucrative business plan that has been well evaluated, the less lucrative venture must be harvested to mobilise funds to finance the lucrative business opportunity. Some SME owners were also quick to emphasise that the culture among SME owners was such that as long as the venture is still viable, there is no reason for harvesting the entity.

- Retirement plan. A few SME owners pointed out they would consider the outright sale as their harvesting strategy and completely retire from the entrepreneurial life. The outright sale harvesting option would provide them with enough funds to sustain them when they are no longer actively involved in business markets.

- Uncertain business environment. A significant number of SMEs particularly those found in the mining sector pointed out that for them, their businesses are largely affected by ever-changing government policies around mineral ownership and the processes involved in the selling of the minerals. The SMEs in the mining sector felt that they are the least protected by regulations. Mining operations are severely threatened by artisanal miners who continuously invade mining shafts and plants. In all this chaos, SME owners blame governments for doing very little to protect SMEs in the mining sector and their employees. When the rule of law is compromised as is the case in the mining sector, an outright sale was the preferred harvesting strategy. This enables the entrepreneur to invest capital in countries where the rule of law is known to be uncompromised.

- Failure of the business turnaround strategy. Unlike some other SMEs who would harvest once symptoms and signs of failure start being noticed, some prefer to try and resuscitate the firm. However, when these efforts fail, they then choose to practice the outright sale harvesting option. The disadvantage of this strategy is that the business may have hit rock bottom a long time ago without the owner noticing. As such, when the new buyer comes, he or she has more bargaining power and the entrepreneur may receive proceeds that are far below the market value of the entity.

4.3 Business merger

The findings reveal that entity merger was the third preferred harvesting option, M = 3.8, SD = 1.30. A study conducted in India by Mantravadi and Reddy [13] found out that firm profitability levels behaved differently depending on the sector after the merger, with some having their profitability levels increasing yet others experienced a decline. Generally, mergers are known to result in improved profitability for firms that were experiencing a sharp decline in profits. It was therefore very much anticipated for SME owners in Sub-Saharan Africa to at least consider business merger as a harvesting method given its tremendous benefits which include, improved revenues and profitability, faster growth in scale and quicker access to markets, acquisition of new technology, elimination of competition and increased market share [4]. Also, through mergers, firms enjoy tax shields and investment savings.

In this research, SME owners who opted merging with other firms as a harvesting technique cited lack of operating and growth capital as the major reason.

- Lack of operating and growth capital. SME owners pointed out that if the firm is experiencing liquidity challenges, merging with a financially stable firm is the only route to preserving the legacy of the founder and keep initial business ideas, products, or services for a reasonable time in the market. Some of the SME owners pointed out that they had undertaken this harvesting practice before. For the previous mergers to occur, SME owners pointed out that the underlying reason that led to those mergers was liquidity problems. However, family and friends played an influential role in choosing the harvesting option. Other SME owners pointed out that they consider a business merger as it is a welcome opportunity to come out of financial distress without having to approach banks for funding.

4.4 Buyout

The research sought the respondents' views on different types of buyouts they would consider as their harvesting options. The findings imply that buyout options are widely used by SMEs. Buyouts involve a transition from one set of owners to another where the previous owners lose control over the firm and the new ones pay a premium for shares that gives them a controlling interest in the firm. The results on the different types of buyouts as entity harvesting options preferred by SMEs owners show that management buy-in is the second most preferred entity harvesting option, M = 4.4, SD = 0.89.

The findings reveal that SME owners are willing to surrender their businesses to external management for considerable value than their internal ones. Investor-led buyout (ILBO) was identified as the fourth preferred entity harvesting option, M = 3.6, SD = 1.67. SME owners argued that if the business is taken over by some investor institutions and is rejuvenated, their peers judge them better than if the same happens with former employees. Leveraged build-ups (LBUs) were identified by SME owners as the fifth preferred entity harvesting option, M = 3.4, SD = 1.51, whereas management buyout (MBO) was the sixth preferred entity harvesting option, M = 3, SD = 1.41.

4.4.1 SME justification for preferring various buyout options

SME owners identified the unavailability of a successor, de-risking and entity owner poor health as major drivers for preferring various buyout entity harvesting options.

- No suitable family member to take over the firm. Similar to the outright sale harvesting option, the MBI, ILBO, LBU and MBO entity harvesting options were identified as harvesting options by SME owners citing unavailability of a suitable family member to drive the firm forward when they quit. SME owners experienced displeasure in the idea that a distant relative would inherit the estate in case their close relatives are not business focused. Hence, SME owners preferred to settle for either the MBI, ILBO, LBU or MBO entity harvesting options.

- De-risking. Some SME owners singled out the LBO entity harvesting option. They cited de-risking as their motivation for preferring this strategy. SMEs owners pointed out that the ILBO by design brings in the much-needed capital to fund business growth initiatives, in the process guaranteeing business continuity. In other words, a portion of SME owners is not interested in total entity harvesting but partial harvest.

- Poor health. Some SME owners opted for the ILBO harvesting option citing deteriorating health conditions. In this case, the owner sells a division of a firm instead of the entire firm. Health failure means that the SME owner is no longer able to participate in business affairs daily. In certain instances, the entrepreneur remains hopeful that he or she would recover and be actively involved in the affairs of the entity and possibly buy out the investor. For the hopeful entrepreneur, it is better to have somebody taking care of the firm until the entrepreneur's recovery point, and by design, the ILBO from the SME owner's perspective, it provides this opportunity.

4.5 Employee share ownership scheme (ESOS)

The research findings reveal that the ESOS is the least preferred entity harvesting options among SME owners, M = 2.8, SD = 1.30. SME owners who preferred this option pointed out that because they would have succeeded in building a strong performance-oriented culture, it was more strategically important for them to involve entity employees in the entity's succession plans. From the SME owner's perspective, having employees who are best performers to own a stake in the firm and participate in running the affairs of the entity would make it easier to pass on the performance-oriented culture to all incoming employees. This is critical in ensuring that the firm's competitive advantage is sustained and the firm's profitability abilities maintained for a foreseeable future.

5. Discussion of the findings

The findings presented in this chapter indicate that both macro- and micro-environmental factors play a significant role concerning the SME owner's preferred entity harvesting strategy. The majority of SME owners in Sub-Saharan Africa pointed out that they prefer an outright sale as an entity harvesting strategy. The results show that this decision is largely influenced by the absence of an heir (macro-environmental factor). SME owners have little control over this aspect and as much as business skills can be learned, people's interest differs upon realising and accepting this reality, SME owners are left with the option of disposing of the entity and salvage the value they may have added to the firm.

The results further reveal that among buyout options, the ILBO is more popular with SME owners as it was more preferred compared to all other buyout options. The findings further reveal that SME owners are worried about the volatility, uncertainty, chaos and unpredictability of the business environment. From the findings, the majority of SMEs are either declining or static and very few are making significant profits as most economies are in a recession. The present circumstances do not help SME owners in Zimbabwe who have consistently braved the economic downturn for over a decade and with the global economy in recession owing to the Covid-19 pandemic, this situation will drastically affect preferred entity harvesting options, possibly from an outright sale to mergers including some of the buyout options.

Despite the global recession that is very likely to have a bearing on preferred entity harvesting options, SME owners are somewhat hopeful that their businesses can have a second life. This is why apart from an outright sale, they believe that through MBI and mergers, their entities or entity offerings are still relevant to the market. What also can be learned from the findings is that such decisions are not being made only in light of the bad economic situation but it appears they were made right from the start as part of the business plan and continue to be adjusted as the economic situation changes.

However, from findings, it has been observed that SMEs owners appear not ready to give current employees and management a chance to own shares and to run the business as a harvesting option. In contrast to extant literature which pointed out that the ESOS is meant to spread the wealth between entity employees and entity owners, the findings reveal that entity owners are utilising this strategy to secure entity profitability for a longer period by extending share ownership to best-performing employees who in turn will have the obligation to pass on the performance-oriented culture to newly recruited employees.

6. Implications for studying entity harvesting strategies

6.1 Theoretical implications

The chapter explained SME owner preferred entity harvesting strategies making use of primary data collected from four Southern African countries and to the author's best knowledge, by the time of writing, this research is the first to adopt such a strategy. More importantly, this chapter calls for more research to be done in this area and advance the debate on SME owner business exit strategies as they are critical in guiding the owner in achieving the entity's mission. Also, the findings presented in this chapter contribute significantly to the gap in extant literature in the Sub-Saharan Africa region and beyond.

6.2 Practical implications

The findings presented in this chapter point to the notion that the preferred SME owner entity harvesting strategies are largely reactionary. This means that SME owners respond to macro- and micro-environmental factors and by so doing they are more of spectators rather than influencers of the business environment. The only way SMEs can succeed in practicing their original entity harvesting plan without being reactionary is to work diligently and make sure that micro-environmental factors are aligned to their needs. As a result, business consultants, policy-makers and business support institutions can help SMEs in training their employees to be the best performers and ensure that all employees with funds can participate in ESOS. Currently, the practice is that only best performing employees benefit from this initiative defeating the original purpose which it was designed for. Other training activities can be held to help SMEs with risk management skills which would help when the de-risking time comes. SME owner-preferred entity harvesting options are influenced by the unavailability of an heir to take over the reins of the entity. This affects mostly family-owned SMEs. It should be acknowledged that succession is not a short-term endeavour but a long-term issue. Therefore, the search and training for a potential successor should start early to ensure the continuity of the firm. The critical aspect of the succession plan is raising awareness among the current SME owner/managers to kick start the search and preparation for succession early. This will enable them to identify the needed support tools, measures and the relevant infrastructure to enhance the success chances of the incoming an heir. When this is done on time, the thinking is that succession plans would have less effect on the SME owner's preferred entity harvesting strategy.

7. Limitations of the study

The research is exploratory and descriptive. Although this is a stepping stone in trying to answer complex questions around SME owner-preferred entity harvesting strategies, considering that this was a cross-country analysis, issues related to culture and economic outlook were not controlled to determine if they had a major bearing on entity harvesting strategies reported. The reader should, therefore, exercise caution in the interpretation and application of the findings.

8. Future research

Future research should focus on similar harvesting strategies to establish causal relationships and also identifying boundaries in which the SME owner's choice of entity harvesting strategy is directly or indirectly influenced by country characteristics, age of the business and economic outlook. Given that this was an exploratory research, the author further advocates for more studies making use of both simple and complex multivariate statistical analysis to establish definite relationships on this phenomenon.

9. Conclusion

The chapter outlined SME owner-preferred entity harvesting strategies and determined why the given option is preferred. Relying on cross-country data, the chapter concludes that the majority of SME owners prefer the outright sale option when harvesting their entities. This option is mainly influenced by the absence of an heir to take over the reins of the business implying that most SMEs are family-owned businesses. The chapter also concludes that SMEs do prefer other entity harvesting strategies such as mergers and buyout which includes among them ILBO, MBI, LBU and MBO as well as employee share ownership schemes. Mergers and buyout options are largely influenced by deteriorating economic conditions among other factors. The chapter further concludes that SMEs also prefer ESOS as a harvesting strategy but solely to secure the entity's competitive advantage and profitability for as long as they can. This is evident in their willingness to sell entity stake to best performing employees who in turn have the duty to pass on the performance-oriented culture to recruits. However, among all other harvesting strategies that SMEs do prefer, the IPO was not one of them. The reason could be that SMEs are still battling with issues related to entity control and autonomy.

Author details

Herring Shava
Department of Business Management, Faculty of Management and Commerce, University of Fort Hare, Alice, South Africa

*Address all correspondence to: herringshava@gmail.com

References

[1] Meyer N, Hamilton L. Female entrepreneurs' business training and its effect on various entrepreneurial factors: Evidence from a developing country. International Journal of Economics and Finance Studies. 2020;**12**(1):135-151

[2] Ahmed T, Chandran VG, Klobas JE, Liñán F, Kokkalis P. Entrepreneurship education programmes: How learning, inspiration and resources affect intentions for new venture creation in a developing economy. The International Journal of Management Education. 2020;**18**(1):100327

[3] Maziriri ET, Chivandi A. Modelling key predictors that stimulate the entrepreneurial performance of small and medium-sized enterprises (SMEs) and poverty reduction: Perspectives from SME managers in an emerging economy. Acta Commercii. 2020;**20**(1):1-5

[4] van Rooyen D, Van Zyl JH. The role of the business environment in harvesting strategies. The Southern African Journal of Entrepreneurship and Small Business Management. 2010;**3**(1):16-31

[5] DeTienne DR. Entrepreneurial exit as a critical component of the entrepreneurial process: Theoretical development. Journal of Business Venturing. 2010;**25**(2):203-215

[6] Nieman G, Nieuwenhuizen C. Entrepreneurship, a South African Perspective. 2nd ed. Pretoria: Van Schaik Publishers; 2019

[7] Houck TE. The great escape. Accounting Today. October 2008. p. 32

[8] Flanagan C. Help small business customers develop an exit strategy. North Western Financial Review. January 2009;7:5

[9] Chaniwa M, Nyawenze C, Mandumbu R, Mutsiveri G, Gadzirayi CT, Munyati VT, et al. Ending poverty through affordable credit to small-scale cotton farmers: The case of the cotton company of Zimbabwe. In: Scaling up SDGs Implementation 2020. Cham: Springer; 2020. pp. 115-127

[10] Elouadi S. The promotion of partnership value through employee share ownership and customer share ownership. In: Corporate Governance Models and Applications in Developing Economies. Hershey PA, USA: IGI Global; 2020. pp. 192-204

[11] Honjo Y. Public or perish? From founding to initial public offering. Review of Managerial Science. 2020;**20**:1-38

[12] Souitaris V, Zerbinati S, Peng B, Shepherd D. Should I stay or should I go? Founder power and exit via initial public offering. Academy of Management Journal. 2020;**63**(1):64-95

[13] Mantravadi DP, Reddy AV. Post-merger performance of acquiring firms from different industries in India. International Research Journal of Finance and Economics. 2008;**22**:192-204

Chapter 3

Domination of Value Creation Networking and Closeness to the Market Dimensions on Entrepreneurial Marketing Behavior: An Analysis from the Perspective of Start-Up Companies and Scale-Up Companies

Christina Whidya Utami and Hendro Susanto

Abstract

The aim of this study is to bridge the gap in literature by studying how far do growth orientation, opportunity orientation, total customer focus, value creation networking, informal market analysis, and closeness to the market dimensions in start-up companies and scale-up companies have impact on entrepreneurial marketing (EM) behavior. Therefore, the goals in this study are: analyzing whether there is any difference in EM behavior for start-up company and scale-up company? The questionnaires were distributed to 406 business owners in Indonesia, spread throughout eight provinces. Start-up companies are companies that have been operating for less than 6 years, and scale-up companies are companies that have been operating for more than 6 years. Snowball sampling was used to select the chosen respondents, using the entire firms in Indonesia, be it services or manufacturing. The result of the study suggests that there is no difference in entrepreneurial marketing behavior between start-up companies and scale-up companies. Value creation networking is shown to be the most dominant dimension for start-up companies in terms of its impact on entrepreneurial marketing behavior, as for scale-up company, the most dominant dimension is closeness to market dimension in its impact on entrepreneurial marketing behavior.

Keywords: entrepreneurial marketing, growth orientation, opportunity orientation, total customer focus, value creation networking, informal market analysis, closeness to the market

1. Introduction

During the development stage, which is around year 1980, there were discussions about the pros and cons of EM [1]. The surfacing of EM was sparked from the critique towards customer centric model in marketing, which caused the lack of innovation and therefore resulted in process and replication of relatively similar products and services, and not very innovative results [2]. For years, EM research was focused on companies; moreover, researchers and practitioners tried to identify the success factors of a company, but were not fully focused on EM problem [3]. In addition, EM domain at the time has not become a developed field of study with established ideas.

Discussion about Entrepreneurial Marketing (EM) surfaced as a marketing practice that can help companies operating in fast changing environments. EM originates from an intercept between marketing and entrepreneurship, and integrates marketing and entrepreneurship through the common concepts that the two fields possess [4]. EM approach can proactively take advantage of innovation and help manage risk as long as marketing process is intended to "create, communicate, and give added value to customers" [5].

Several previous studies identified several characteristics of EM behavior, such as decision making [6], resources decision making and decision based on intuition and experience [7], focus on opportunity recognition, flexible approach on market and exploiting smaller niche market [8]. From initial discussions conducted, there was a phenomenon where EM behavior is proven to be different between companies that have been operating longer (scale-up companies) and start-ups. This conclusion is based on several initial researches that show that startup companies were more successful in implementing entrepreneurial marketing, and scale-up company would also be more successful in implementing entrepreneurial marketing. Despite that, there was still no study that explicitly studied the implementation of EM on scale-up companies compared to start-up companies. Majority of EM studies depended on case study, and as a result, although it gave an overview of the companies' experience in detail, but it could not be generalized to various samples. Several studies conducted previously also tend to be unable to decide on the dimension that is most dominant that would contribute to the entrepreneurial marketing behavior if the researcher decided to research companies with certain characteristics.

Based on the reasons above, researcher will attempt to analyze the difference in entrepreneurial marketing behavior of start-up companies compared to scale-up companies. The unit of this study is companies located in Indonesia, and operating in eight provinces. Start-up company is defined as a company that has been conducting business operation for less than 6 years, whereas scale-up company is a company that has been operating for more than 6 years. Snowball sampling was used to select the respondents with the entirety of firms in Indonesia, be it services or manufacturing, as the population. Furthermore, this study is aimed to bridge the gap in literature by analyzing how far the difference is in the implementation of entrepreneurial marketing behavior between start-up company and scale-up company.

2. Literature review

In the study on EM definition [9], expanded it to a wider version by combining the definition of entrepreneurship and the definition of marketing of American Marketing Association (page 27): EM is an organizational function and a series of processes to create innovation, communicate, and give value to customer and to manage relationship with customer in a way that benefits the organization and its stakeholders, and this can be indicated by innovation, risk taking, proactive, that can be done without the currently existing resources. However in the initial conception, EM was often seen as reactive, not advanced and limited to individual's wants [4, 9, 10]. EM practice is describes as "an entrepreneur's unplanned action, not linear and visionary." Conceptualized EM as "proactive identification and exploitation of opportunities to obtain and maintain customers that is beneficial through innovative approach on risk management, increasing resources, and value creation," a more recent definition proposed in the literature [9, 10]. Researcher realized the two definitions are in accordance with the core concept of EM, and this article focuses on the dimension that underlies both definitions.

Several studies have explored various combinations of EM dimensions. Though fragmented, several researchers collectively formed EM paradigm [11, 12]. Several further studies were conducted by focusing on the understanding of the reciprocal relationship between the main constructs (for example, encouraged opportunity, proactive, focus on innovation, customer intensity, risk management, resource development and value creation) of Entrepreneurial Marketing. EM scale recently developed and tested it for convergent, discriminant and nominative validity. The latest development shows that EM is a multidimensional construct [9].

Therefore, based on the results of various studies, it can be suggested that EM dimensions are as follows: growth orientation, opportunity orientation, total customer focus, value creation networking, informal market analysis, and closeness to the market whereby each EM dimension will be explained briefly below.

EM is often linked with growth. Entrepreneur marketers often have long term goal in their marketing activity and aim to generate sales growth through long term relationship. Marketer's ambition to grow the company will eventually determine the company's business model, competitive strategy and resource management. To grow, marketers adopt several ways to grow their business, including increasing repeated business and creating a community of customers who are dedicated and loyal to the product. Several researchers suggested that on EM characteristic dimension is encouraging growth in the identified target market.

EM puts emphasis on pursuing opportunities, regardless of consideration to the existing resources. Marketers respond to the opportunities that arise by improvising and allocating their resources [13]. Even though opportunities can arise randomly, but EM is known to be proactive and to always look for new opportunities. Entrepreneurial marketers are able to see and have the willingness to be a pioneer in serving unfulfilled needs and capturing arising opportunities before their competitors. Therefore, innovation and creativity are important processes that help EM to change opportunity to reality. Companies that adopt EM often focus on creating new product category and directing their customer to respond to the result of company's innovation continuously [14]. Innovation is to be understood not only limited to the product or service, but also including the process or marketing strategy.

EM make their customers their main priority and treat customers as active participants in their marketing decision making process. Marketers integrated their customers to their operation and accept regularly recommendations from customers. Customers' preference directly plays an important role in determining product approach, price, distribution, and communication of a company. In order to follow the change, EM behavior prioritizes customers' preference, using very focused, flexible approach that can be adjusted to the market [4, 13]. They are willing to make new promises to customers, modify their product design and change price to give the most satisfactory product or service for the customers.

Value creation through networking is an important concept in EM. EM collects market information and gain access to potential customer through their network.

The information from network is also what's helping marketer to give product with the best quality to the customers, and to create a competitive advantage compared to the competitors [15]. Resources from network can help companies to manage their risks and allocate their resources more efficiently. This is especially applicable to small companies with marketing activities that are usually limited by their lack of resources. Note that entrepreneurial marketer's network is not limited to suppliers and customers, but also including competitors.

Entrepreneurial marketers often follow their intuition when making marketing decision and consider intuitive assessment as a very important part in assessing market potential [16]. Marketing decision under EM does not always depend on formal planning process. Company's marketing strategy can also appear and adjusted during implementation. Marketers have the tendency to not conduct formal market research since they believe that they gain intuitive understanding that is rich about the market through their constant contact with the customers. By taking into consideration customers' perception during the interaction, marketer can gain valuable market information and identify appropriate market opportunity.

EM often have decision-making process that is tightly related to the customer. They make decisions based on customer's feedback or information that they gain during the direct interaction or face-to-face conversation with the customer. Through relationship with suppliers and trade partners, marketers can gather information about the market and customer's change in preference. This information enables them to more effectively implement marketing strategy and communication. Several EM rely on experience when making decision about new product and service because they believe that experience helps make competent marketing decision.

Previous entrepreneurial studies consider 6 years or less as the conventional operational definition of start-up companies [17, 18]. This research also explored the validity of the results using different cut off, whereby the company has been operating for 6 or 7 years, but it did not make any difference. This further ensures that the cut off for start-up companies operating for 6 years has a strong judgment (**Figure 1**).

The relationship between EM and company's characteristic needs to be explored, two hypotheses about the relationship between the practice of EM in company and characteristic was beginning to be developed. Considering entrepreneurial behavior is often found in small companies, start-up companies and scale-up companies, this research studies the relationship between the practice of EM and company's characteristic, which is the operating age of the company. In the context of EM practices being related to company's age, several researchers admitted that company's age has significant impact towards the strategy and performance of the company [19]. Previous studies stated that entrepreneurial process usually happens at the beginning stages of company development [20]. Several studies have also provided evidence that shows that start-up companies have several characteristics that enables it to be more entrepreneurial than scale-up companies. Start-up companies are not limited by certain structures and routines that prevents them from thinking creatively. As a result, they can use their resources more innovatively and make more innovation. Several studies also found that start-up companies have slight advantage compared to scale-up companies in exploring new technology [21], and that start-up companies tend to have more innovation activities compared to scale-up companies. The lack of routine also enables start-up company to react more readily to rising market opportunity in unknown region better than scale-up companies. In a study, start-up company can make use of their knowledge from the international market and expand their business through the launch of new product or service, whereby scale-up companies are unable to do that [22]. For companies at

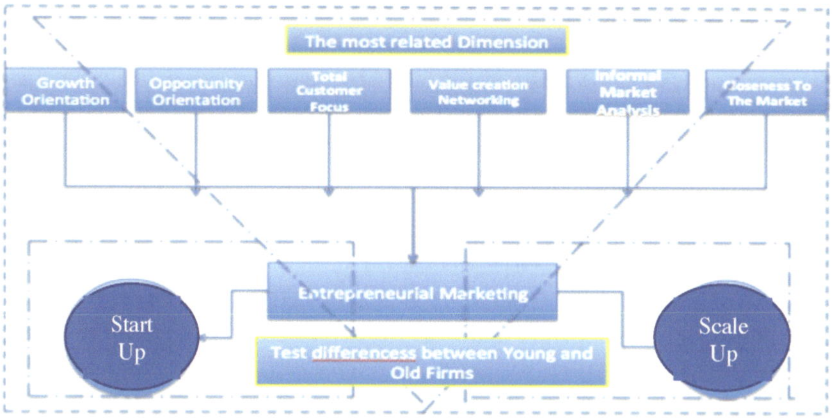

Figure 1.
Conceptual model. Source: Christina [1].

the beginning of the life stages (start-up), they do have a very well-defined knowledge management process. Start-up companies are more informal in their planning and marketing analysis [23] and often improvise to make or implement a solution [24]. Improvisation enables them to be more customer oriented by adjusting their product/service rapidly based on customer's preference and by using innovative marketing strategy that might not be thought up of by scale-up companies. Start-up companies emphasize more on network creation and relationship through using more of information from their network compared to scale-up companies. Network and alliances help companies to plant themselves in their market and gather important market information through direct interaction with their customers. Researchers believe that network not only helps start-up companies identify new market opportunities, but also helps them to survive [25]. This might be the reason why start-up companies are able to grow in small market and in environments that do not require wide production asset [26]. Based on the discussion from the studies, therefore the hypotheses are as follows:

H1. Start-up companies have higher entrepreneurial marketing behavior than scale-up companies.

H2. Value creation networking will be the dominant dimension in start-up companies and scale-up companies.

3. Research methodology

This research used quantitative approach, since it examined the significance of EM dimension in determining the dominant dimension among start-up companies and scale-up companies. In quantitative approach, the study uses rationalization process of a phenomenon that occurred and measured the variable (indicator variable) that is being studied, and would subsequently try to make a generalized conclusion. The population of the study is companies in eight provinces in Indonesia. Snowball sampling was used to select the chosen respondents. Questionnaires were distributed to national sample from 406 business owners in Indonesia, spread throughout eight provinces. Start-up companies are companies that have been operating for less than 6 years, whereas scale-up companies are companies that have been operating for more than 6 years. The analysis technique to test the hypotheses proposed is by the use of multiple regression analysis and t-test difference test.

4. Variable identification

The dependent variable in this study is EM behavior, measured using 6 questions. Five points Likert scale is used as follows: agree, slightly agree, disagree, slightly disagree, and strongly disagree. The independent variables are categorized according to the EM dimensions, which are growth orientation, closeness to the market, value creation networking and informal market analysis, each measured through three questions, as for opportunity orientation and total customer focus are each measured through four questions (**Figure 2**).

From the sample of 406 companies there are 185 (45.56%) start-up companies and 221 (54.43%) scale-up companies that were the respondents. In terms of the company asset, there are 23% companies with asset between 200 and 500 million, 37% companies with assets more than 500 million to 10 billion, and 40% companies with assets more than 10 billion. The sample characteristics are based on the type of industries as follows: 3% service, 10% manufacturing, 3% real estate, 7% retail, 3% health tools industry, 3% biotechnology, 3% sugar refination, 3% property, 3% food and beverage, 3% retail houseware, 3% coffee processing, 3% trading company, 3% hospitality, 7% freight forwarding and logistic, 3% fishery, 7% batik industry, 3% paint company, 3% agency, 7% furniture, 10% digital industry, and 7% branding and graphic design.

All 406 companies have launched new product or service in their business with details as follows: 58% of the companies have launched new product or service in its business within ≤2 years, 26% of the companies have launched a new product or service within 2.5 ≤ 5 years, 13% of the companies have launched a new product or service within 5.5 ≤ 10 years and 2% of the companies have launched a new product or service within ≤10.5 tahun. Therefore, more than half of the sample has launched new product or service in less than 2 years. A total of 96% of the sample agreed and strongly agreed to appreciate process related to innovation and only 4% slightly disagreed or disagreed with innovation process.

In addition, below is the observation of respondents' answers for each of the questionnaires questions that can be seen in **Table 1** as follows:

Almost all responses from respondents for all questions have the mean of above 4, only the mean for the answers to opportunity orientation dimension question, which is "Our marketing effort leads the customer, and not to respond" and the three questions for all dimensions of informal analysis dimension that have answers mean between 3 and 3.5, which are "Introducing new product or service usually only involves limited research and formal market analysis," "Our marketing decisions are based more on informal customer feedback rather than formal market research," "It is important to rely on intuition when making marketing decision."

Figure 2.
Research model. Source: Christina [1].

Code	Question	Mean	Std. deviation
G1	Long term growth is more important than immediate gain	4.5	0.7593
G2	Our main purpose is to grow the business	4.633	0.5405
G3	We aggressively try to expand our customer base	4.1601	0.9514
O1	We keep searching for new business opportunities	4.4113	0.73419
O2	Our marketing effort leads the customer, and not to respond	3.4704	1.33809
O3	Adding innovative product or service is very important to our success	4.5	0.73954
O4	Creativity stimulates good marketing decision	4.5739	0.65032
T1	Majority of our marketing decisions is based on what we learnt from daily contact with the customers	4.2833	0.80189
T2	Our customers require us to act flexibly and according to their specific needs	4.0739	0.97851
T3	Everyone in this company make customers their main priority	4.5123	0.71912
T4	We adjust ourselves quickly to fulfill our customers' everchanging expectations	4.4532	0.67515
V1	We learn from our competitors	4.4039	0.81612
V2	We use our friends and main industry partners extensively to help us in developing and marketing our products and services	4.2931	0.86084
V3	Majority of our marketing decisions is based on information exchange with people in our personal and professional network	4.1897	0.81103
I1	Introducing new product or service usually only involves limited research and formal market analysis	3.1059	1.41635
I2	Our marketing decisions are based more on informal customer feedback rather than formal market research	3.4631	1.16634
I3	It is important to rely on intuition when making marketing decision	3.2217	1.25122
C1	Customer demands are usually the reason why we introduce new product and/ or service	4.9012	0.90122
C2	We usually introduce new product and service based on the recommendation from our suppliers	4.9831	0.98316
C3	We highly rely on experience when making marketing decision	4.7436	0.74367
EM1	Growth orientation is an important factor in building business success	4.5148	0.63131
EM2	Opportunity orientation is an important factor in building business success	4.4852	0.60739
EM3	Total customer focus is an important factor in building business success	4.5	0.63148
EM4	**Value Creation Through Networking** is an important factor in building business success	4.5	0.67678
EM5	**Informal Market Analysis** is an important factor in building business success	4.3374	0.67909
EM6	**Closeness To The Market** is an important factor in building business success	4.4113	0.71372

Source: data processing, 2020.

Table 1.
Mean and standard deviation of respondents' answers.

5. Analysis and discussion

5.1 Validity and reliability test

Validity test using Pearson correlations shows that the value of calculated r is > table r, based on the significance test 0.01 (two-tailed), which means that the items above are valid. As for the reliability test, it was conducted using Cronbach's alpha that shows value of 0.876, higher than 0.6 which means that it is reliable, that the instrument used in the study to obtain information used can be relied on as a tool to collect data and can reveal actual information in the field.

5.2 Hypothesis testing

t-Test differences test is used to prove that there is a difference in the entrepreneurial marketing behavior between start-up and scale-up companies, based on **Tables 2** and **3** as follows.

Table 2 shows that there are 185 (45.56%) start-up companies and 221 (54.43%) scale-up companies as respondents, with mean of 4.45 for start-up companies and mean of 4.45 for scale-up companies. The standard deviations for the two are 0.51 and 0.47 respectively, which indicates that the respondents' responses tend to be homogeneous.

Table 3 shows EM differences test analysis for companies managed by founders and companies managed by professionals by using Levene's test in independent t-test. Sig value (two-tailed) or p value. In the test below the p value is 0.96, whereby it is >0.05. Since it is >0.05, then there is no statistically meaningful or significant difference between entrepreneurial marketing behavior of start-up companies and scale-up companies on the 0.05 probability level.

As for **Tables 4–6**, multiple regression tests were conducted to analyze whether the six dimensions have significant impact on entrepreneurial marketing behavior of start-up companies compared to scale-up companies.

According to **Table 4**, R value is 0.767 and R square value is 0.588 for start-up companies, and as for scale-up companies, the R is 0.606 and the R square is 0.444, which suggests that the percentage contribution of the independent variables (which are: growth orientation, opportunity orientation, total customer focus, value creation networking, informal market analysis, and closeness to the market) on EM behavior is 58.8% for start-up companies and 37.0% for scale-up companies.

According to **Table 5**, it shows that the significance is 0.000 be it for start-up companies and also for scale-up companies, which means that there is a significant impact of growth orientation, opportunity orientation, total customer focus, value creation networking, informal market analysis, and closeness to the market simultaneously on EM behavior of start-up companies and also for scale-up companies.

According to **Table 6**, it can be analyzed that the six dimensions have significant impact on entrepreneurial marketing behavior. For start-up companies, there are only two dimensions that are significant, which are opportunity orientation and value creation networking. As for scale-up companies, all dimensions are

	Start_Scale		Mean	Std. deviation	Std. error mean
Antremark2	Start-up	185	4.4595	0.51224	0.03766
	Scale-up	221	4.457	0.47518	0.03196

Table 2.
Group statistic.

		Levene's test for equality of variance								
		F	**Sig**	**t**	**df**	**Sig. (2-tailed)**	**Mean difference**	**Std. error difference**	**95% confidence interval of the difference**	
									Lower	**Upper**
Entre mark2	Equal variance assume of	2.763	0.097	0.05	404	0.96	0.00245	0.04907	−0.09402	0.09891
	Equal variance assume of			0.05	379.758	0.961	0.00245	0.0494	−0.09468	0.09957

Table 3.
T-test difference testing.

Model	R	R square	Adjusted R square	Std. error of the estimate
Young (<6 years)	0.767	0.588	0.579	0.33896
Old (>6 years)	0.608	0.370	0.352	0.38244

Table 4.
Model summary.

Type of companies		Sum of squares	df	Mean square	F	Sig.
Young (start-up)	Regression	36.250	6	6.042	89.404	0.000
	Residual	12.029	178	0.068		
	Total	48.279	184			
Old (scale-up)	Regression	18.376	6	3.063	20.940	0.000
	Residual	31.299	214	0.146		
	Total	49.675	220			

Table 5.
ANOVA.

Type of companies	Unstandardized coefficients	Std. error	Standardized coefficients	t	Sig.
	B		Beta		
	Young Old	Young Old	Young Old	Young Old	Young Old
(Constant)	0.983	0.164		6.01	0
	1.713	0.311		5.516	0
GrowthOrient1	0.165	0.051	0.194	3.227	0.001
	0.119	0.058	0.142	2.063	0.04
OpportunityOrient2	0.053	0.055	0.061	0.976	0.33
	−0.106	0.055	−0.141	−1.933	0.055
TotasCustFocus3	0.065	0.044	0.087	1.463	0.145
	0.254	0.059	0.268	4.334	0.00
ValueCreationNetwork4	0.46	0.055	0.568	8.352	0.0
	0.178	0.049	0.25	3.669	0
InformalMarketAnalysis5	-0.006	0.025	-0.012	-0.24	0.811
	-0.18	0.031	-0.412	-5.888	0
ClosnessToTheMarket6	0.076	0.102	0.117	0.743	0.459
	0.345	0.063	0.384	5.472	0

Table 6.
Coefficient.

significant, which are growth orientation, opportunity orientation, total customer focus, value creation networking, informal market analysis, and closeness to the market. They are deemed significant because the significance value is smaller than 0.05. Value creation networking variable is the most dominant dimension for start-up companies, with beta value of 0.46, and as for scale-up companies, the most dominant dimension is closeness to the market, with beta value of 0.345.

6. Discussion

The result of the study shows that there is no difference in entrepreneurial marketing behavior between start-up companies and scale-up companies. For both start-up and scale-up companies, value creation networking seems to be the most dominant dimension. For start-up companies, they use difference approach in pursuing their market opportunity. Start-up companies pursue opportunity by relying on speed, flexibility, and ability to satisfy market niche, whereas scale-up companies pursue opportunity by relying on financial resources and human resources [27]. Start-up companies have opportunistic, flexible and innovative marketing decision making process with clear target. Company can improvise and make sudden changes in their decision making pattern when involved with their market. As a result, they have the ability to react rapidly to environmental changes and tend to capture new opportunities at a faster rate than scale-up companies [6, 28]. Start-up companies have less decision makers that dominate compared to scale-up companies. As a result, decision and strategy in start-up companies will be directly impacted by the personal intention of the decision maker [29].

Finally, start-up companies have a more flat organizational structure compared to scale-up companies, and it makes them closer with the customers. Members of the company at all levels in start-up companies have potential to be involved in interactions at individual level and direct face to face interaction with the customers [6]. Also, it is relatively easy for start-up companies to access market information through direct means [30]. As a result, start-up companies have the tendency to invest in creating personal relationship with their main customers to build strong customer contact compared to scale-up companies.

In detail, this research found that start-up companies are more oriented to value creation to build networking in marketing. As for scale-up companies, closeness to the market dimension is shown to be the dimension with the most dominant impact on entrepreneurial behavior.

7. Conclusion

Various studies suggested that the EM behavior is common in start-up companies, and this suggests the assumption that scale-up company type is not suited for Entrepreneurial Marketing. However, this study has systematically found that there is not difference between the entrepreneurial marketing behavior of start-up and scale-up companies. However, it was found that for start-up companies, value creation networking is the most dominant dimension, and as for scale-up companies, closeness to the market dimension is the most dominant dimension.

In the context of EM practices, the findings of this study, which are the characteristics of start-up and scale-up companies, are the right determining factor for EM practices. Therefore, this study gives important theoretical contribution, whereby EM behavior cannot be conceptualized only through the activities of start-up companies and scale-up companies, but should also use other steps that will represent the entrepreneurial level of a company better, such as analyzing the entrepreneurial organization aspect.

This study offers several implications for future studies. Whereby, the result of this study illustrates that start-up companies do not have well defined market or established customer base, therefore they rely less on market demand/market information compared to scale-up companies when introducing new products. These findings suggest that future studies need to analyze how far EM can help in reducing effect of responsibility for newness within the company and to identify the best EM practices that should be adopted by the company so that they can survive in the long run.

Acknowledgement

The research was financially funded by the Ministry of Research, Technology, and Higher Education Directorate General of Research and Development (Kementerian Riset, Teknologi, dan Pendidikan Tinggi Direktorat Jenderal Penguatan Riset dan Pengembangan).

Author details

Christina Whidya Utami* and Hendro Susanto
Ciputra University, Surabaya, Indonesia

*Address all correspondence to: whidyautami@ciputra.ac.id

References

[1] Christina WU, Susanto H. Perilaku entrepreneurial marketing (Sebuah Tinjauan dari Skala Perusahaan). Business and Finance Journal. 2019;**4**(2):93-104. DOI: 10.33086/bfj.v4i2.1365. ISSN: 2527-4872 dan E-ISSN: 2477-393X c

[2] Sheth JN, Newman BI, Gross BL. Why we buy what we buy: A theory of consumption values. Journal of Business Research. 1991;**22**(2):159-170. DOI: 10.1016/0148-2963(91)90050-8

[3] Scott M, Rosa P. Has firm analysis reached its limits? Time for a rethink. International Small Business Journal: Researching Entrepreneurship. 1996;**30**(8):81-89. DOI: 10.1177/02F0266242696144006

[4] Morris M, Schindehutte M, LaForge R. Entrepreneurial marketing: A construct for integrating emerging entrepreneurship and marketing perspectives. Journal of Marketing Theory and Practice. 2002;**10**(4):1-19. DOI: 10.1080/10696679.2002.11501922

[5] Miles MP, Darroch J. Large firms, entrepreneurial marketing processes, and the cycle of competitive advantage. European Journal of Marketing. 2006;**40**(5/6):485-501. DOI: 10.1108/03090560610657804

[6] Carson D, McCartan-Quinn D. Non-practice of theoretically based marketing in small business: Issues arising and their implications. Journal of Marketing Theory and Practice. 1995;**3**(4):24-32. DOI: 10.1080/10696679.1995.11501702

[7] Thomas LC, Painbéni S, Barton H. Entrepreneurial marketing within the French wine industry. International Journal of Entrepreneurial Behavior & Research. 2013;**19**(2):238-260. DOI: 10.1108/13552551311310392

[8] Stasch S. Guerilla marketing in new venture marketing strategies. In: Hills GE, Siu W, Malewicki D, editors. Research at the Marketing/Entrepreneurship Interface. Chicago, IL: University of Illinois at Chicago; 1999. pp. 57-67

[9] Kraus MW, Cote S, Keltner D. Social class, contextualism, and empathic accuracy. Psychological Science. 2010;**21**(11):1716-1723. DOI: 10.1177/2F0956797610387613

[10] Hills GE, Hultman C. Entrepreneurial marketing: Conceptual and empirical research opportunities. Entrepreneurship Research. 2013;**3**(4): 437-448. DOI: 10.1515/erj-2013-0064

[11] Collinson E, Shaw E. Entrepreneurial marketing – A historical perspective on development and practice. Management Decision. 2001;**3**(4):761-766. DOI: 10.1108/EUM0000000006221

[12] Jones R, Rowley J. Entrepreneurial marketing in small businesses: A conceptual exploration. International Small Business Journal. 2011;**29**(1):25-36. DOI: 10.1177/2F0266242610369743

[13] Becherer RC, Haynes PJ, Fletcher LP. Paths to profitability in owner-operated firms: The role of entrepreneurial marketing. Journal of Business and Entrepreneurship. 2006;**43**(1/2):17-31

[14] Hacioglu G, Eren SS, Eren MS, Celikkan H. The effect of entrepreneurial marketing on firms' innovative performance in Turkish SMEs. Social and Behavioral Sciences. 2012;**58**:871-878. DOI: 10.1016/j.sbspro.2012.09.1065

[15] Gilmore A, Carson D, Grant K. SME marketing in practice. Marketing Intelligence & Planning. 2001;**9**(1):6-11. DOI: 10.1108/02634500110363583

[16] Li Y-H, Huang J-W, Tsai M-T. Entrepreneurial orientation and firm performance: The role of knowledge creation process. Industrial Marketing Management. 2009;**38**(4):440-449. DOI: 10.1016/j.indmarman.2008.02.004

[17] Brush CG, Vanderwerf P. A comparison of methods and sources for obtaining estimates of new venture performance. Journal of Business Venturing. 1992;**14**(3):157-170. DOI: 10.1016/0883-9026(92)90010-O

[18] Robinson K, McDougall P. Entry barriers and new venture performance: A comparison of universal and contingency approaches. Strategic Management Journal. 2001;**22**(6/7):659-685. DOI: 10.1002/smj.186

[19] Stinchcombe AL. Social structure and organizations. In: March JG, editor. Handbook of Organizations. Chicago, IL: Rand McNally; 1965. pp. 142-193

[20] Cunningham J, Lischeron J. Defining entrepreneurship. Journal of Small Business Management. 1991;**29**(1):45-61

[21] Nooteboom B, Haverbeke WV, Duysters G, Gilsing V, Van den Oord A. Optimal cognitive distance and absorptive capacity. Research Policy. 2007;**36**(7):1016-1034. DOI: 10.2139/ssrn.903745

[22] Naldi L, Davidsson P. Entrepreneurial growth: The role of international knowledge acquisition as moderated by firm age. Journal of Business Venturing. 2013;**29**(5):687-703. DOI: 10.1016/j.jbusvent.2013.08.003

[23] Covin JG, Slevin DP. New venture strategic posture, structure, and performance: An industry life cycle analysis. Journal of Business Venturing. 1990;**5**(2):123-135. DOI: 10.1016/0883-9026(90)90004-D

[24] Zahra SA, Sapienza HJ, Davidsson P. Entrepreneurship and dynamic capabilities: A review, model and research agenda. Journal of Management Studies. 2006;**43**(4):917-955. DOI: 10.1111/j.1467-6486.2006.00616.x

[25] Watson J. Modeling the relationship between networking and firm performance. Journal of Business Venturing. 2007;**22**(6):852-874. DOI: 10.1016/j.jbusvent.2006.08.001

[26] Katila R, Shane S. When does lack of resources make new firms innovative? Academy of Management Journal. 2005;**48**(5):814-829. DOI: 10.5465/amj.2005.18803924

[27] Dean TJ, Brown RL, Bamford CE. Differences in large and small firm responses to environmental context: Strategic implications from a comparative analysis of business formations. Strategic Management Journal. 1998;**19**(8):709-728. DOI: 10.1002/(SICI)1097-0266(199808)19:8%3C709::AID-SMJ966%3E3.0.CO;2-9

[28] Chen MJ, Hambrick DC. Speed, stealth, and selective attack: How small firms differ from large firms in competitive behavior. Academy of Management Journal. 1995;**38**(2):453-482. DOI: 10.5465/256688

[29] Brush CG, Chaganti R. Businesses without glamour? An analysis of resources on performance by size and age in small service and retail firms. Journal of Business Venturing. 1998;**7(2)**:233-257. DOI: 10.1016/S0883-9026(97)00103-1

[30] Hisrich R. The need for marketing in entrepreneurship. Journal of Business & Industrial Marketing. 1992;7(3):53-57. DOI: 10.1108/08858629210035427

Chapter 4

Measuring a Blended Performance: Managerial Insights from the Field of Impact Entrepreneurship

Irene Bengo, Veronica Chiodo and Valentina Tosi

Abstract

The commitment to generating a blended value is increasingly spreading in the business sector. At the forefront of this movement, impact ventures are organizations born to produce value for the society, i.e. social impact, while engaging in commercial activities to sustain their operations. On the other end, we have observed an increased emphasis on more responsible, sustainable practices that traditional for-profit businesses have been called to establish. Accounting for and reporting on social impact has become increasingly of interest to a range of institutions and sectors, with the result that many competing methodologies, approaches, guidelines and standards have been introduced. The chapter performs a comprehensive review of existing approaches for impact measurement and management implemented by socially-oriented ventures (both not for profit organizations and for-profit businesses) focusing on both methodological, governance and operational barriers and enabling factors of the practices. Then, it drafts a framework which helps any ventures to structure a process and methodology to measure its blended performance. The research not only contributes to the scant literature on impact entrepreneurship but impact ventures might offer a compelling laboratory to disentangle the obstacles posed by the combined achievement of financial and social objectives and how organizations might address these challenges.

Keywords: social impact, performance measurement, blended value, social ventures, social reporting

1. Introduction

The commitment to generating a blended value, which produces positive effects on society alongside economic returns, is spreading in the business sector. Corporations are increasingly asked to produce not only economic but also social value. Recently, Hart and Zingales have promoted this idea, stating that, companies should maximize shareholders welfare, not value [1].

Therefore, on one end, the organization delivering social services has progressively acquired the know-how, tools, and models which usually characterize the business world, leading to the establishment of new enterprises defined as *social ventures* [2]. Social ventures (SVs) are hybrid organizations where their primary aim is to provide solutions to the most wicked problems – such as aging, climate change, refugee's crisis – leveraging on forms of entrepreneurship to sustain their operations

[3]. On the other end, we have observed an increased emphasis on more responsible, sustainable and inclusive practices that traditional for-profit businesses have been called to establish or observe. Companies have started to consider the integration of social and environmental concerns no more as initiatives needed to be compliant with mandatory regulations but as a strategic part of the core business and they are moving from a responsive to a proactive approach [4]. Corporate Social Responsibility (CSR) has shifted from being a side-unit of the company to strategic leverage for the creation of economic value [5].

Within this context, social impact assessment has emerged as an endogenous practice to improve accountability and transparency of a large range of organizations, as well as to enhance communication among various actors, both aspects being essential to foster the growth of the whole sector [6]. Moreover, several contextual elements are raising the need to include the practice of measuring social impact in the organizations' operations: the attempt of public administrations to reengineer their procurement schemes according to the outcome-based paradigm; diffusion of evidence-based practices in philanthropy as well as in public policies; the emergence of the so-called social impact finance; and national governments are bringing in guidelines for measuring social impact [7]. Therefore, these elements increase the urgency for organizations to quantify and make explicit the social value generated. Indeed, social impact measurement and reporting can be strategic to improve their performance, access resources, and build organizational legitimacy.

Standards for measuring social value are still underdeveloped to date [8]. In fact, during the years, a large number of approaches, methods, frameworks and tools have been developed as an attempt to meet the diverse information needs of stakeholders in the sector. This ongoing proliferation of models is due to the fact the term social impact describes a very heterogenous array of effects on several users, different scales and type of activities [9].

However, such heterogeneity in approaches has not yet been fully systematized [10] and there is still an open debate on whether and how to find a common standard on social impact measurement. Those supporting the idea of a *golden standard*, used by all the organizations and harmonized among countries, state that it would allow the comparability of results and support the development of this domain. On the other end, the skeptical claim that this standard would lead to an excessive simplification losing the true soul of the social impact they try to measure. This would be detrimental for the sector because it raises the risk of the so-called *purpose washing* [11], namely when a business or financial institution claims to be impact-oriented without having any substantive social or environmental effects but just to leverage the momentum of the phenomenon for marketing purposes. Instead, they posit a transaction-based approach (a custom method and KPIs for each deal) is the most appropriate way to measure the real social changes an organization produces. However, this customized effort very often requires an organization to design a measurement infrastructure and gather specialized data from scratch. Therefore, specialized expertise is needed and this makes impact measurement and management very costly and time consuming especially for small impact ventures already operating in a resource-constraint environment.

Against this lack of a prevalent approach, organizations have many difficulties to surf this huge pool of methods, metrics, framework and processes.

Therefore, the purpose of this paper is to analyze existing practices of social impact measurement, with a specific focus on emerging ones, and discuss their characteristics. To this aim, we performed a broad review of academic and gray literature that focuses on social impact measurement and searched existing databases collecting relevant practices in the field. Based on the analysis of specific dimensions, we formulated a conceptual framework to provide a more clearly articulated view of the state of this domain and highlight the evolving trends to support organization approaching this practice to find their way.

2. Literature review

The goal of fulfilling a social mission raises the question of how the impact that these organizations have on society should be assessed to understand if and how they are achieving their objectives and contributing to the well-being of society. Moreover, enterprises blended social and business logics have multiple stakeholders to account to, raising the quest for transparency and accountability [12, 13].

First, the definition of what social impact means is still controversial and differently translated based on the domain it is applied [14].

Scholars have also used terminology such as social value [15, 16], social performance [17, 18], social returns [19] to express similar concepts. Different definitions could be found in literature as:

> *"Social Impact Assessment includes the processes of analysing, monitoring and managing the intended and unintended social consequences, both positive and negative, of planned interventions (policies, programs, plans, projects) and any social change processes invoked by those interventions." [20], p. 5*

> *"Impact only if it increases the quantity or quality of the enterprise's social outcomes beyond what would otherwise have occurred." [21], p. 1*

> *"The process of transforming patterns of thought, behavior, social relationships, institutions, and social structure to generate beneficial outcomes for individuals, communities, organizations, society, and/or the environment beyond the benefits for the instigators of such transformations." [22], p. 1252.*

In this paper, we use a broad conceptualization of social impact to include considerations on the organizations' capacity to deliver social and environmental value and of specific methods to measure it.

Concerning social impact measurement, a comprehensive review of the literature indicates two historical trends: one addressing *social accounting* and *audit*, and the other on *social impact assessment* [23]. Social accounting and audit is defined as "a systematic analysis of the effects of an organization on its communities of interest or stakeholders" [24], p. 309 and has become a commonly used label for what has been named, among others, *corporate social reporting* or *social responsibility accounting* [25]. Essentially, it includes reporting on an organization's social activities, environmental impact, interactions with the employees, the community, customers and other stakeholders and, possibly, their consequences [26]. Social impact assessment "includes the processes of analysing, monitoring and managing the intended and unintended social consequences, both positive and negative, of planned interventions (policies, programs, projects) and any social change processes invoked by those interventions." [27], p. 5. [9], p. 1174 stressed that assessing social impact consists of "providing evidence that an organization is providing a real and tangible benefit to the community or the environment".

The field has grown to use a diverse terminology to indicate slightly differing approaches within the same field, including *impact assessment*, *impact measurement*, *outcome measurement*, *performance evaluation*, *performance measurement*, *social accounting*, *social and environmental reporting*, *social impact measurement*, *social performance*, and, *triple bottom line reporting*. These terms typically cover a range of approaches that have their roots in program evaluation and performance measurement in the public and non-profit sectors [28].

More recently, in a seminal article on the Stanford Social Innovation Review, [29], p. 6 stressed the fact that "an impact evaluation should help determine why something works, not merely whether it works."

We use the terms social impact measurement in the manner employed by [30], to encompass the broad range of practices adopted by an organization to measure its progress towards its social goals.

Measuring social impact is crucial for many reasons. Lall [31] distinguishes between two fundamental factors: external, or *measuring to prove*, and internal, or *measuring to improve*.

On one end, the measurement process is thought to be capable to improve an organization's performance, because it allows a deep understanding of how to best allocate resources and efforts to maximize social outcomes. On the other end, the practice of social impact assessment may be seen as the process of providing validated evidence that the organization is generating a real and tangible benefit to the community or the environment [9]. [31, 32] also observe that the purpose and perceptions of impact measurement in impact investing processes actually change from legitimacy to learning in the course of time. Whereas [33] underlined that investor-investee relationships negotiated through the impact measurement process are generating a new set of impact measurement practices, which are relational and non-transactional in nature with an evolving and ongoing learning process for both. Trends in corporate sustainability have further enhanced the emphasis on impact measurement needs.

Therefore, social impact measurement and reporting are considered to be strategic to improve performance of the organization, access resources, and build organizational legitimacy [34].

However, the lack of a well-established framework for social and environmental accountability may prevent organizations, and particularly social ventures, to operate at their best capacity in the economy. In fact, the absence of reliable metrics may limit the investors' willingness to provide funding to the enterprise, due to the fact that they may not be able to make informed decisions on how to channel their funding in the most effective way to generate social value [6]. Moreover, the lack of a consolidated measurement system may be detrimental for the organization's management which may not have adequate information to support effective decision making and maximize social outcomes [32].

In recent years, there has been considerable progress in developing measurement and evaluation methods with numerous approaches being developed at the practitioners' level and a prominent role being played by foundations and impact investors [30]. Indeed, attention to impact has been often driven by funders who want to know whether their financial resources are making a difference on society, and the growing field of responsible, sustainable and impact investing has highly contributed to developments in this area. Other practitioners such as social analysts and managers of social ventures have also repeatedly tried to develop an appropriate framework for measuring and comparing social value creation [35].

Despite, the practice of social impact measurement has evolved quite rapidly in the last decades, scientific research has lagged behind. Therefore, a proper theorization of how to measure and compare the results of social value creation processes is still missing in the academic community [36]. The most sophisticated approaches in impact evaluation are experimental and quasi-experimental research designs, such as randomized control trials (RCTs) or the difference-in-differences technique have been rarely employed (e.g., [37, 38]). On the other hand, some of the most consolidated approaches have been developed by practitioners. For example, the

Balanced Scorecard [39] was initially developed for corporates and it has been adapted for the non-profit and the social enterprise sectors [40]; the Social Return on Investment (SROI) has been widely used by a large range of actors [41]. The impact investors' community, especially in the United States, has widely adopted the Impact Reporting and Investment Standards (now IRIS+) developed by the Global Impact Investing Network (GIIN) to report on the impact of their investment in the sector. In the business world, a lot of companies have started to assess their social impact through the B Impact Assessment developed by B Lab, to obtain the B Corp certification. Simultaneously, sustainability and Environmental, Social, and Governance (ESG) accounting practices for businesses have been largely shaped by the Global Reporting Initiative (GRI) and the Sustainability Accounting Standards Board (SASB). These few examples clearly highlight how the various perspectives of organizations in the sector resulted in an increasing number of models being developed but a comprehensive and systematic vie of them has not been yet developed.

3. Methodology

3.1 Data collection

The chapter performs a review of the existing social impact measurement models through data collected on secondary sources.

The practice of social impact measurement, as already underlined, is still emerging and very dynamic therefore we built our database from scratch merging different sources.

To select the models to be included in the analysis, we performed a search through Scopus and Google Scholar to search for the academic papers in the last five years that performed a review of approaches or described one single, well defined, method specific to measure social impact. We also carried out desk research of gray literature to find practitioner reports illustrating specific approaches, guidelines, tools and metrics to assess social and environmental impact. The search used the keywords listed in **Table 1**.

The process yielded to 647 academic papers published between 2016 and 2020, and 123 practitioner reports. To further ensure the relevance of our sample, we reviewed the abstracts and excluded documents that did not discuss the measurement of social or environmental impact. From the documents, we identified 116 social impact measurement models. We excluded from the selection of those models that were either found to no longer be used or those that were not consistent with the objectives of our research. The most robust attempts to classify existing social impact measurement models used are [6, 9, 42] from which we identified 63 models (10 of them were no longer in use and were therefore excluded by the analysis). The other relevant a cluster of sources were papers and report belonging to the domain of social impact investing. For example, the [43] 12 modes as the most spread among social impact investors. Lastly, the analysis includes different efforts implemented by the corporate sector to measure ESG performance, sustainability and social responsibility.

Table 7 (in the Appendix) outlines all the identified models and which type of organizations generated the social impact measured by the specific model.

3.2 Data analysis

After selecting the sample, we identified a number of variables through which we classified the models relying on previous studies. The dimensions used in the

Keywords	
Social impact measurement	Social return evaluation
Social impact assessment	Social return metrics
Social impact evaluation	Impact investing measurement
Social impact metrics	Impact investing assessment
Social performance measurement	Impact investing evaluation
Social performance assessment	Impact investing metrics
Social performance evaluation	ESG assessment
Social performance metrics	ESG standard assessment
Nonfinancial performance measurement	ESG assessment framework
Nonfinancial performance assessment	ESG rating
Nonfinancial performance evaluation	ESG measurement
Nonfinancial performance metrics	ESG evaluation
Social return measurement	ESG certification
Social return assessment	ESG label

Table 1.
Keywords.

	Description
Type [44]	
Method	Provide a specific procedure to perform the measurement, often through a step-by-step approach. These are able to guide the organization conducting the evaluation all the way to a final result.
Framework	Provide a way for organizations to think about, design, plan, implement and embed performance measurement into a project, program or organization as a whole. They do not prescribe a particular method or indicators to use to assess social impact or performance
Dashboard	Dashboards provide a predefined "set of indicators and metrics to cover different performance dimensions, that are considered representative of the results of the organization" [6], p. 13
Set of metrics	Databases or catalogs of indicators to be chosen and used autonomously by the evaluator, but they do not include any specific consideration on how to implement the measurement process.
Driver [45]	
External	Approaches developed or used to serve the needs of internal stakeholders and primarily decision-makers within the organization.
Internal	The latter identifies those approaches, which are used to support a transparent reporting process towards external stakeholders.
External; internal	
Purpose of the measurement [46, 47]	
Accountability	Approaches intended to achieve transparency towards stakeholder through dedicated reporting and disclosure.

	Description
Assess strengths and weaknesses	Focus on assessing the organization's structural and operational capacity to deliver social impact, without evaluating specific end results.
Measure approach effectiveness	Models which have been explicitly developed to measure the effectiveness of a specific programmatic or sectoral approach (e.g. in the case of microfinance at its beginning).
Performance measurement	Approaches that have as primary objective to assess how well the organization, program or project is achieving its social or environmental results.
Performance improvement	Approaches which, in addition to the purpose of assessing results, are used to make the organization, program or project more effective.
Portfolio management	Support the investment process of capital providers (i.e. funders, investors, etc.) when evaluating investment opportunities and allocating funding.
Scope [48]	
Sectoral	Measurement approaches can be developed with a specific sectoral scope or they can be used for evaluating results in multiple sectors.
Multi-sectoral	
Target stakeholder of the measurement process [45]	
Managers	This category identifies the main type of stakeholder which will use the results of the evaluation. The category "Sector Stakeholders" refers to those cases where there is no specific focus on a single category of stakeholders.
Funders/investors	
Sector stakeholders	
Public administrations	
Others	

Table 2.
Dimensions and categories.

analysis are listed in **Table 2**. The categories identified for each dimension have been used to conduct a coding analysis of documents, websites and academic articles describing the approaches. Therefore, the approach was then assigned to one or more category of each dimension. Lastly, a frequency analysis was conducted for each variable included, aiming to have a better understanding of the characteristics of the approaches under study.

4. A decision-making framework for social impact measurement

4.1 Results of the frequency analysis

The analysis conducted identified 126 approaches to impact measurement developed over time by academia and practitioners in the sector. Among these, 10 were found to be no longer in use and were therefore excluded from the sample. A frequency analysis was conducted for each variable discussed in the methodology, aiming to have a better understanding of the characteristics of the approaches under study. Findings are shown in **Table 3**.

Most of the identified approaches were Methods, followed by frameworks (20,7%) and dashboards (20,7%) still representing a large part of the sample. Finally, 6 sets of metrics (5,2%) were identified. Concerning the driver of the

Variable	Value	Frequency (%)
Type	.	
Method	62	53.4
Framework	24	20.7
Dashboard	24	20.7
Set of metrics	6	5.2
Driver		
Internal	31	26.7
Externa	65	56.1
Internal; external	20	17.2
Purpose		
Accountability	22	19
Assess strengths and weaknesses	7	6
Measure approach effectiveness	5	4.3
Performance measurement	42	36.2
Performance improvement	12	10.3
Portfolio management	53	45.7
Scope		
Sectoral	18	15.5
Multi-sectoral	98	84.5
Thematic	28	24.1
ESG	21	75
Employees	1	3.6
Environment	3	10.7
Sustainability	3	10.7
Target audience		
Managers	28	24.1
Funders and investors	66	56.9
Sector stakeholders	24	20.7
Public administrations	2	1.7
Others	1	0.9

Table 3.
Frequency analysis.

measurement, most models analyzed have a primarily external focus (56%), while 26,7% have an internal focus. Some models are suited to serve both internal and external interests (17,2%). With respect to the ultimate purpose of the measurement approach, most models were designed to support portfolio management (45,7%), performance measurement efforts (36,2%) or accountability (19%). Some were particularly suited to support performance improvement (10,3%), assess organizational strengths and weaknesses (6%) or measure the effectiveness of a specific programmatic or sectoral approach (4,3%). Clearly, some models were able to respond to multiple purposes and were therefore present in more than one category. Most of the models analyzed have a multi-sectoral scope (84,5%), while only 15,5% of the models in the sample have a specific sectoral focus. As far as the target audience is concerned, we found that most models were structured to inform funders and investors (56,9%) or managers (24,1%). A large part of the sample was targeted at general sector stakeholders (20,7%), while one model was aimed at informing other categories of stakeholders such as the organization's staff or customers.

After reviewing the distribution of the sample within the categories identified on the basis of our conceptualization, we suggest that an organization should consider what to measure (the *unit of analysis of the measurement process*) or for whom to measure (the target audience). Therefore, an organization approaches the measurement practice might consider which its main unit of analysis of the measurement and building on this to identify the other features fitting to the process. Therefore, we set these two variables as the main driver of the analysis and we investigated how they interact with the other categories interact (**Tables 4** and 5).

Referring to activities *Social Ventures* as the main unit of analysis, the organization can mostly rely on specific procedure able to guide the organization conducting the evaluation all the way to a final result. The method might help in the managing performance of the organization, functioning as a decision-making tool. Indeed, the main purpose of the identified approaches is performance measurement, followed by portfolio management in case the organizations, is an investor. It is interesting that very few approaches are seen as an accountability tool or enable them to reach a deep level of analysis to really improve the performance of the organization. Almost all the approaches are multi-sectoral and they mainly target investors and managers of the organization. Interestingly, the same holds once we consider *For-profit Companies*; the only crucial difference is that the prevalent target audience is the managers of the organizations and no more investors.

The third category we analyzed is Investors. In this case, we see a greater number of dashboards in the Type of approach, supporting the idea that they favor synthetic measures. The main driver of measurement is to serve internal stakeholders and in particular, we see from the prevalent purpose that is Portfolio management that it is used by investment managers to assess the performance of their portfolio to make the allocation of capital more efficient.

Lastly, the analysis reveals a low presence of approaches considering the social impact of policy.

Once we read the frequency analysis using the Type of approach as the main lens (**Table 5**), we can notice that Method and Dashboards are mostly used to produce information targeting external stakeholders; while, Frameworks, helping organizations to think about, design, plan, implement and embed performance measurement into a project, program or organization as a whole and Set of metrics are meant for internal stakeholders. Considering the scope, for performance measurement, Frameworks are the most appropriate; both Methods and Dashboards are mostly used for portfolio management. Set of metrics and Dashboards should be considered reporting and disclosure.

Lastly, we can consider the audience the social impact measurement approaches are supposed to target (**Table 6**). Social impact measurement targeting the managers and other internal stakeholders is mainly used as a decision making instrument to improve the performance; once, the target is the financiers, the analysis confirms that about half of the approaches are used for portfolio managers followed by performance measurement. Few of the approaches are then really used to provide information to other relevant external stakeholders in the forms of social reporting or other types of disclosure.

	Unit of analysis of the measurement process							
	Social ventures		For-profit companies		Investors		Public institutions	
	Value	(%)	Value	(%)	Value	(%)	Value	(%)
Type								
Method	27	23.3	25	21.6	20	17.2	2	1.7
Framework	14	12.1	10	8.6	4	3.4	—	—
Dashboard	8	6.9	12	10.3	8	6.9	—	—
Set of metrics	2	1.7	5	4.3	1	0.9	—	—
Driver								
External	28	24.1	29	25	19	16.4	2	1.7
Internal	17	14.7	10	8.6	6	5.2	—	—
External; internal	5	4.3	13	11.2	8	6.9	—	—
Purpose								
Accountability	9	7.8	11	9.5	4	3.4	—	—
Assess strengths and weaknesses	3	2.6	2	1.7	2	1.7	—	—
Measure approach effectiveness	2	1.7	—	—	1	0.9	—	—
Performance measurement	24	20.7	17	14.7	11	9.5	1	0.9
Performance improvement	9	7.8	5	4.3	1	0.9	—	—
Portfolio management	16	13.8	27	23.3	22	19	1	0.9
Scope								
Sectoral	6	5.2	3	2.6	12	10.3	1	0.9
Multi-sectoral	44	37.9	49	42.2	21	18.1	1	0.9
Target audience								
Managers	17	14.7	10	8.6	4	3.4	—	—
Funders/investors	22	19	34	29.3	25	21.6	1	0.9
Sector stakeholders	10	8.6	12	10.3	4	3.4	1	0.9
Public administrations	2	1.7	—	—	—	—	—	—
Others	1	0.9	—	—	—	—	—	—

Table 4.
Frequency Analysis by the unit of analysis.

	Type							
	Method		Framework		Dashboard		Set of metrics	
	Value	(%)	Value	(%)	Value	(%)	Value	(%)
Driver								
External	35	30.2	11	9.5	13	11.2	6	5.2
Internal	13	11.2	11	9.5	7	6	—	—
External; internal	14	12.1	2	1.7	4	3.4	—	—
Purpose								
Accountability	4	3.4	5	4.3	9	7.6	4	3.4

	Type							
	Method		Framework		Dashboard		Set of metrics	
	Value	(%)	Value	(%)	Value	(%)	Value	(%)
Assess strengths and weaknesses	1	0.9	3	2.6	3	2.6	—	—
Measure approach effectiveness	4	3.4	1	0.9	—	—	—	—
Performance measurement	27	23.3	8	6.9	5	4.3	2	1.7
Performance improvement	4	3.4	4	3.4	4	3.4	—	—
Portfolio management	37	31.9	5	4.3	10	8.6	1	0.9
Scope								
Sectoral	11	9.5	5	4.3	2	1.7	—	—
Multi-sectoral	51	44	19	16.4	22	19	6	5.2
Target audience								
Managers	12	10.3	10	8.6	6	5.2	—	—
Financiers	41	35.3	9	7.6	13	11.2	3	2.6
Sector stakeholders	10	8.6	4	3.4	7	6	3	2.6
Public administrations	2	1.7	—	—	—	—	—	—
Others	—	—	1	0.9	—	—	—	—

Table 5.
Frequency Analysis by type.

	Target audience									
	Managers		Financiers		Sector stakeholders		Public administrations		Others	
	Value	(%)	Value	(%)	Value	(%)	Value	(%)	Value	(%)
Driver										
External	1	0.9	48	41.4	14	12.1	2	1.7	1	0.9
Internal	22	19	7	6	3	2.6	—	—	—	—
External; internal	5	4.3	11	9.5	7	6	—	—	—	—
Purpose										
Accountability	2	1.7	9	7.6	10	8.6	—	—	1	0.9
Assess strengths and weaknesses	5	4.3	2	1.7	2	1.7	—	—	—	—
Measure approach effectiveness	3	2.6	1	0.9	1	0.9	—	—	—	—
Performance measurement	8	6.9	23	20	10	8.6	2	1.7	—	—
Performance improvement	9	7.6	1	0.9	2	1.7	—	—	—	—
Portfolio management	3	2.6	50	43.1	3	2.6	—	—	—	—
Scope										
Sectoral	3	2.6	11	9.5	4	3.4	—	—	—	—
Multi-sectoral	25	21.6	55	47.4	20	17.2	2	1.7	1	0.9

Table 6.
Frequency Analysis by the target audience.

Leveraging on the frequency analysis, we developed a framework to support impact-oriented organizations to select to the most appropriate model based on their needs and objective.

We suggest that the first two steps of the analysis to be considered are the Unit of analysis and the Target Audience. The second step is to select models that are appropriate respect to the purpose of the measurement and the driver of the measurement. Third, the scope and type of approach help refine the process.

4.2 How to implement a social impact measurement

The analysis of the 116 approached identified also enabled to outline a reference process that an organization approaching the design of its social impact measurement might follow. The process presented in this section emerged from the review of the implementation procedures and tools entailed by the existing methodologies. Indeed, for each of the step, we also provided a reference to one or more methods that the organization can look at.

The process foresees the steps outlined in **Figure 1** and described in the following sections.

4.2.1 Measurement objectives and internal boundaries

The scope of this first phase is setting the objectives of impact analysis (why and for whom), the level (e.g. portfolio of social investments/individual social enterprise), the available resources, the motivation for measuring social impact, the leader of the process (internal resource or a consultant).

More suitable models for the needs of this phase are *EY Total Value*, *EPIC methodology* and *WBCSD Measuring Impact Framework*.

4.2.2 Impact statement and impact Mission

In this phase, the organization defines what the impact perspective and the impact ambition are. First of all, it is fundamental to analyze social needs and their relevance linked to the context. This analysis implies the study of the effects and changes that could be generated in the long term by the activities of the

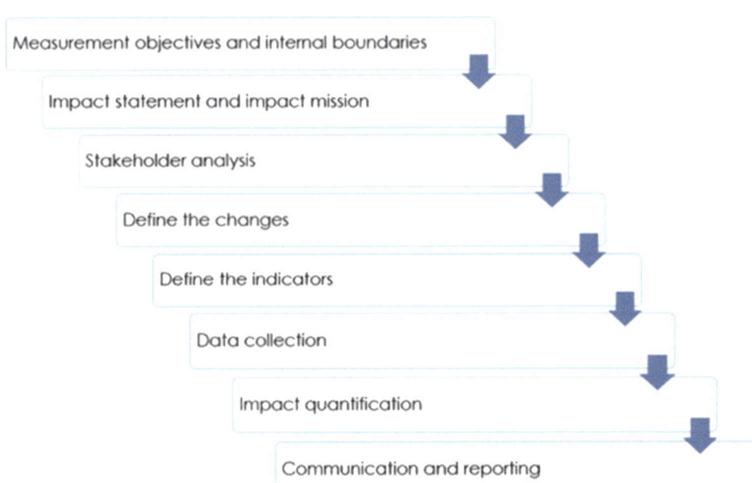

Figure 1.
Social impact measurement process.

organization. In this part of the process, stakeholders will understand the needs, the type of impact and the approach of measurement (social, environmental or integrated).

To achieve this objective, the actors could agree on several founding principles to guide their work as proposed by the *UNPRI Operating Principles for Responsible Investment*, one of the approaches that could be used to develop the impact statement and impact mission. Other principles, for example, are developed by the *EY Total Value* and the *EPIC methodology*.

4.2.3 Stakeholder analysis

Stakeholder analysis implies the identification of the main actors that can affect or be affected in some way by project activities [49]. This analysis should start with the mapping of internal and external stakeholders. Once the most relevant stakeholders have been identified and classified according to their nature, it would be crucial to investigate, one by one, their specific interests or needs, the main capabilities they can devote to the project and all the possible actions the organization can implement in order to involve them, foster their participation into the project and satisfy their needs [50].

Finally, it is interested to assign priority to stakeholders in order to classify them according to their level of power to influence the project and the level of interest in the service/product offered by the project. A reference to undertaking this step is the *Power and Interest Grid* [51].

Social impact measurement models that better interpret this phase are the *Social Return On Investments (SROI)* and the *Social Impact Assessment (SIA)*.

4.2.4 Define the changes

The further step of the social impact measurement process is the definition of the Social Value Chain [52]. This tool allows to graphically represent the process of change that a project can generate in relation to a specific social problem. The main objective of this step is to identify the logical framework and the cause and effect links between the different elements that compose it.

By developing the Social Value Chain it is possible to understand the social value's creation process. Moreover, it is an easily understandable representation of the logic through which the short-term results on beneficiaries lead to the generation of long-term impacts on the community of reference.

Theory of Change and *Impact Management Project* are two models that well describe this phase.

4.2.5 Define the indicators

Once defined the outcomes and impacts that the organization's activity is generating, it is possible to define the indicators (KPIs) to use in order to assess the generated social change. The and international institution such as *IRIS +*, *GRI* and *SASB Standards*, provide a huge repository of indicators that can be consulted, nevertheless, sometimes the impact dimensions do not coincide with those present on the existing repositories and therefore it is necessary to conceive ad-hoc indicators.

4.2.6 Data collection

After the definition of the indicators, there is the data collection phase.

Once identified which stakeholder to involve, there is the definition of the modality of the collection (interviews, focus group, questionnaire, observation) which is chosen according to the nature of the data to gather, the number of stakeholders to involve, and the available resources, and the mean of the collection (digital platforms, email, pa56per questionnaire, phone call) that should be consistent with the modality of collection selected. The last aspect to define is the timing of the collection, namely when the data collection phase should take place. According to the overall measurement process, data could be collected periodically, or at the beginning and at the end of a project or a pilot, etc.

Acumen Lean Data approach uses the power of low-cost technology to collect high-quality data at a fraction of the time and cost of other methods.

4.2.7 Impact quantification

After collecting data, and verify their reliability, it is necessary to analyze them, calculate the quantitative indicators and describe the qualitative ones, according to the defined times and methods.

If it was not already available, the first assessment will provide the baseline or, in other words, the identification of the starting point. Then, it's important to periodically repeat the measurement, evaluating the results by comparing them with the defined targets and historical values.

Therefore, in this stage an attempt is made to go beyond the measurement of the simple output - the immediate result produced in terms of product/service - and to understand how the changes on the beneficiary directly produced by the organization/project activity (outcome) contribute to generating wider effects and over a longer time horizon (impact) and finally to understand, and possibly purify, the "collateral" effects (deadweight, attribution, drop off, displacement, etc.) that are difficult to trace back to the organization's activity. To overcome (or partially overcome) these impact measurement challenges (deeply explained into the fourth chapter), there are some analytical approaches like the counterfactual analysis that can be used in order to more precisely assess social impact.

Models that best suit the needs of this phase are, for examples the *Impact Weighted Accounts* and the *Social Return On Investments (SROI)*.

4.2.8 Communication and reporting

The final stage of the social impact measurement process is reporting to stakeholders, communicating and using the results, and embedding the measurement process in the organization.

This phase is strongly addressed within the *SDGs Compass approach*.

5. Discussion and conclusions

This chapter contributes to theory and practice in different ways. It fills the gap in the academic literature of systematizing the existing heterogeneous pool of approaches to conduct social impact measurement. Indeed, we first identify 116 approaches (see the **Table** 7 in the Annex) which the most used so far; second, we suggest several dimensions that can be employed to analyze and classify these approaches. Third, we combine these dimensions to create a framework able to support organization eager to design their own social impact measurement infrastructure in selecting the proper instruments, metrics and approach.

Moreover, the findings support the idea that so far it has not been possible to establish a *golden standard* in the practice of social impact measurement. Indeed, we found several approaches with different characteristics to meet the heterogeneous needs of many stakeholders. Indeed, there seem to be tradeoffs between the scope of application of standards and the validity of comparison. Thus, it may be difficult for researchers and practitioners to develop direct social impact measurement standards that are universally applicable. Therefore, the chapter provides a contribution to practice by outlining a reference process that an organization can follow to design its own methodology.

In addition, our analysis confirmed to a certain extent that recent developments in impact measurement have been largely driven by impact investors. This clearly emerged by the results showing that most models in our sample, and particularly the most recently developed one, are designed to have funders and investors as their primary audience.

The analysis also reveals some open issues that should need to be addressed to advance the practice of social impact measurement and might represent avenues of further research.

The first challenge that hinders the practice of social impact measurement is the availability of **suitable data.** It should be crucial to increase the quality of data, where quality refers not only to availability but also to homogeneity, interoperability and standardization. Scholars pinpointed the lack of database that directly observes the provision of social impact across multiple sectors and locations [53]. Second, there has been a global effort in recent years towards **harmonizing** indicators, instruments, and methods for assessing and analyzing results, assisted by international networks for data sharing and learning. Among them, we highlight the development of the Impact Management Project (IMP), spearheaded by Bridges Ventures, which has put together a structured network including the most influential organization in the field, such as the GIIN, B Lab, the Global Steering Group for Impact Investing, Social Value International, the International Finance Corporation, the World Benchmarking Alliance, UNDP, the Sustainability Accounting Standards Board, etc. The IMP is aiming to put forward a comprehensive framework, comparable to those used for financial analyses of traditional investing decisions, to be widely used to articulate considerations concerning impact.

Second, a recent trend is the emergence of a new generation of **open-source platforms** that generate opportunities for complex projects that enable real-time data entry and analysis, as well as the data processing, analysis, and visualization facility. Leveraging on latest technologies, artificial intelligence algorithms and big data analytics, combined with large and small data [54], is seen from many [55–57] as one of the possible paths to improve the usability of SIM both in finance and in the social sector. Although the recognized potential, there are still many aspects hampering the ability to leverage the power of data and technology to tackle societal challenges [58] and particularly their application to social impact measurement as well as to program and policy evaluation. According to the literature, these issues concern different aspects i.e. data ownership and accountability ethical issues like risk of doubling down on bias, reproduce inequalities or gender or race discrimination [59]; methodological issues like the importance of realizing safety mechanisms that can complement the algorithmic decision-making process or the trade-off between big data analysis and the work on the field [54]. Many specific elements that should be complemented with a broader and multi-actors effort finalized to the construction of a proper data analysis infrastructure, an essential element to share data and resources as many [60] have been affirming in recent years.

To conclude, the analysis presented in this chapter adds to the debate on whether there is a need of a standard method in social impact measurement by underlining that the most promising path is not standardization, but harmonization to enable a minimum level of comparability and platforms to enhance the open sharing of data on social aspects.

Conflict of interest

The authors declare no conflict of interest.

A. Appendix

#	Approach	Unit of analysis of the measurement process			
		Social ventures	For-profit companies	Investors	Public institutions
1	AA1000AP		x		
2	Acumen Lean Data	x			
3	Acumen scorecard	x			
4	Aeris CDFI Ratings System			x	
5	Anticipated Impact Measurement and Monitoring (AIMM)			x	
6	Atkisson compass assessment for investors		x		
7	Barclays Sustainability Impact Framework		x		
8	Best available charitable option	x			
9	Bridges Ventures Impact Radar		x		
10	Business Reporting on the SDGs: An Analysis of the Goals and Targets		x		
11	CERISE-IDIA			x	
12	Charity analysis framework	x			
13	Cost per impact	x			
14	Cradle to Cradle certification		x		
15	Dalberg Approach	x			
16	DTA Fit for purpose	x			
17	Echoing green midyear and year-end report	x			
18	Eco-mapping		x		
19	EFQM		x		
20	EMAS		x		
21	ENVIRONMENTAL, SOCIAL AND GOVERNANCE (ESG) SCORES		x		
22	EPIC		x		
23	ESG Disclosure score		x		
24	ESG Relevance Score		x		
25	ESG Risk Rating		x	x	
26	European Impact Investing Luxembourg	x			
27	Expected return	x			

#	Approach	Unit of analysis of the measurement process			
		Social ventures	For-profit companies	Investors	Public institutions
28	Family of measures		x		
29	Finance Initiative Impact Radar	x		x	
30	Financial Instruments for Social Impact	x			
31	Financial Products for Specified Use of Proceeds project-related finance (Equator principles scope)		x		
32	Financial Products for Unspecified Use of Funds		x		
33	FMO ESG Toolkits		x		
34	FTSE ESG Ratings		x	x	
35	Global Alliance for Banking on Values			x	
36	Global Impact Investing Rating System		x		
37	GOGLA Impact Metrics	x	x		
38	GRESB Infrastructure Fund Assessment			x	
39	GRESB Real Estate Assessment		x	x	
40	GRI sustainability reporting framework		x		
41	HIP Rating		x	x	
42	HIPSO Harmonized Indicators for Private Sector Operations	x	x		
43	Il Metodo VALORIS	x			
44	Impact Analysis for Corporate Finance & Investments (Tool prototype)		x		
45	Impact Due Diligence Tools	x			
46	Impact Identification & Assessment for Bank Portfolios			x	
47	Impact Management Project (IMP) Five Dimensions	x	x	x	
48	Impact Measurement - A practical guide to data collection		x		
49	Impact multiple of money (IMM)	x			
50	Impact Risk Classification (IRC)	x		x	
51	Impact-Weighted Accounts		x		
52	Inrate ESG Country Ratings				x
53	Inrate ESG Impact Rating Methodology		x	x	
54	Inrate ESG Real Estate Assessment		x	x	
55	Inventory of Business Indicators (SDG Compass)		x		
56	Investing for Impact: operating principles for impact management Guide to Investing for impact: Operating Principles for Impact Management			x	
57	Investors in people		x		
58	IRIS + (and IRIS)		x	x	

#	Approach	Unit of analysis of the measurement process			
		Social ventures	For-profit companies	Investors	Public institutions
59	ISS ESG Corporate Rating		x		
60	ISS SDG Impact rating		x		
61	LM3	x			x
62	Logic model builder	x			
63	LuxFLAG ESG Label			x	
64	Measuring impact framework		x		
65	Methodology for impact analysis and assessment	x			
66	MetODD-SDG	x			
67	MicroRate			x	
68	Movement above the US$1 a day threshold			x	
69	MSCI ESG Ratings Methodology		x	x	
70	Omidyar Network Lean data	x	x	x	
71	Outcome star	x			
72	Practical quality assurance system for small organizations (PQASSO) / Trusted Charity	x			
73	Progress out of poverty index			x	
74	Prove it!	x			
75	Public value scorecard	x			
76	Quality first	x			
77	RobecoSam 3 steps SDG Framework		x		
78	S&P Global Ratings ESG Evaluation Sam Corporate Responsibility Assessment		x		
79	SASB Standard SASB Materiality Map and Standard Navigator		x	x	
80	SDG Impact Indicators: A Guide for Investors and Companies		x		
81	SDG Impact Practice Standard	x			
82	SOCIAL			x	
83	Social accounting and audit	x			
84	Social Business Scorecard	x			
85	Social enterprise balanced scorecard	x			
86	Social enterprise mark	x			
87	Social Impact Assessment (SIA)	x			
88	Social Impact Measurement for Local Economies (SIMPLE)	x			
89	Social rating			x	
90	Social return assessment		x		
91	Social return on investment	x			
92	Social Value Maturity Index	x			
93	Social value metrics	x			

#	Approach	Unit of analysis of the measurement process			
		Social ventures	**For-profit companies**	**Investors**	**Public institutions**
94	Sopact - tool	x	x		
95	SPI4			x	
96	SPI4 - Alinus			x	
97	Standard Ethics Rating (SER)		x		
98	Star social firm	x			
99	Success measures data system	x			
100	The B impact rating system		x		
101	The big picture	x			
102	The Committee on Sustainability Assessment (COSA) Methodology		x		
103	The FINCA client assessment tool			x	
104	The Impact Due Diligence Guide	x			
105	The SRI LABEL		x	x	
106	Third sector performance dashboard	x			
107	TIMM	x			
108	Towards Common Metrics and Consistent Reporting of Sustainable Value Creation		x		
109	Trucost		x		
110	UK social housing Sector Standard Approach for ESG Reporting	x			
111	Vital Capital's Impact Diamond			x	
112	Volunteering impact assessment toolkit	x			
113	Wallace assessment tool			x	
114	WBA's benchmarks		x		
115	What did we learn from listening to 4800+ customers in Omidyar Network's Education portfolio?	x		x	
116	Y Analytics	x			

Table 7.
List of approaches classified by unit of analysis.

Author details

Irene Bengo, Veronica Chiodo* and Valentina Tosi
Department of Management, Economics and Industrial Engineering (DIG), Politecnico di Milano, Milan, Italy

*Address all correspondence to: veronica.chiodo@polimi.it

References

[1] Hart, O, Zingales, L. Companies Should Maximize Shareholder Welfare Not Market Value. 2017; ECGI - Finance Working Paper No. 521/2017.

[2] Harris, M. Nonprofits and business toward a subfield of nonprofit studies. Nonprofit and Voluntary Sector Quarterly. 2012;41:892–902. DOI: 10.1177/0899764012443735

[3] Margiono, A, Zolin, R., Chang, A. A typology of social venture business model configurations. International Journal of Entrepreneurial Behavior & Research. 2018;24(3):626–650. DOI: 10.1108/IJEBR-09-2016-0316

[4] Wood, DJ, Logsdon, JM. Social issues in management as a distinct field: Corporate social responsibility and performance. Business & Society. 2019; 58(7):1334–1357. DOI: 10.1177/0007650316680041

[5] Arena, M, Azzone, A, Mapelli, F. What drives the evolution of Corporate Social Responsibility strategies? An institutional logics perspective. Journal of Cleaner Production. 2018;171(10): 345–355. DOI: 10.1016/j.jclepro.2017.09.245

[6] Bengo, I, Arena, M, Azzone, G, Calderini, M. Indicators and metrics for social business: a review of current approaches. Journal of Social Entrepreneurship. 2016;7(1):1–24. DOI: 10.1080/19420676.2015.1049286

[7] Bengo, I. Debate: Impact measurement and social public procurement. Public Money & Management. 2018;38(5):391–392. DOI: 10.1080/09540962.2018.1471817

[8] Salazar, J, Husted, BW, Biehl, M. Thoughts on the evaluation of corporate social performance through projects. Journal of Business Ethics. 2012;105(2): 175–186. DOI: 10.1007/s10551-011-0957-z

[9] Grieco, C, Michelini, L, Iasevoli, G. Measuring value creation in social enterprises: A cluster analysis of social impact assessment models. Nonprofit and voluntary sector quarterly. 2015;44 (6):1173–1193. DOI: 10.1177/0899764014555986

[10] Braig, P, Edinger-Schons, LM. From Purpose to Impact - An Investigation of the Application of Impact Measurement and Valuation Methods for Quantifying Environmental and Social Impacts of Businesses. Sustainable Production and Consumption. 2020;23:189–197. DOI: 10.1039/c9pp90009h

[11] Findlay, S, Moran, M. Purpose-washing of impact investing funds: motivations, occurrence and prevention. Social Responsibility Journal. 2019;15(7):853–873. DOI: 10.1108/SRJ-11-2017-0260

[12] Bagnoli, L, Megali, C. Measuring performance in social enterprises. Nonprofit and Voluntary Sector Quarterly. 2011;40(1):149–165. DOI: 10.1177/0899764009351111

[13] Arena, M., Azzone, G., Bengo, I. Performance measurement for Social Enterprises. International Journal of Voluntary and Nonprofit Organizations. 2015;26(2):649–672. DOI: 10.1007/s11266-013-9436-8

[14] Rawhouser, H, Cummings, M, Newbert, SL. Social impact measurement: Current approaches and future directions for social entrepreneurship research. Entrepreneurship Theory and Practice. 2019;43(1):82–115. DOI: 10.1177/1042258717727718

[15] Moss, TW, Short, JC, Payne, GT, Lumpkin, GT. Dual identities in social ventures: An exploratory study. Entrepreneurship theory and practice.

2011;35(4):805–830. DOI: 10.1111/j.1540-6520.2010.00372.x

[16] Santos, FM. A positive theory of social entrepreneurship. Journal of business ethics. 2012;111(3):335–351. DOI: 10.1007/s10551-012-1413-4

[17] Husted, BW, de Jesus Salazar, J. Taking Friedman seriously: Maximizing profits and social performance. Journal of Management studies. 2006;43(1):75–91. DOI: 10.1111/j.1467-6486.2006.00583.x

[18] Mair, J, Marti, I. Social entrepreneurship research: A source of explanation, prediction, and delight. Journal of world business. 2006;41(1):36–44. DOI: 10.1016/j.jwb.2005.09.002

[19] Emerson, J. The blended value proposition: Integrating social and financial returns. California management review. 2003;45(4):35–51. DOI: 10.2307/41166187

[20] Vanclay, F. International principles for social impact assessment. Impact assessment and project appraisal. 2003; 21(1):5–12. DOI: https://doi.org/10.3152/147154603781766491

[21] Brest P, Born K. Unpacking the Impact in Impact Investing. Stanford Social Innovation Review. 2013;11(4):22–31.

[22] Stephan U, Patterson M, Kelly C, Mair J. Organizations driving positive social change: A review and an integrative framework of change processes. Journal of Management. 2016;42(5):1250–81. DOI: 10.1177/0149206316633268

[23] Dufour, B. State of the art in impact measurement: methods for work integration social enterprises measuring their social value in a public context. In: 5th EMES International Research Conference on Social Enterprise "Building a scientific field to foster the social enterprise eco-system; 30 June – 3 July 2015; Helsinki.

[24] Richmond, BJ, Mook, L, Quarter, J,. Social Accounting for Nonprofits. Nonprofit Management & Leadership; 2003; 13(4): 308–324.

[25] Gray, R. Current developments and trends in social and environmental auditing, reporting and attestation: a review and comment. International journal of auditing. 2000;4(3):247–268. DOI: 10.1111/1099-1123.00316

[26] Lisi IE. Determinants and performance effects of social performance measurement systems. Journal of Business Ethics. 2018;152(1):225–51. DOI: 10.1007/s10551-016-3287-3

[27] Vanclay F. International principles for social impact assessment. Impact assessment and project appraisal. 2003; 21(1): 5–12. DOI: https://doi.org/10.3152/147154603781766491

[28] Hatry, HP. Sorting the relationships among performance measurement, program evaluation, and performance management. New Directions for Evaluation. 2013;137:19–32. DOI: https://doi.org/10.1002/ev.20043

[29] Gugerty. M K, Dean Karlan, D. Ten Reasons Not to Measure Impact—and What to Do Instead Impact evaluations are an important tool for learning about effective solutions to social problems, but they are a good investment only in the right circumstances. Stanford Social Innovation Review. 2018.

[30] Ebrahim, A, Rangan, VK. What impact? A framework for measuring the scale and scope of social performance. California management review. 2014; 56 (3): 118–141.

[31] Lall, S. Measuring to improve versus measuring to prove: Understanding the adoption of social performance measurement practices in nascent social

enterprises. VOLUNTAS: International Journal of Voluntary and Nonprofit Organizations. 2017;28(6):2633–2657. DOI: 10.1007/s11266-017-9898-1

[32] Ormiston J. Blending practice worlds: Impact assessment as a transdisciplinary practice. Business Ethics: A European Review. 2019;28(4): 423–40. DOI: 10.1111/beer.12230

[33] Chen S, Harrison R. Beyond profit vs. purpose: Transactional-relational practices in impact investing. Journal of Business Venturing Insights. 2020; 14: e00182. DOI: 10.1016/j.jbvi.2020.e00182

[34] Nicholls, A. "We do good things, don't we?": 'Blended Value Accounting' in social entrepreneurship. Accounting, organizations and society. 2009; 34(6–7): 755–769. DOI: 10.1016/j.aos.2009.04.008

[35] Rawhouser H, Cummings M, Newbert SL. Social impact measurement: Current approaches and future directions for social entrepreneurship research. Entrepreneurship Theory and Practice. 2019; 43(1):82–115. DOI: 10.1177/1042258717727718

[36] Kroeger, A, Weber, C. Developing a conceptual framework for comparing social value creation. Academy of Management Review. 2014; 39(4): 513–540. DOI: 10.5465/amr.2012.0344

[37] Duflo, E, Kremer, M. Use of randomization in the evaluation of development effectiveness. Evaluating development effectiveness. 2005; 7: 205–231.

[38] Meyer, BD. Natural and quasi-experiments in economics. Journal of business & economic statistics. 1995; 13 (2): 151–161.

[39] Kaplan, RS, Norton, DP. Using the balanced scorecard as a strategic management system. Harvard business review. 2007; 74(1): 75–85.

[40] Somers, AB. Shaping the balanced scorecard for use in UK social enterprises. Social Enterprise Journal. 2005;1(1): 43–56. DOI: 10.1108/17508610580000706

[41] Arvidson, M, Lyon, F, McKay, S, Moro, D. Valuing the social? The nature and controversies of measuring social return on investment (SROI). Voluntary sector review. 2013; 4(1): 3–18. DOI: 10.1332/204080513X661554

[42] Olsen, S, Galimidi, B. Catalog of Approaches to Impact Measurement - Assessing social impact in private ventures. The Rockfeller Foundation. 2008.

[43] Global Impact Investor network report (GIIN). The State Of Impact Measurement And Management Practice. The Rockfeller Foundation 2020.

[44] Zappalà, G, Lyons, M. Recent approaches to measuring social impact in the Third sector: An overview. Centre for Social Impact Sydney. 2009.

[45] Migliavacca, AM. Social impact measurement practices; A meta-analysis. International Journal Series in Multidisciplinary Research. 2016; 2(3): 1–17.

[46] Clark, C, Rosenzweig, W, Long, D, Olsen, S. Double Bottom Line Project Report: Assessing Social Impact in Double Line Ventures, Methods Catalog. Columbia Business School: Rise-Project. 2004.

[47] Rinaldo, H. Getting Started in Social Impact Measurement: A guide to choosing how to measure social impact. Norwich: The Guild. 2010.

[48] Grieco, C, Michelini, L, Iasevoli, G. Measuring value creation in social

enterprises: A cluster analysis of social impact assessment models. Nonprofit and voluntary sector quarterly. 2015; 44 (6): 1173–1193. DOI: https://doi.org/10.1177/0899764014555986

[49] Goodpaster, KE. Business ethics and stakeholder analysis. Business ethics quarterly. 1991; 1:53–73. DOI: 10.2307/3857592

[50] Bryson, JM. What to do when stakeholders matter: stakeholder identification and analysis techniques. Public management review. 2004; 6(1): 21–53. DOI: https://doi.org/10.1080/14719030410001675722

[51] Eden C, Ackermann F. Making strategy: The journey of strategic management. London, UK: Sage; 2013. DOI: 10.4135/9781446217153

[52] Funnell, SC, Rogers, PJ. Purposeful program theory: Effective use of theories of change and logic models. John Wiley & Sons; 2011: 31.

[53] Soleimani, A, Schneper, W D, Newburry, W. The impact of stakeholder power on corpor- ate reputation: A cross-country corporate governance perspective. Organization Science. 2014; 25(4): 991–1008. DOI: 10.1287/orsc.2013.0889

[54] York, P, Bamberger, M. Measuring results and impact in the age of big data: The nexus of evaluation, analytics, and digital technology. The Rockefeller Foundation. 2020.

[55] Letouzé, E, Sangokoya, D. How To Use Big Data? Data Pop Alliance. 2017.

[56] OECD. Social Impact Investment 2019: The Impact Imperative for Sustainable Development. Paris: OECD Publishing; 2019.

[57] Coulton, C J, George, R, Putnam-Hornstein, E, De Haan, B. Harnessing Big Data for Social Good : A Grand Challenge for Social Work. American Academy of Social Work and Social Welfare. 2015.

[58] Niño, M, Zicari, R V, Ivanov, T, Hee, K, Mushtaq, N, Rosselli, M., ... Underwood, H. Data Projects for " Social Good ": Challenges and Opportunities. 2017; 11(5), 896–906. DOI: doi.org/10.5281/zenodo.1130095

[59] Lepri, B, Nuriam O, Letouze, E F, Pentland, A P, Vinck, P. Fair, Transparent, and Accountable Algorithmic Decision-Making Processes. Philosophy & Technology. 2018; 31(4): 611–627. DOI: 10.1007/s13347-017-0279-x

[60] Varshney, K R, Mojsilovi'c, A, Mojsilovi´. Open Platforms for Artificial Intelligence for Social Good: Common Patterns as a Pathway to True Impact. In: International Conference on Machine Learning AI for Social Good Workshop; 2019; Long Beach.

Section 2

Entrepreneurial Education and Opportunities

Chapter 5

The Role of Prior Knowledge in the Process of Recognizing Entrepreneurial Opportunities

Felipe Baeta and Tales Andreassi

Abstract

Recognizing opportunities has often been raised as a crucial aspect of the entrepreneurial process. It seems that the ability to identify, analyze and develop entrepreneurial opportunities is what differentiates entrepreneurs from those who are not. This assertion highlights the relevance of understanding in greater depth the variables that have an influence on the process of recognizing opportunities. In this context, an entrepreneur's prior knowledge and experience, which can be broken down into three domains, have an impact on the dimensions of recognizing opportunities, such as the scope of the opportunity and the intensity of the process. Deriving from this dynamic, the objective of this study is to understand the role of prior knowledge in the process of recognizing entrepreneurial opportunities. By way of in-depth interviews with ten entrepreneurs, it was concluded that those who have limited professional experience attribute greater relevance in the process to their educational activities. When it comes to recognizing opportunities, however, these same entrepreneurs have a broader scope and approach the process in a more intense way. Entrepreneurs who have a better-defined mental framework, on the other hand, which results from their vast professional experience, tend to channel any opportunities they recognize towards the industry in which they operate and this results in fewer potential businesses.

Keywords: entrepreneurial opportunities, processo of recognizing opportunities

1. Introduction

The emergence of the recognition of opportunity as a central issue in the entrepreneurial process has been shifting the subject and unit of analysis of the research in this particular area [1]. One of the conclusions that derives from this is the understanding that entrepreneurship is a process of creating value, which is based on solid concepts involving a combination of resources, in order to exploit a particular opportunity after it has been identified.

Literature, in particular, has attempted to answer the question of why some people recognize entrepreneurial opportunities, while others do not. In order to answer to this question, studies have presented a series of characteristics and interactions. The characteristics of entrepreneurs are divided between the psychological and the non-psychological, including, for example, their social networks and the quality and depth of the resultant ties; family role models; an ability to recognize patterns; a state of alertness; and the ability to assess information. As for interactions, it is worth mentioning the reservation raised by [2], that any response that differentiates people based on their ability to recognize opportunities must also consider entrepreneurial motivation, the opportunity sources and the degree of deliberation of the process of searching for opportunities, which is sometimes active and sometimes emerging.

This said, previous knowledge and past experiences have been configured as one of the fundamental factors on the horizon of non-psychological variables. It is also assumed that accumulated knowledge and experiences, especially previous career experiences, provide the conditions for forming a more assertive judgment of entrepreneurial opportunities. Basically, it is claimed that the accumulation of knowledge and experiences favors the creation of cognitive structures that in some way affect the scope of the opportunities and the intensity of their recognition process [3].

Literature presents three aspects of the origin of prior knowledge: knowledge that comes from activities that are of special interest to the entrepreneur; the professional experiences of the entrepreneur; and the formal education of the entrepreneur [4].

This work sought to understand the role of prior knowledge in the recognition of opportunities, which was broken down into its three dimensions. Specifically these dimensions are identifying how: the activities that fascinate entrepreneurs, their professional background, and their studies influence the scope of the business opportunities and the intensity of the process. It is understood that the scope of the opportunities has to do with the extent and divergence of the entrepreneur's experiences and the potential opportunities that are recognized as existing. The intensity of the process is related to the number of opportunities that emerge during the process.

2. Theoretical reference

The concept of entrepreneurial opportunities has become central to the conceptual definition of entrepreneurship. This affirmation and the procedural approach applied to studies in the field highlights the need for more in-depth studies into the opportunity recognition process that entrepreneurs adopt when creating any new business.

A central dimension of the approach to entrepreneurship is the process of identifying and economically exploiting new opportunities, either by creating new companies, or within the scope of existing organizations [1]. Using this same line of reasoning, [5] define entrepreneurship as the process of creating value based on combining resources for exploiting an opportunity.

Despite its relevance, the definition of entrepreneurial opportunities in literature is highly fragmented. Another point that arises from the conceptual distortions and that must be considered is the difficulty in determining the boundary between an idea and a real opportunity [6]. We use, however, the definition proposed by [7], in which opportunities for entrepreneurs are moments when there is a possibility of introducing a profitable product, i.e. one that generates more revenue than the costs associated with the process of producing or developing it.

In line with the emergence of research in the area and the increasing indication of the importance of opportunities in this field of study, seeking opportunities and continuously and creatively recognizing them as such has been shown to be important [8]. Recognizing opportunities is often also suggested as both the starting point and, indeed, the main point of the entrepreneurial process.

Several authors, such as [9–11], stress that recognizing opportunities is actually the first critical step in the entrepreneurial process. With this same understanding, [12] also suggest that entrepreneurship is mainly driven by the perception and recognition of opportunities. Likewise, the work by [13] had already suggested that recognizing and exploiting opportunities was the central point of studies about entrepreneurship.

The identification process - the recognition of opportunities - is guided by three central activities: perception or identification, discovery or evaluation, and creation or development [14]. When developing each of them, it is evident that perception induces the act of feeling the demands of the market, or perceiving any underutilization of resources; discovery is related to the fit between the needs of the market and specific resources; while creation is the consolidation of resources in a well-defined business concept as a solution that responds to discoveries.

In view of the objectives of this study, we need to understand the mechanisms and *locus* of the recognition of opportunities in literature.

Assuming and observing that entrepreneurship is a process in which opportunities are recognized when they are beginning, even before the undertaking is formalized, [10] undertook an empirical study aimed at identifying the different behaviors of successful entrepreneurs with regard to their recognition of opportunities.

The recognition and exploitation of opportunities from a theoretical perspective and propose a radical change in the direction of the research into entrepreneurship [1]. These authors believe that entrepreneurial behavior is transitory, the result of the ability certain people have of responding to signals from the environment about opportunities, and this is not related to any stable, permanent characteristic that differentiates some people (entrepreneurs) from others (non-entrepreneurs) in all situations. The study of entrepreneurship, therefore, should have as its main focus an analysis of the nature and process of identifying and exploiting opportunities.

Empirical evidence shows that entrepreneurs have special resources and the ability to perceive and reason differently from other people. In general terms, it seems to be due to this point that they are able to identify innovative business opportunities before others do.

This vision is shared for some researchers who argue that studies should focus on examining the entrepreneurial process in the connection between the individual and the opportunity [7]. The connection in question can be interpreted as being the interaction between the individual, their characteristics and the environment. The dialog between them is the result of the resources that entrepreneurs have at their disposal and the resources provided and existing in the environment, plus other aspects that have an influence on the entrepreneurial process.

Whether discovering opportunities, or evaluating and exploiting them, entrepreneurs individually commit both personal and psychological factors and non-psychological characteristics, namely, their prior knowledge, social networks, the ability to recognize patterns, their alertness, and others.

One of the first explanations of the way in which entrepreneurs recognize business opportunities was proposed by [15], who suggested that opportunities are the result of the tacit knowledge of each individual.

Prior knowledge and social networks as points that favor the recognition of opportunities: jobs that allow access to the most recent information that is closely linked to the market; the varied experiences of life and work that enable the knowledge base to be expanded; an extensive social network facilitating access to information that is otherwise difficult to obtain; and the active search for opportunities, particularly in places that others ignore [16].

Narrowing our analysis to consider just prior knowledge, there is a wealth of evidence indicating that information gathered from life experiences, both in its quality and diversity, can be of great advantage to entrepreneurs in terms of their recognizing potentially lucrative opportunities. As an example, prior knowledge that focuses on the needs of customers and, consequently, on ways of addressing them, greatly reinforces the ability of entrepreneurs to provide innovative solutions and, as a result, favors the emergence of opportunities that are potentially valuable for creating new businesses [7].

It is important to stress that although life experience can be of great advantage to recognize opportunities, no necessarily elder entrepreneurs are more successful in this process than younger entrepreneurs. According to [17], countries whose populations are excessively skewed towards old or young cohorts may experience low levels of entrepreneurial activity. [18] studied start-ups systematically in the United States and found that successful entrepreneurs are middle-aged, not younger or older. The mean age at founding for the 1-in-1000 fastest growing new ventures is 45 years old.

In this particular context, literature provides evidence of three different types of prior knowledge that are identified as coming from an entrepreneur's background. The first type of prior knowledge has to do with fascination and fun [4], and is described as an area that an entrepreneur dominates, or that is of special interest to them. The second type concerns the experiences that arise from work positions they have held. Finally, the third type of prior knowledge has to do with the educational activities undertaken by the entrepreneur. It is worth mentioning that the three perspectives listed above consider that there is a close relationship between access to information and the emergence of the perception of opportunities.

In addition to the role of each of the variables that have an influence on the process of recognizing opportunities, we now need to understand in greater detail the dynamics of this relationship.

The entrepreneur's background, including their prior knowledge, has an impact on the recognition of opportunities based on the dimensions of the process. Here we highlight the consequences of the variables on the scope of the opportunity and the intensity of the process. Scope concerns the peculiarities and sectoral and functional attributes of the undertaking, while intensity is related to the number of opportunities that emerge during the process. **Figure 1** shows the dynamics of this relationship.

As potential inferences of this framework, it is presumed that very high levels of prior knowledge may reduce the need for active research, since a large stock of knowledge contributes to the formation of broad and rich connections of cognitive structures, and this again makes participation in formal search activities a less crucial task [19].

Based on their comparative analysis of experienced and novice entrepreneurs, these same authors identified that these two profiles have distinct cognitive structures, which provide experienced entrepreneurs with a cognitive advantage because of their greater clarity and the depth of their experience.

Based on the results of the literature, it is possible to argue that as entrepreneurs acquire a particular knowledge, they become more skilled at perceiving meanings based on new data and information, and at exploring the links between existing items of information [20].

In the positions entrepreneurs hold within a company, they have potential access to various pieces of information they would not have access to if they were not in the company. This information ranges from unexplored ideas and discontinued projects to proprietary technological knowledge, and can serve as a driver of the process of recognizing an entrepreneurial opportunity.

The entrepreneur also has access to specific information from the sector in which they work, such as customer needs and demands, or changes in consumption

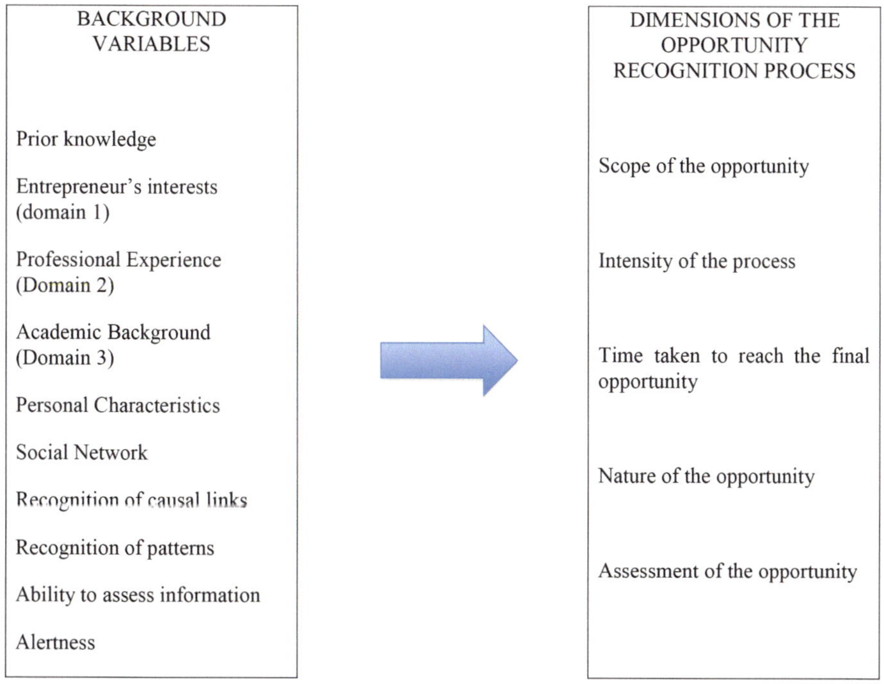

Figure 1.
The dynamics of the relationship between the entrepreneur's background and the dimensions of the process of recognizing opportunities. Source: Prepared by the author.

habits. Alsos and Kaikkonen [20] also argue that entrepreneurs who have access to a vast network of contacts through a company or the market in which they operate will probably have access to a large number of good but "hidden options," in other words, latent business ideas.

Based on the simple act of starting a new business, entrepreneurs can observe opportunities that they would be unable to recognize or develop had they not started their own venture [21].

This dependence, as expressed in the literature and that is related to the entrepreneur's previous activities with the possibilities of recognizing new opportunities, is the basis of this study.

3. Research methodology

The questions that guided this research relate to the field of entrepreneurship, its approach being recognizing opportunities. The research problem, therefore, can be summarized in the following question: What is the role of prior knowledge in the process of recognizing entrepreneurial opportunities?

Deriving from the research problem, the general objective is to identify the relevance and dynamics of the influence of prior knowledge and past experiences in the process of recognizing entrepreneurial opportunities. The specific objectives of this study are: to understand how prior knowledge and past experiences influence the recognition of opportunities; to identify the relationships between the three types of prior knowledge and the process of recognizing entrepreneurial opportunities; and to analyze the interactions between each type of prior knowledge and the dimensions of the opportunity recognition process, in particular the scope of opportunities and the intensity of the emergence of potential new businesses and their interactions.

With regard to the nature of the research, it can be classified as exploratory. Exploratory research is usually undertaken when there are few previous studies related to the research question. Rather than testing hypotheses, this type of research looks for patterns, ideas and insights in order to carry out a more rigorous and qualitative investigation in the future.

In order to operationalize this investigation, we chose a research strategy that involved carrying out a basic qualitative study [22]. This is justified because of the nature of the problem, the objectives that guided the research and, in particular, the fact that there are few alternative methodological processes in this field of research. The framework was based on a qualitative phenomenological paradigm [22].

It is also worth noting that qualitative research starts from an extensive interest or a broad question that becomes narrower as the investigation progresses. In this sense, it does not demand that observed events are measured or listed, nor does it base its analysis on statistical tools [23].

A thorough bibliographic review was initially undertaken on those topics that were relevant to this research. The objective of this initiative was to become familiar with the literature and gain an understanding from the perspective of prior knowledge as applied to recognizing opportunities, thus giving rise to insights into potential research problems. Bringing together this theoretical reference point helped us develop the methodological processes behind this research and supported the framework that involves prior knowledge and the dimensions of scope and intensity.

Based on the research object, and from the point of view of the approach to the problem being researched, we chose in-depth interviews as the data collection source of the empirical material of this study. An in-depth interview technique is recommended for understanding a single meaning when various agents are being used [22].

A semi-structured interview script was used for this purpose, which was developed on the basis of the objectives of this research and the literature that was consulted when establishing the theoretical point of reference. The purpose of these interviews was to obtain as much information as possible about the topics being addressed in the research from the oral reports of the respondents. The use of interviews is justified since they are the ideal way to obtain responses to the objectives proposed by this study.

The initial suggestion was to approach ten entrepreneurs. The selection of respondents was not intended to be statistically representative, but to include as much diversity as possible. The age profile of the seven men and three women who were interviewed was quite different and ranged from 23 to 55 years old. It is worth adding that the activity sectors and the professional and academic backgrounds of the entrepreneurs were also diverse.

4. Result and discussions

The results we obtained corroborate the result proposed by [15], who states that previous experience facilitates recognition of the value of new information and, consequently, favors the process of recognizing entrepreneurial opportunities. In other words, the different dimensions of prior knowledge apparently interfere in a positive way in the process of recognizing entrepreneurial opportunities.

One notable aspect that all entrepreneurs mentioned during the research is that what they are and what they know were, in some way or another, a starting point and served as orientation in their process of recognizing opportunities. This sentence reaffirms the belief expressed in the literature that the entrepreneur's background has an impact, regardless of its extent, in the way they recognize opportunities and even in the opportunity itself.

Family aspects, involving both relationship ties and the intrinsic knowledge that derives from this aspect, were also repeatedly mentioned by the entrepreneurs during the interviews, and certainly they can condition even the relevance of an entrepreneur's experiences and knowledge when it comes to recognizing opportunities.

It is essential to highlight that the third variant of prior knowledge, which is related to fascination and the hobbies of the entrepreneur, plays a relevant role in the process. It seems, however, that this aspect is much more closely related to the fact that it provides the legitimate motivation for a more in-depth search for knowledge in this field of interest rather than to the direct accumulation of the knowledge necessary for discovering an opportunity. This is what the following extract from an interview shows:

> *I always liked flying... I've got an uncle and a cousin who are pilots and I've always been influenced by that. Since I was little, I've built model airplanes. I fly model planes and I've always liked flying a flight simulator. On weekends an outing for me was to go to the airport. It's a big hobby... I studied mechanical engineering because I liked airplanes, and my dream was to work for Embraer. (Entrepreneur A).*

In short, this domain of prior knowledge drives the entrepreneur to outline the boundaries of his potential opportunities, thereby influencing the reach and scope of his entrepreneurial opportunities.

Another latent result obtained from this study was the fact that younger entrepreneurs tend to attribute greater value to knowledge gained by way of a formal education process. They recounted during the interviews that practically every experience they had had before starting their venture generated some kind of buzz in them or had a positive influence on them. This respondent profile repeatedly presented social ties - especially with those closest to them - as being important in the process of recognizing their opportunities.

In a clear correlation, another profile, of the entrepreneur who attributes great relevance to dominating the type of prior knowledge that is aligned with education and academic studies, is comprised of those entrepreneurs who have a narrow professional experience. From a conceptual point of view, discussions focus on the relationship between having little professional experience and the greater importance of knowledge that comes from the education of the entrepreneur, as shown in the following extracts:

> *Yes, I think I can find a link between the opportunities I've already recognized and those that appeared... Since I had a more technical education, I see things from their more technical side, and opportunities too... Perhaps my education in mechanical engineering influenced the opportunities (Entrepreneur A).*

> *I used to work as a cashier for Itaú Bank and then my career started to take off sharply. I got several promotions in a short space of time in the bank for something I did not like doing. After all, I had a degree in marketing... because it was short and had little focus on my area, it was not an experience that helped a lot when it came to identifying an opportunity... The opportunities I saw were always linked to my college, to publicity and marketing... I always wanted to do an internship in my area, in the area of creation, and I always asked [myself] how I could do this little by little without giving up my job... And what if I had an advertising agency completely on-line? (Entrepreneur E).*

> *I'd not had a lot of professional experience, just an internship... There's no doubt at all that the things I learned in college helped me a lot. They gave me the technical basis for understanding the subject... I was doing my end of course work in the same business area. It was when I was preparing the work that I saw it was a promising business. (Entrepreneur F).*

It is worth noting that these same entrepreneurs, who have a smaller stock of knowledge resulting from their professional experiences, tend to have a broader opportunity recognition process in terms of scope. In other words, there is a greater diversity in the profile of the opportunities that these entrepreneurs recognize, especially with regard to the branches of industry in which an opportunity might occur.

It is believed, therefore, that as private entrepreneurs with a lot of professional experience build their wealth of information based on their educational activities or as a result of their hobbies, they tend to have a smaller focus, but a consequently broader scope of opportunities. This is in line with what [19] proposed. As a result, entrepreneurs with less experience in business, which is the result of the work they did, tend to spend more time on a variety of potential opportunities.

For entrepreneurs with a low cognitive structure as a result of their professional experiences the intensity of the process is greater, with a much higher number of entrepreneurial opportunities springing up. The following extracts from the transcribed interviews corroborate this situation:

> *There were various opportunities. I tried several times to do other things. I tried opening a home automation company with the same partner I have today, but it was a market that was just beginning. I'm always having new business ideas... I cannot see any coherence between them; few of them are in the same market. Perhaps my technical background because of engineering conditions me in some way, but generally I cannot especially see any relationship with a market or a sector (Entrepreneur A).*

> *I looked on my own at everything from physiotherapy clinics, distance learning financial courses, etc.; I do not even remember any more, there were a lot of markets. There were undoubtedly more than ten in completely different sectors (Entrepreneur B).*

> *I could see various business possibilities, from a store selling scarves, which was a franchise, to technology for the textile industry... I looked at a lot of things (Entrepreneur F).*

> *Various others [opportunities] appeared in a wide variety of sectors... one that was fairly relevant was in the functional food sector. Because of my family I had contact with some functional products, but the investment was too high for me. That's why I left it for a later stage (Entrepreneur H)*

On the other hand, those entrepreneurs with more robust professional experiences tend to identify and develop opportunities that are much more focused on their previous field of activity, either from the point of view of functional position, or as a branch of industry. In this situation, these entrepreneurs find it more difficult to move away from the ties they have. We draw this conclusion from the interviews, but it is also based on inferences taken from the above literature. (XIX) infer and suggest a more in-depth study into the suspicion that entrepreneurs who are just beginning should look at opportunities in a less focused way. Those who are experienced, however, should channel their analyses towards a smaller thematic area that has opportunities that focus on the experiences and knowledge that come from their past.

Finally, another conclusion derived from this profile of entrepreneurs is that, in contrast to the great intensity presented by those who have low cognitive structures as a result of their professional experiences, they usually recognize a smaller number of opportunities and consequently the process is less intense. This is what the extracts from the interviews transcribed below show:

> *There were not a lot of businesses that I thought about establishing, and they always were in some way related to my work experience [...]. (Entrepreneur D).*

> *In fact, I was in the insurance industry for many years. Even though I spent some time in advertising, my origin and my major interest was in the insurance market... I used to know the market. I had a lot of relationships in it. I knew the problems and I was already imagining an ideal business model... As a result, I looked on this market more kindly, and it was natural for me to decide to set up an insurance broker, with a focus and the differentials that I thought were ideal (Entrepreneur G).*

> *I worked my whole professional life in the building management (condominium) area. I started in a large company and then I set up my own company... I began to get interested in technology, which is when I imagined that the operation I knew well could be automated by way of a web application environment... That was basically the only opportunity I identified (Entrepreneur J).*

5. Conclusions

Due to the increasing relevance of the concept of opportunities as a central point in defining the entrepreneurial process, the ability to identify, evaluate and develop opportunities emerges as a potential item that differentiates entrepreneurs from non-entrepreneurs.

It is also believed that the experiences and knowledge accumulated in a wide variety of activities in some way mean that certain people are capable of acting better when faced with a combination of disconnected items of information. In other words, the cognitive structures derived from these past experiences facilitate and guide people towards recognizing an entrepreneurial opportunity.

In order to explain the relationship between prior knowledge and past experiences when recognizing opportunities, this work adopted a theoretical framework that draws a parallel between three domains of knowledge, namely: i) subjects of special interest to the entrepreneur, professional experiences and formal education activities, and the dimensions of the opportunity recognition process, and specifically for this study, ii) the scope of entrepreneurial opportunities and iii) the intensity of the process.

The scope of opportunities has to do with the characteristics of the business, which are related to its line of activity and the functional role of its work. Meanwhile, the intensity of the process is based on the number of opportunities that appear to the entrepreneur.

By adopting a qualitative research approach, this study carried out ten in-depth interviews with entrepreneurs using a semi-structured script.

This allowed us to reach some conclusions. The first concerns endorsing the literature on the relevance of past knowledge in the process of identifying, evaluating and developing an entrepreneurial opportunity.

Another conclusion was the fact that in the process of recognizing an opportunity those entrepreneurs who had had less time in their professional careers attribute the relevance of their prior knowledge to their educational activities.

Along these same lines, entrepreneurs who have little professional experience present a very wide field of opportunities, making it clear that they have little detailed knowledge of a particular sector or industry. This can be justified by the fact that experiences that originate from formal education are much less restrictive than professional experiences. These same entrepreneurs are endowed with enormous intensity when it comes to the process of recognizing opportunities; in other words, business ideas that become opportunities and potential ventures are constantly emerging.

On the other hand, those entrepreneurs with greater and better constructed work experience, both in an industry and in a functional position, have less scope; in other words, in most cases they direct their past experiences to a connected and very narrow thematic horizon. These entrepreneurs also have a less intense opportunity recognition process, which is directly justified by the fact that the possibilities in terms of thematic fields are narrower.

The limitations of this study are, in particular, the potential correlation that exists between robust professional experiences and the age of the entrepreneur. In other words, the question remains as to how much their deliberation in terms of their little professional experience is based on the limitations of their professional experiences, or on their age, in view of the little time they have had to form a stronger set of experiences.

As a suggestion for future research, there is a need for a detailed study of the interactions, not only between the domains of prior knowledge, but of other variables that try to explain the differences in the ability to recognize an entrepreneurial opportunity.

Author details

Felipe Baeta and Tales Andreassi*
FGV EAESP, Brazil

*Address all correspondence to: tandreassi@gmail.com

References

[1] SHANE, S.; VENKATARAMAN S. The promise of entrepreneurship as a field of research. Academy of Management Review, v. 25, p. 217-226, 2000.

[2] FUDURIC, N. The sources of entrepreneurial opportunities. Aalborg: Aalborg University, 2008.

[3] FAASSEN, W. Recognition and development of the entrepreneurial opportunity by novice entrepreneurs: influenced by their background? Enschede: University of Twente, 2010.

[4] ARDICHVILI, A.; CARDOZO, R.; RAY, S. A theory of entrepreneurial opportunity identification and development. Journal of Business Venturing, v. 18, n. 1, p. 105-123, 2003.

[5] STEVENSON, H. H.; JARILLO-MOSSI, J. C. Preserving entrepreneurship as companies grow. Journal of Business Strategy, v. 7, p. 10-23, 1986.

[6] SINGH, R. P. Entrepreneurial opportunity recognition through social networks. Londres: Garland Publiching, 2000.

[7] SHANE, S. A general theory of entrepreneurship. Cheltenham: Edward Elgar, 2003.

[8] ALVES, R. D. Empreendedorismo e o processo de identificação de oportunidades. Master Thesis – Pontifícia Universidade Católica do Rio de Janeiro, Rio de Janeiro, 2005.

[9] CHRISTENSEN, P. S.; MADSEN, O. O.; PETERSON, R. Conceptualizing entrepreneurial opportunity recognition. In: HILLS, G. E. (Ed.). Marketing and entrepreneurship: research ideas and opportunities. Westport: Quorum Books, 1994. p. 61-75.

[10] HILLS, G. E. Opportunity recognition by successful entrepreneurs: a pilot study. In: ZAHRA S. A. et al. (Ed.). Frontiers of entrepreneurship research. Wellesley: Babson College, 1995.

[11] TIMMONS, J. A. et al. Opportunity recognition: the core of entrepreneurship. In: CHURCHILL, N. C. et al. (Ed.). Frontiers of entrepreneurship research. Wellesley: Babson College, 1987.

[12] STEVENSON, H. H.; ROBERTS, M. J.; GROUSBECK, H. I. New business ventures and the entrepreneur. Homewood: Irwin, 1985.

[13] KIRZNER, I. M. Competition and entrepreneurship. Chicago: University of Chicago Press, 1973.

[14] HILLS, G. E.; SHRADER, R. C. Successful entrepreneurs: insights into opportunity recognition. In: ZAHRA S. A. et al. (Ed.). Frontiers of entrepreneurship research. Wellesley: Babson College, 1998.

[15] SHANE, S. Prior knowledge and the discovery of entrepreneurial opportunity. Organization Science, 2000

[16] BARON, R.; SHANE, S. Entrepreneurship: a process perspective. Nelson Education, 2007

[17] LÉVESQUE, M.; MINNITI, M. Age matters: how demographics influence aggregate entrepreneurship. Strategic Entrepreneurship Journal, September 2001.

[18] AZOULAY, P.; JONES, B.F.; KIM, J.D.; MIRANDA, J. 2020. "Age and High-Growth Entrepreneurship." American Economic Review: Insights, 2 (1): 65-82.

[19] BARON, R.; ENSLEY, M. Opportunity recognition as the detection of meaningful patterns: evidence from comparisons of novice and experienced entrepreneurs. Management Science, v. 52, p. 1331-1344, 2006.

[20] ALSOS, G. A.; KAIKKONEN, V. Opportunities and prior knowledge: a study of experienced entrepreneurs. In: ZAHRA S. A. et al. (Ed.). Frontiers of entrepreneurship research. Wellesley: Babson College, 2004. p. 300-314.

[21] RONSTADT, R. The corridor principle. Journal of Business Venturing, v. 3, n. 1, p. 31-40, 1988.

[22] MERRIAM, S. B. Case study research in education: a qualitative approach. San Francisco: Jossey-Bass, 1988.

[23] GODOY, A. S. Introdução à pesquisa qualitativa e suas possibilidades. Revista de Administração de Empresas, v. 35, n. 2, p. 57-63, 1995.

Chapter 6

International Entrepreneurship: An Entrepreneurial Behavior Oriented to the Pursuit of International Opportunities

Alexander Tabares

Abstract

International entrepreneurship (IE) research draws on the notion that internationalization is an entrepreneurial behavior oriented to the discovery, enactment, evaluation, and exploitation of opportunities across national borders to create value and get a competitive advantage. Based on the clear emphasis on opportunity-focused behaviors, IE research has made progress and extended its domain and boundaries to an extent that the mechanisms operating throughout the international opportunity process can be described. The present chapter aims to depict antecedents, mechanisms, and outcomes of this entrepreneurial behavior oriented to the pursuit of international opportunities and it offers directions for future research. As such, the chapter makes four contributions. First, it outlines antecedents at three levels (individual, firm, and environmental) as driving aspects that lead to the international opportunity-related behavior. Second, it reveals the mechanism by which different actors discover, enact, evaluate, and exploit international opportunities. Third, it describes the outcomes of this opportunities process. Fourth, it suggests establishing a conceptual basis around one previously proposed definition incorporating a notion of a social context that would enable IE scholarly community to set the objective criteria around opportunities and go beyond the legal entity of the focal firm and consider multiple actors, resources, processes, history, and context. Finally, the chapter offers some theoretical contributions by proposing directions for future research.

Keywords: international entrepreneurship, international opportunities, opportunity discovery, opportunity creation, international performance

1. Introduction

International entrepreneurship (IE) is an intersectional domain [1, 2] combining international business and entrepreneurship areas of knowledge. The IE field emerged in the early 1990s when different studies indicated that some small and young new ventures could go into international markets from inception at their early years [3], which was different from the traditional Uppsala perspective which argued that firms, especially multinationals, could become international following a specific-regular, slow, and evolutionary process to become international. Thus, this early and rapid internationalization theoretical framework challenged the validity of the Uppsala model prevailing so far, and it opened avenues for IE research to study and focus on features of early internationalizing firms and their innovative and new internationalization process [4, 5]. Consequently, most IE research concentrated on studying the internationalization of newly founded ventures that are necessarily small and young and it restricted for years the study of bigger companies [2].

Nonetheless, over the last years, IE research has moved on toward studying a variety of internationalization entrepreneurial behaviors [2, 6] of different actors—organizations, groups, or individuals [7]; and then, it has considered not only the entrepreneurial behaviors of small and young firms but also the entrepreneurial behaviors of large and established companies [2]. Hence, IE has evolved over the years, and it has incorporated progressively new insights that address the field as a behavioral process of pursuing opportunities across national borders [2, 8–12] to create value and get a competitive advantage [2, 12].

In the evolving IE field, different definitions have determined common conceptual elements suggesting that the IE field implies a dynamic process or behavior of discovering, evaluation, and exploitation of opportunities across national borders to achieve value creation to different stakeholders [2]. First, McDougall and Oviatt [13] defined IE as a combination of innovative, proactive, and risk-seeking behavior that crosses national borders and is intended to create value in business organizations. Then, Zahra and George [12] defined IE as the process of creatively discovering and exploiting opportunities that lie outside a firm's domestic markets in the pursuit of competitive advantage. Afterward, Dimitratos and Plakoyiannaki [14] defined IE as an organizational-wide process that is embedded in the organizational culture of the firm and which seeks through the exploitation of opportunities in the international marketplace to generate value. Next, Oviatt and McDougall [7] defined IE as the discovery, enactment, evaluation, and exploitation of opportunities—across national borders—to create future goods and services. Later, Styles and Seymour [11] defined IE as the behavioral processes associated with the creation and exchange of value through the identification and exploitation of opportunities that cross-national borders. Afterward, Zahra et al. [15] defined IE as the discovery, formation, evaluation, and exploitation of opportunities across national borders to create new businesses, models, and solutions for value creation, including financial, social, and environmental. Finally, Tabares, et al. [2] defined IE as the socially constructed behavioral processes associated with the discovery, enactment, evaluation, and exploitation of opportunities across national borders to create new businesses, models, and solutions for value creation, including financial, social, and environmental.

Based on the clear emphasis on opportunity-focused behaviors, IE research has made progress and extended its domain and boundaries to an extent that the mechanisms operating throughout the international opportunity process can be described [2]. In this sense, the international opportunity process has been described as a dynamic and iterative phenomenon [2] that develops over time and interacts with the outside world [2, 16, 17] in a complex system that embraces numerous dimensions and various levels (individual, firm, and environment) [2, 18, 19]. Over the years, IE research has also depicted antecedents, mechanisms, and outcomes of this entrepreneurial behavior oriented to the pursuit of international opportunities [2, 20].

2. Antecedents influencing the international opportunities process

IE research has outlined antecedents at three levels (individual, firm, and environmental) as driving aspects that lead to the discovery, enactment, evaluation, and exploitation of international opportunities.

2.1 Individual-level analysis

Three significant variables have been identified in the process of discovering, enacting, evaluating, and exploiting international opportunities [2]. They have been related to cognition, human capital, and social capital features that determine why some individuals, and not others, pursue specific international opportunities and behave differently toward these opportunities [2]. Thus, different studies illustrate the importance of cognitive features and mental models in the discovery, enactment, evaluation, and exploitation of international opportunities [2, 21–23]. Specifically, individuals with high entrepreneurial intention—perceived desirability and self-efficacy—are psychologically equipped to pursue international opportunities successfully [24–26]. Similarly, individuals with high levels of commitment [16, 27], alertness [28, 29], imagination [22, 30, 31], willingness, and flexibility [16, 27] can sense and exploit opportunities more efficiently. Other cognitive schemas driving to opportunity-related behaviors are also related to higher levels of proactiveness, risk-taking propensity [16, 21, 23], and global mindset [25, 32, 33] that enable individuals to pursue specific international opportunities. Accordingly, the mentioned cognitive schemas serve individuals to make decisions involving international opportunity capture and growth in foreign markets [2]. Such mental schemas serve to acquire and process information to resolve problems and respond to dynamic and changing market conditions [2].

Regarding individuals' human capital, some studies suggest that the constant investment of individuals in training, education, and other types of learning, namely the English language acquisition, are determinant factors in the pursuit of international opportunities [2, 21, 28, 34–36]. Similarly, different studies indicate that prior experiential knowledge of individuals in the form of entrepreneurial experience [37], market experience—the business with clients, market, and competitors [28, 31, 37], internationalization experience—resources, capabilities, strategies [27, 38–41], and cross-cultural experience—institutional rules, norms, and cultural values [31, 42–45] enables individuals to identify a broader range of opportunity types and hence pursue better international opportunities.

About individuals' social capital, scholarly research observes that this social capital offers sources of learning and provides information that enables individuals to obtain strategic knowledge on providers, clients, and institutions in foreign countries and then pursues international opportunities [2, 16, 46–49]. Furthermore, this social capital enables individuals to gain financial resources and learn where to find them for continued internationalization [40, 50]. Some studies point out that personal ties with international trade intermediaries, export promoting agencies, local and international distributors, and trade exhibitions are fundamental to discover, enact, evaluate, and exploit international opportunities [31, 36, 44, 47, 51, 52]. Similarly, other ties related to family, social, and business contexts benefit individuals to get access to critical resources, including knowledge that assists them in pursuing and exploiting international opportunities [25, 26, 46, 52–55]. Interestingly, casual ties with overseas distributors and customers through word of mouth are also triggers of international opportunities [39, 47, 56–60].

2.2 Firm-level analysis

The previous individual-level analysis asserted that the person's traits are vital factors to pursue international opportunities [2]. However, these features alone cannot be considered as sufficient to handle the complexities and challenges of discovering, enacting, evaluating, and exploiting international opportunities [2]. Influenced by the individual's unique characteristics, the firm must be able to embed the entrepreneurial vision and orientation of the founders into the company and build up an organizational structure that can facilitate the pursuit of international opportunities and thus achieve a competitive advantage [2]. At this firm-level, four significant variables have been identified in the process of discovering, enacting, evaluating, and exploiting international opportunities. They have been related to the firm's culture, the firm's knowledge-based resources, the firm's networks, and the firm's strategy [2].

Substantial IE research indicates the relevance of the firm's culture as a set of shared values and beliefs (a collective cognition) that help firms' members to understand organizational performance and thus provide norms for their behavior and actions in the organization [14, 61–64]. Such collective cognition (collective knowledge structures or articulated heuristics) serves the firm to pursue international opportunities and respond to external events they face [61, 64]. Thus, the firm's culture becomes a source of sustainable competitive advantage, and, most importantly, it enables the employees to pursue and exploit foreign market opportunities [14, 62, 63, 65–68].

Regarding the firm's knowledge-based resources, some findings suggest that access and control of unique resources, in particular, knowledge, enable the firm to gain competitive advantage by pursuing opportunities in international markets [2, 39, 69–71]. Although these knowledge-based resources are grounded on the individual's human capital capabilities [2], they are integrated into the firm through collective routines and processes by which the firm combines and reconfigures new and existing resources to pursue international opportunities and achieve competitive advantage [2, 24, 61, 71]. Furthermore, the firm leverages its capacity to discover, enact, evaluate, and exploit international opportunities through prior organizational knowledge acquired through experiential knowledge within international networks [72–74], international industry and market-specific knowledge [35, 56, 75, 76], internationalization knowledge [40, 47, 75, 77], technological knowledge [33, 35, 39, 78], and institutional knowledge [31, 40, 42, 44, 79].

About the firm's networks, different studies contend that the firm's alliances and relationships provide better access to international opportunities [40, 41, 44, 47, 48, 72] and abilities to overcome the liabilities of newness and foreignness [40, 80, 81]. Some findings indicate that the firm's networks are sources of learning that offer information on risks, consumers, suppliers, politics, economics, and competitive resources leading to superior knowledge and incremental commitment that, in turn, enable the firm to pursue international opportunities successfully [34, 56, 65, 73]. Interestingly, some findings reveal that bonding—close ties offering trust and security—and bridging networks—open and weak ties offering new information)—enable firms to discover, enact, evaluate, and exploit international opportunities [57, 72, 82–86].

Some IE research underscores that the firm's strategy is also essential because it defines a roadmap to deal with the uncertain events which constitute the dynamic and changing business environment [2]. Some studies remark that the firm's strategy has three dimensions: an entrepreneurial posture-oriented strategy, a decision-making rule-oriented strategy, and organization capabilities reconfiguration-oriented strategy [2]. Through the firm's entrepreneurial orientation (understood as the posture to be risky, proactive, and innovative), the firm is alert and prepared to discover and enact international opportunities [39, 61, 63, 70, 77, 79, 87, 88]. Through the firm's decision-making rules (causal logic or effectual logic), the firm evaluates and exploit international opportunities [39, 44, 59, 89–92]. Through the firm's capabilities reconfiguration, the firm responds to changing environments and then combines, modifies, and deploys efficiently existing and new asset base are likely to pursue and exploit other opportunities across national markets [31, 61, 70, 71, 78, 89, 93, 94].

2.3 Environmental-level analysis

At this level, different studies show that three main environmental conditions act as a moderator force that shapes the way different individuals or firms pursue international opportunities [2]. The first factor spins around a technological advancement context that comprises the Internet and other information-and-communication-technologies. The other two factors gravitate around a national and international context that includes legal, political, economic, social, and cultural features [2]. Specifically, these environmental factors are classified into formal institutions (laws, regulations, and government apparatuses enforcing social acceptability) and informal institutions (socio-cultural values and beliefs defining behavior legitimacy) that enable or constrain the way different actors pursue international opportunities [2].

Some studies highlight the moderating role of the technological advancement context that provides individuals and firms with new ways to pursue international opportunities [2, 33, 95]. The rapid pace of technological change has opened vast opportunities not only to big and established firms but also to smaller and younger-entrepreneurially oriented-competitive firms that efficiently exploit emerging opportunities facilitated by the liberalization of barriers to internationalization [2, 33, 96]. In general, these technological revolutions provide firms with new ways to conduct international business, acquire information and knowledge, communicate ideas, and co-create with others facilitating the pursuit of international opportunities quicker and more successfully [2, 22, 25, 33, 56, 95, 97].

Regarding national and international contexts, some findings underscore the moderating role of formal institutions that enable or constrain different actor-specific behaviors, particularly how they discover, enact, evaluate, and exploit international opportunities [2, 98, 99]. Specifically, economic liberalization opens frontiers and allows firms to pursue international opportunities in an accelerated way [2, 22]. Likewise, nations' property rights protection and transparent laws [100] and regulations promote institutional stability leading to more opportunity-related behaviors [99]. Likewise, the lack of laws, regulations, and government agencies or inefficient and unregulated markets constrain different actors to pursue international opportunities [84, 100, 101]. According to some relevant IE research, institutional voids or weak formal institutions may eventually trigger opportunity-related behaviors oriented to solve social problems worldwide [2, 15, 36].

Regarding informal institutions, relevant IE research suggests that socio-cultural values and beliefs strongly influence how different individuals and firms pursue international opportunities [8, 23, 60, 69, 102] and that relationship [2]. Specifically, cultural values around the formation of social communities such as joint ventures or agglomerations influence individuals and firms in their opportunity development [43, 91, 100, 103]. Similarly, collective beliefs carrying with them societal and cultural expectations and a country's education system shape the way different actors discover, enact, evaluate, and exploit international opportunities [23, 60, 102, 104]. On the other hand, the social and structural stratification processes—a nation's labor division—[100] and the nation's socio-cultural structures [23] increase the likelihood that individuals and firms discover, enact international opportunities, as well as evaluate the types of costs and benefits [23], and exploit them due to the knowledge gap between the cultures [47, 105]. Other studies highlight that global wealth disparity and corporate social responsibility movements encourage individuals and firms to pursue international opportunities [15, 95], specially oriented to solve social problems originated from institutional voids in inactive governments [106].

3. Mechanism in the international opportunities process

A systematic literature review conducted in IE literature indicates that the international opportunities process can begin with an opportunity discovery—by serendipity or by active search—or with an opportunity enactment—by creation or co-creation as a continuum of behaviors of decision logics that are intertwined and complemented each other [2]. Different from the hot debate in the IE research around the nature and the conditions of the opportunity existence in which the discovery-creation-opportunity-related behaviors are considered as exclusive and contradictory, some findings reveal that both behaviors are indeed complementary and intertwined in entrepreneurial action [2, 6, 7, 88, 107–110]. Instead of making ontological or epistemological differentiation of the concepts, IE research has paved the way to enrich opportunity research theory by considering discovery and creation of opportunities as interdependent [9] and mutually enabling [88, 108, 110, 111] in a multilayer reality.

Broadly, the international opportunities process is an iterative entrepreneurial action moving between discovery and enactment as a continuum of behaviors of decision logics where it is involved not only individuals' and firms' activities but also the collaboration with other business and market firms, entrepreneurs, partners, customers, competitors, and institutions [2]. Regarding opportunity discovery, international opportunities can be discovered by serendipitous (accidental) encounters where individuals and firms are usually receptive to international opportunities, but they do not necessarily carry out a systematic search [35, 39, 74, 90, 112–114]. Thus, individuals and firms discover international opportunities through unplanned encounters initiated by inbound inquiries or others who find the focal firm [26, 37, 47, 57, 74, 77, 80, 90, 115, 116].

Similarly, international opportunities can be discovered by active search where individuals and firms discover international opportunities through a purposeful and deliberate exploration process and use trusted information sources and channels, prior knowledge, and networks to limit the length of the search [39, 51, 77, 78, 84, 112–114, 117]. Hence, individuals and firms strategically direct efforts via a formal planning process (Ciravegna, Majano, et al., 2014; [2, 65, 91]). This indicates that opportunity discoveries fluctuate between effectual and causal decision-making depending on different circumstances and entrepreneurial intentions [2, 7, 8, 37, 69, 110, 112].

Regarding opportunity enactment, international opportunities can be created through proactive [61, 77, 87] and imaginative thinking [6, 22, 56, 118, 119] where individuals and firms combine available resources in novel and productive ways [2, 51, 59, 88]. Thus, opportunities are created as a result of an iterative process of action and reaction, where individuals and firms learn by doing under conditions of high uncertainty, flexibility, and adaptability [2]. Similarly, international opportunities can be co-created through constant interaction with different actors in experimental and mutual learning [8, 15, 24, 27, 31, 34, 37, 56, 80, 83, 91, 93, 120] rather than by acting alone [44]. In general, international opportunity enactment implies an iterative and incremental decision-making process in which the opportunity is actualized and constructed through social interaction with others and in which individuals and firms are continually evaluating information to weigh up the risks, gains, and losses [8].

Once an international opportunity is discovered or enacted, then, individuals and firms move to a development stage where the opportunity is evaluated to determine if it is valid and substantial enough to be exploited [2] overall, the way individuals and firms evaluate opportunities is not absolute [104, 115]. Arguably, some authors posit that the decision rules of individuals and firms fluctuate between causal logic and effectual logic [2] depending on a set of contingency factors such as experience [61, 72], resource availability (e.g., knowledge networks), time availability, type of stakeholders [115], or type of business conditions [34, 112, 119]. What is evident is that whether the opportunity is discovered or enacted, the opportunity requires a continual development process [2] in which individuals and firms gain more knowledge and experience about international opportunities and can then assess them more objectively [5, 115].

Chandra [115] gives evidence that individuals (firms) evaluate opportunities as a result of the interaction of time and experience where they deploy simple (unstructured, minimalist simple rule-based reasoning), revised (elaborated rule-based reasoning oriented to choose the best opportunities), and complex rules (finer rule-based reasoning oriented to maximize expected returns). Consequently, not all the opportunity ideas survive in this evaluation process [2, 22], and only some of them are likely to be exploited, while others are likely to be abandoned due to insufficient resource support [2, 61].

On the other hand, international opportunities exploitation requires various individuals' abilities and firms' capabilities where actions and behaviors oscillate from nonstrategic planning to deliberate and rational planning [2, 34, 59, 88], depending on the level of foreign market uncertainty and the kind of opportunity. Broadly stated, international opportunities can be exploited through various individuals' abilities, namely cognitive heuristics [23, 61], proactive and risk-taking behavior [51, 65, 79], self-efficacy [118], and firms' capabilities such as international market knowledge, international experience, information-and-communication-technology competencies, linguistic, cultural and experiential knowledge [33, 39, 51, 54, 63, 78, 79], as well as active participation in international networks [47, 48, 52, 55, 75, 80, 93, 94, 121].

Similarly, international opportunities can be exploited through specific and specialized knowledge-based resources leveraged with other market partners [2], namely via joint-ventures [90], multinational subsidiary stakeholders [42], business partners [55, 80, 93], clients [22, 27, 56, 83], industry agglomerations [100], government agency officials [15, 27, 101], and via financial resources in the form of venture capital [35, 116].

3.1 Outcomes of the international opportunities process

The IE literature research reveals that different from two common proxies capturing outcomes (e.g., international growth and performance), there is a broader set of outcomes that can be classified into financial and nonfinancial performances [2]. Regarding financial performances, some studies reveal that prevalent indicators of international profitability [16, 33, 37, 42, 46, 58, 122], sales growth and sales volume [69, 75, 76, 83, 101, 123], operational efficiency [38, 124], opportunity selling [27, 42, 69], venture capital [39, 46], licensing [125, 126], tax incentives and grants [98, 99], new ventures [37, 127].

Regarding nonfinancial performances, other studies found intangible and immaterial benefits at the individual level and the firm level [2]. At the individual level, the international opportunities process generally enables individuals to expand their cognitive schemas and enhance heuristic decisions to face uncertainty [21, 128]. As such, individuals address international market uncertainties with better perceptions of self-efficacy and perceived-desirability and they are equipped with a greater entrepreneurial behavior [87] characterized by high-risk propensity [43], personal proactiveness and commitment [26] that elevates motivation and willingness to face and tolerate uncertainty [21, 51]. Furthermore, individuals improved their evaluation reasoning [115] through trial-and-error learning [23, 43]. International opportunities also improve individuals' human capital and social capital traits [2]. Specifically, individuals enhance social capital in foreign market networks, which results in new opportunities in the form of new business, access to information, new knowledge [75, 80], and superior opportunity development [37].

At the firm level, the international opportunities process leads the firm to achieve better and sophisticated organization capabilities and routines [31, 33, 61, 71, 94, 125, 129], stronger organizational culture [75], more innovative strategies [78, 123], novelty [37], and new products and services [73], early internationalization [31, 122], firm's growth and market diversity [47, 71, 75, 76, 87, 101], success [16, 31, 37, 76], competitive advantage [31, 125], survival [83], more efficient entry modes [58, 115, 130, 131], and international expansion [34, 75, 123, 132].

4. Conclusions

International entrepreneurship (IE) research draws on the notion that internationalization is an entrepreneurial behavior oriented to the discovery, enactment, evaluation, and exploitation of opportunities across national borders to create value and get a competitive advantage [2, 12]. Hence, the international opportunity process has become a central concept in the IE literature and then it leads the IE field to advance to a point where the field has broadened its territory and boundaries with a robust conceptual basis that should consider not only the entrepreneurial behaviors of small and young firms but also the entrepreneurial behaviors of large and established companies [2].

Abundant IE research reveals that this international opportunity discovery-enactment-evaluation-exploitation process is a multidimensional, dynamic, and iterative phenomenon [2] that develops over time and interacts with the outside world [2, 6, 8, 16, 17, 100] in a complex system that embraces numerous dimensions and various levels (individual, firm, and environment [2, 18, 19]. Broadly stated, individual, organizational, and institutional level aspects interact in the market to enable or constrain the pursuit of new international opportunities [2, 102]. As Reuber et al. [5] suggest, the pursuit of international opportunities can be assessed by an individual-level cognitive activity, constructed by a firm-level innovative activity and shaped by an institutional-level structuring activity [5] in a notion of a distributed, global ecosystem of opportunities and opportunity seekers.

In the evolving IE field, different definitions have determined common conceptual elements suggesting that the IE field implies a dynamic behavioral process oriented to the pursuit of international opportunities to achieve value creation to different stakeholders. Interestingly, the last definition in the IE research proposed by Tabares et al. [2], who extend and acknowledge previous conceptualizations, suggest that "IE is a socially constructed behavioral processes associated with the discovery, enactment, evaluation, and exploitation of opportunities across national borders to create new businesses, models, and solutions for value creation, including financial, social, and environmental." With this definition, IE research has a robust conceptual basis around opportunity-related behaviors and then incorporates a notion of a social context that influences and shapes the way individuals, firms, organizations discover, enact, evaluate, and exploit to create value not only financial but also social and environmental. Second, the definition makes the IE domain independent of firm size and age analysis and enable scholarly studies to set the objective criteria around opportunities that could encourage researchers to go beyond the legal entity of the focal firm and consider multiple actors, and resources, processes, history, and context [2, 5, 102], giving a 360° view of opportunity-related behaviors [133].

5. Suggestions for future research

As Reuber [5] stated in her JIBS collections, IE research, like any social science research, has been cumulative with successive studies building on past insights, resulting in an impressive body of findings that can be integrated and interpreted based on shared assumptions about what constitutes interesting and relevant research questions. The potential downside to such consensus is that it is difficult to move away from it and consider alternate perspectives and prospects [20]. Hence, all the antecedent and outcome factors identified in this chapter and classified within each proposed level do not represent either a fixed or complete list. Neither do the mechanisms that describe the international opportunities process. Rather, this chapter opens critical directions for future research.

Future research could explore other antecedents, mechanisms, and outcomes of this entrepreneurial behavior oriented to the pursuit of international opportunities. One direction is to call for scholarly studies that could increase our understanding of how individuals (managers and entrepreneurs) pursue international opportunities to reconfigure firm resources and capabilities to respond to dynamic and changing market environments. Specifically, future research can examine in greater detail the effect of the three individuals' aspects—cognition, human capital, and social capital—and their corresponding performance patterns under a dynamic managerial capability perspective and/or use a broader interdisciplinary approach [2]. Further, research is needed to develop a deeper theoretical understanding of the cognitive approach and expand the scope of the analysis on risk-taking, proactiveness, and innovativeness aspects of their international entrepreneurial orientation and their actions within the different phases of the international opportunities process and their ultimate performance [2].

While much research has been conducted on social capital aspects, it is crucial to focus on how individuals (managers) develop weak and strong ties with strategic networks and what impact these ties have on the international opportunities process [2]. Future research might also focus on the precise ways in which trust and commitment are developed in these types of ties. One of the most fertile areas for future analysis is to clarify the sectors, markets, and circumstances in which networks generate superior performance [2]. Furthermore, future researchers could also explore the role of political network actors and institutional settings in this process. About this institutional networking, one interesting avenue is to analyze how the institutional actors vary across countries and how they contribute or constrain their discovery, evaluation, and exploitation of international opportunities [2]. In line with this, another avenue is to examine why some individuals do not gain access to institutional networks or gain other network resources in the same way others do.

In respect to human capital, future studies could better examine the impact of information-and-communication-technology capabilities on the international opportunities process, which in turn drives firms' international market performance [2]. Given that language skills seem to play a specific role in the international opportunities process and firm performance, research in this stream is needed to develop a deeper theoretical understanding of this managerial capability [2]. Forthcoming research could also explore how managers assess and reconfigure their learning capabilities and how they affect learning at the firm level, and how this affects firm performance [2]. Other research areas where scholarship could advance in human capital capability include international market orientation, branding decisions, marketing communication, pricing, product design, and customer equity [2].

At an environmental-level analysis, future research needs to understand better how different economies and political contexts influence opportunity-related behaviors and how social, cultural, and institutional settings shape distinctively the way different actors pursue international opportunities and exploit them. Increasingly, there is a need to explore how different actors from emerging economies pursue international opportunities and deal with turbulent and dynamic markets to achieve international performance. For instance, more research from emerging economies is required to understand how different actors overcome their resource constraints and pursue international opportunities under uncertainty and institutional voids. Related, there is a need for further research on how formal and informal institutions shape and influence international opportunity-related behaviors.

As for future research in the international opportunities process, one fruitful line would be to analyze the international entrepreneurial process on different types of individuals (one-shot, drop-out, nascent, novice, serial, and portfolio entrepreneurs) or firms and understand their opportunity-related behaviors and their decision-making rule process through the evaluation and exploitation of international opportunities [2]. Specifically, further research is needed to understand the best type of reasoning that entrepreneurial decision-makers should use to deal with different types of uncertainty and how managers respond to serendipitous encounters or unexpected discoveries. As for the development phase of the international opportunities process, further research is required to understand how individuals and firms evaluate opportunities and their decisions to exploit opportunities [2].

A promising line would be to explore decision-making models—effectuation or causation—individuals and firms utilize to evaluate international opportunities [2, 20]. Future research could examine the international opportunities process under the effectuation theory and understand the transition from effectual reasoning to causal reasoning to provide a connection between entrepreneurship and strategy through a decision-making rule process [2, 20]. Different from current research studies on failed international attempts and their evaluation process would also provide rich insights. Also, there is a need to understand why international opportunities that are discovered are not successfully exploited. Along with this line, researchers could explore how individuals and firms can exploit new international business opportunities through different entry modes. It is worth noting that the operationalization of the international opportunities process—discovery, enactment, evaluation, and exploitation—is at an embryonic stage and needs further operationalization [2].

As for methodology, further research is needed to explore the contexts, dynamics, and types of international entrepreneurial firms. Specifically, a diverse sample of firms, including ranges in age, size, sector, internationalization pace, and scope, are promising and needed research lines [2]. Future research could explore how micro-multinationals and multinationals pursue international opportunities and what entrepreneurial behaviors they deploy in that process. They behave in different ways facing diverse challenges [2]. Also, future studies from agriculture-based and low-value-adding commodity-based industries, as well as from emerging economies, would enrich the debate and deepen our understanding of international entrepreneurial behavior and its antecedents and outcomes [2]. The field would also benefit from additional tools and techniques based on simulation methods (e.g., agent-based modeling and ethnographic and system dynamics), as well as contingency models (structural equation modeling). Future quantitative and qualitative data analyses can be used to capture development over time. Along with this line, further qualitative studies with longitudinal approaches could follow up with international performance and depict a more holistic picture of the effects of international opportunities [2].

Additionally, knowledge in this stream needs to be extended to other antecedents for international opportunities; for instance, studies could investigate the moderator and/or mediator roles of the different driving factors (e.g., managerial capabilities and environmental aspects as examined in this study) with international performance [2]. Future research could investigate the various indicators analyzed here regarding international performance as an outcome of the international opportunities process. Moreover, further studies are needed to explore the links between financial and nonfinancial performance, as well as the relationship between exporting performance and other dimensions of business performance [2]. Lastly, another potentially fruitful area could be to amply the variety of subjective and objective indicators and contrast them for reliability purposes [2].

Author details

Alexander Tabares
Universidad de Medellín, Medellin, Colombia

*Address all correspondence to: atabares@udem.edu.co

References

[1] Jones MV, Coviello N, Tang YK. International Entrepreneurship research (1989-2009): A domain ontology and thematic analysis. Journal of Business Venturing. 2011;**26**(6):632-659. DOI: 10.1016/j.jbusvent.2011.04.001

[2] Tabares A, Chandra Y, Alvarez C, Escobar-Sierra M. Opportunity-related behaviors in international entrepreneurship research: A multilevel analysis of antecedents, processes, and outcomes. International Entrepreneurship and Management Journal. 2020:1-48. [In press]. DOI: 10.1007/s11365-020-00636-3

[3] Oviatt BM, McDougall PP. Toward a theory of international new ventures. Journal of International Business Studies. 1994;**25**(1):45-64. DOI: 10.1057/palgrave.jibs.8490193

[4] Coviello N. Re-thinking research on born globals. Journal of International Business Studies. 2015;**46**(1):17-26. DOI: 10.1057/jibs.2014.59

[5] Reuber AR, Knight GA, Liesch PW, Zhou L. International entrepreneurship: The pursuit of entrepreneurial opportunities across national borders. Journal of International Business Studies. 2018;**49**(4):395-406. DOI: 10.1057/s41267-018-0149-5

[6] Mainela T, Puhakka V, Servais P. The Concept of international opportunity in international entrepreneurship: A review and a research agenda. International Journal of Management Reviews. 2014;**16**(1):105-129. DOI: 10.1111/ijmr.12011

[7] Oviatt B, McDougall P. Defining international entrepreneurship and modeling the speed of internationalization. Entrepreneurship Theory and Practice. 2005;**29**(5):537-554. DOI: 10.1111/j.1540-6520.2005.00097.x

[8] Fletcher D. International entrepreneurship and the small business. Entrepreneurship and Regional Development. 2004;**16**(4):289-305. DOI: 10.1080/0898562042000263267

[9] Mathews JA, Zander I. The international entrepreneurial dynamics of accelerated internationalisation. Journal of International Business Studies. 2007;**38**(3):387-403. DOI: 10.2307/4540430

[10] Peiris IK, Akoorie MEM, Sinha P. International entrepreneurship: A critical analysis of studies in the past two decades and future directions for research. Journal of International Entrepreneurship. 2012;**10**(4):279-324. DOI: 10.1007/s10843-012-0096-3

[11] Styles C, Seymour RG. Opportunities for marketing researchers in international entrepreneurship. International Marketing Review. 2006a;**23**(2):126-145. DOI: 10.1108/02651330610660056

[12] Zahra S, George G. International Entrepreneurship: The Current Status of the Field and Future Research Agenda. In: Strategic Entrepreneurship: Creating an Integrated Mindset. Strategic Management Series, Oxford. Oxford: Blackwell; 2002

[13] McDougall P, Oviatt B. International entrepreneurship: The Intersection of two research paths. Academy of Management Journal. 2000;**43**(5): 902-906. DOI: 10.2307/1556418

[14] Dimitratos P, Plakoyiannaki E. Theoretical foundations of an international entrepreneurial culture. Journal of International Entrepreneurship. 2003;**1**(2):187-215. DOI: 10.1023/A:1023804318244

[15] Zahra S, Newey LR, Li Y. On the frontiers: The implications of social

entrepreneurship for international entrepreneurship. Entrepreneurship Theory and Practice. 2014;**38**(1): 137-158. DOI: 10.1111/etap.12061

[16] Jones MV, Coviello NE. Internationalisation: Conceptualising an entrepreneurial process of behaviour in time. Journal of International Business Studies. 2005;**36**(3):284-303. DOI: 10.1057/palgrave.jibs.8400138

[17] Keupp MM, Gassmann OO. The past and the future of international entrepreneurship: A review and suggestions for developing the field. Journal of Management. 2009;**35**(3):600-633. DOI: 10.1177/0149206308330558

[18] Carlsson B, Braunerhjelm P, McKelvey M, Olofsson C, Persson L, Ylinenpää H. The evolving domain of entrepreneurship research. Small Business Economics. 2013;**41**(4): 913-930. DOI: 10.1007/s11187-013-9503-y

[19] Terjesen S, Hessels J, Li D. Comparative international tntrepreneurship. Journal of Management. 2016;**42**(1):299-344. DOI: 10.1177/0149206313486259

[20] Reuber AR, editor. International Entrepreneurship. Cham: Springer International Publishing; 2018. DOI: 10.1007/978-3-319-74228-1

[21] Acedo FJ, Jones MV. Speed of internationalization and entrepreneurial cognition: Insights and a comparison between international new ventures, exporters and domestic firms. Journal of World Business. 2007;**42**(3):236-252. DOI: 10.1016/J.JWB.2007.04.012

[22] Oyson MJ, Whittaker H. Entrepreneurial cognition and behavior in the discovery and creation of international opportunities. Journal of International Entrepreneurship. 2015;**13**(3):303-336. DOI: 10.1007/s10843-015-0156-6

[23] Zahra S, Korri JS, Yu J. Cognition and international entrepreneurship: Implications for research on international opportunity recognition and exploitation. International Business Review. 2005;**14**(2):129-146. DOI: 10.1016/j.ibusrev.2004.04.005

[24] Kauppinen A, Juho A. Internationalisation of SMEs from the perspective of social learning theory. Journal of International Entrepreneurship. 2012;**10**(3):200-231. DOI: 10.1007/s10843-012-0093-6

[25] Muzychenko O, Liesch PW. International opportunity identification in the internationalisation of the firm. Journal of World Business. 2015;**50**(4):704-717. DOI: 10.1016/j.jwb.2014.12.001

[26] Nowiński W, Rialp A. The impact of social networks on perceptions of international opportunities. Journal of Small Business Management. 2016;**54**(2):445-461. DOI: 10.1111/jsbm.12149

[27] Lehto I. International entrepreneurial selling as construction of international opportunities. Journal of International Entrepreneurship. 2015;**13**(3):277-302. DOI: 10.1007/s10843-015-0147-7

[28] Andersson S, Evers N. International opportunity recognition in international new ventures—a dynamic managerial capabilities perspective. Journal of International Entrepreneurship. 2015;**13**(3):260-276. DOI: 10.1007/s10843-015-0149-5

[29] Di Gregorio D, Musteen M, Thomas DE. International new ventures: The cross-border nexus of individuals and opportunities. Journal of World Business. 2008;**43**(2):186-196. DOI: 10.1016/j.jwb.2007.11.013

[30] Butler JE, Doktor R, Lins FA. Linking international entrepreneurship

to uncertainty, opportunity discovery, and cognition. Journal of International Entrepreneurship. 2010;**8**(2):121-134. DOI: 10.1007/s10843-010-0054-x

[31] Karra N, Phillips N, Tracey P. Building the born global firm: Developing entrepreneurial capabilities for international new venture success. Long Range Planning. 2008;**41**(4): 440-458. DOI: 10.1016/j.lrp.2008.05.002

[32] Eriksson T, Nummela N, Saarenketo S. Dynamic capability in a small global factory. International Business Review. 2014;**23**(1):169-180. DOI: 10.1016/J.IBUSREV.2013.03.007

[33] Glavas C, Mathews S, Bianchi C. International opportunity recognition as a critical component for leveraging internet capabilities and international market performance. Journal of International Entrepreneurship. 2017;**15**(1):1-35. DOI: 10.1007/s10843-016-0191-y

[34] Laperrière A, Spence M. Enacting international opportunities: The role of organizational learning in knowledge-intensive business services. Journal of International Entrepreneurship. 2015;**13**(3):212-241. DOI: 10.1007/s10843-015-0151-y

[35] Nordman ER, Melén S, Nordman ER, Melén S. Journal of World Business. Vol. 43. Elsevier Science Inc.; 2008. Available at: http://econpapers.repec.org/article/eeeworbus/v_3a43_3ay_3a2008_3ai_3a2_3ap_3a171-185.htm

[36] Zolfaghari Ejlal Manesh SM, Rialp-Criado A. International ecopreneurs: The case of eco-entrepreneurial new ventures in the renewable energy industry. Journal of International Entrepreneurship. 2019;**17**(1):103-126. DOI: 10.1007/s10843-017-0222-3

[37] Chandra Y, Styles C, Wilkinson IF. Opportunity portfolio: Moving beyond single opportunity explanations in international entrepreneurship research. Asia Pacific Journal of Management. 2015;**32**(1):199-228. DOI: 10.1007/s10490-014-9400-1

[38] Bhatti WA, Larimo J, Coudounaris DN. The effect of experiential learning on subsidiary knowledge and performance. Journal of Business Research. 2016;**69**(5):1567-1571. DOI: 10.1016/J.JBUSRES.2015.10.018

[39] Chandra Y, Styles C, Wilkinson I. The recognition of first time international entrepreneurial opportunities. International Marketing Review. 2009;**26**(1):30-61. DOI: 10.1108/02651330910933195

[40] Johanson J, Vahlne J-E. The Uppsala internationalization process model revisited: From liability of foreignness to liability of outsidership. Journal of International Business Studies. 2009;**40**(9):1411-1431. DOI: 10.1057/jibs.2009.24

[41] Weerawardena J, Mort GS, Liesch PW, Knight G. Conceptualizing accelerated internationalization in the born global firm: A dynamic capabilities perspective. Journal of World Business. 2007;**42**(3):294-306. DOI: 10.1016/j.jwb.2007.04.004

[42] Angeli F, Grimaldi R. Leveraging offshoring: The identification of new business opportunities in international settings. Industry and Innovation. 2010;**17**(4):393-413. DOI: 10.1080/13662716.2010.496245

[43] Muzychenko O. Cross-cultural entrepreneurial competence in identifying international business opportunities. European Management Journal. 2008;**26**(6):366-377. DOI: 10.1016/j.emj.2008.09.002

[44] Schweizer R, Vahlne J-E, Johanson J. Internationalization as an entrepreneurial process. Journal

of International Entrepreneurship. 2010;**8**(4):343-370. DOI: 10.1007/s10843-010-0064-8

[45] Vinogradov E, Jørgensen EJB. Differences in international opportunity identification between native and immigrant entrepreneurs. Journal of International Entrepreneurship. 2017;**15**(2):207-228. DOI: 10.1007/s10843-016-0197-5

[46] Domurath A, Patzelt H. Entrepreneurs' assessments of early international entry: The role of foreign social ties, venture absorptive capacity, and generalized trust in others. Entrepreneurship Theory and Practice. 2016;**40**(5):1149-1177. DOI: 10.1111/etap.12164

[47] Ellis P. Social ties and international entrepreneurship: Opportunities and constraints affecting firm internationalization. Journal of International Business Studies. 2011;**42**(1):99-127. DOI: 10.1057/jibs.2010.20

[48] Leite YVP, de Moraes WFA, Salazar VS. Expressions of relationship networking in international entrepreneurship. Journal of International Entrepreneurship. 2016;**14**(2):213-238. DOI: 10.1007/s10843-016-0166-z

[49] Sharma DD, Blomstermo A. The internationalization process of Born Globals: A network view. International Business Review. 2003;**12**(6):739-753. DOI: 10.1016/J.IBUSREV.2003.05.002

[50] Lindstrand A, Melén S, Nordman ER. Turning social capital into business: A study of the internationalization of biotech SMEs. International Business Review. 2011;**20**(2):194-212. DOI: 10.1016/J.IBUSREV.2011.01.002

[51] Chandra Y, Styles C, Wilkinson IF. An opportunity-based view of rapid internationalization. Journal of International Marketing. 2012;**20**(1):74-102. DOI: 10.1509/jim.10.0147

[52] Kontinen T, Ojala A. Network ties in the international opportunity recognition of family SMEs. International Business Review. 2011b;**20**(4):440-453. DOI: 10.1016/j.ibusrev.2010.08.002

[53] Calabrò A, Brogi M, Torchia M. What does really matter in the internationalization of small and medium-sized family businesses? Journal of Small Business Management. 2016;**54**(2):679-696. DOI: 10.1111/jsbm.12165

[54] Hurmerinta L, Nummela N, Paavilainen-Mäntymäki E. Opening and closing doors: The role of language in international opportunity recognition and exploitation. International Business Review. 2015;**24**(6):1082-1094. DOI: 10.1016/j.ibusrev.2015.04.010

[55] Vasilchenko E, Morrish S. The role of entrepreneurial networks in the exploration and exploitation of internationalization opportunities by information and communication technology firms. Journal of International Marketing. 2011;**19**(4):88-105. DOI: 10.1509/jim.10.0134

[56] Chandra Y, Coviello N. Broadening the concept of international entrepreneurship: Consumers as international entrepreneurs. Journal of World Business. 2010;**45**(3):228-236. DOI: 10.1016/J.JWB.2009.09.006

[57] Crick D, Chaudhry S, Batstone S. An investigation into the overseas expansion of small Asian-owned U.K. firms. Small Business Economics. 2001;**16**(2):75-94. DOI: 10.1023/A:1011180017485

[58] Ellis P. Social ties and foreign market entry. Journal of International Business Studies. 2000;**31**(3):443-469. DOI: 10.1057/palgrave.jibs.8490916

[59] Galkina T, Chetty S. Effectuation and networking of internationalizing SMEs. Management International Review. 2015;**55**(5):647-676. DOI: 10.1007/s11575-015-0251-x

[60] Perks KJ, Hughes M. Entrepreneurial decision-making in internationalization: Propositions from mid-size firms. International Business Review. 2008;**17**(3):310-330. DOI: 10.1016/J.IBUSREV.2007.10.001

[61] Bingham CB, Eisenhardt KM, Furr NR. What makes a process a capability? Heuristics, strategy, and effective capture of opportunities. Strategic Entrepreneurship Journal. 2007;**1**(1-2):27-47. DOI: 10.1002/sej.1

[62] Dimitratos P, Johnson JE, Plakoyiannaki E, Young S. SME internationalization: How does the opportunity-based international entrepreneurial culture matter? International Business Review. 2016;**25**(6):1211-1222. DOI: 10.1016/j.ibusrev.2016.03.006

[63] Dimitratos P, Voudouris I, Plakoyiannaki E, Nakos G. International entrepreneurial culture—Toward a comprehensive opportunity-based operationalization of international entrepreneurship. International Business Review. 2012;**21**(4):708-721. DOI: 10.1016/j.ibusrev.2011.08.001

[64] Kumar N, Sharma DD. The role of organisational culture in the internationalisation of new ventures. International Marketing Review. 2018;**35**(5):806-832. DOI: 10.1108/IMR-09-2014-0299

[65] Dimitratos P, Plakoyiannaki E, Pitsoulaki A, Tüselmann HJ. The global smaller firm in international entrepreneurship. International Business Review. 2010;**19**(6):589-606. DOI: 10.1016/J.IBUSREV.2010.03.005

[66] Kocak A, Abimbola T. The effects of entrepreneurial marketing on born global performance. International Marketing Review. 2009;**26**(4/5):439-452. DOI: 10.1108/02651330910971977

[67] Tuomisalo T. Emergence of an entrepreneurial opportunity: A case within a Finnish telecommunication international new venture. Journal of International Entrepreneurship. 2019;**17**(3):334-354. DOI: 10.1007/s10843-019-00247-2

[68] Zhou L, Barnes BR, Lu Y. Entrepreneurial proclivity, capability upgrading and performance advantage of newness among international new ventures. Journal of International Business Studies. 2010;**41**(5):882-905. DOI: 10.1057/jibs.2009.87

[69] Åkerman N. International opportunity realization in firm internationalization: Non-linear effects of market-specific knowledge and internationalization knowledge. Journal of International Entrepreneurship. 2015;**13**(3):242-259. DOI: 10.1007/s10843-015-0152-x

[70] Jantunen A, Nummela N, Puumalainen K, Saarenketo S. Strategic orientations of born globals—Do they really matter? Journal of World Business. 2008;**43**(2):158-170. DOI: 10.1016/J.JWB.2007.11.015

[71] Jantunen A, Puumalainen K, Saarenketo S, Kyläheiko K. Entrepreneurial orientation, dynamic capabilities and international performance. Journal of International Entrepreneurship. 2005;**3**(3):223-243. DOI: 10.1007/s10843-005-1133-2

[72] Hohenthal J, Johanson J, Johanson M. Network knowledge and business-relationship value in the foreign market. International Business Review. 2014;**23**(1):4-19. DOI: 10.1016/j.ibusrev.2013.08.002

[73] Vahlne J-E, Bhatti WA. Relationship development: A micro-foundation for

the internationalization process of the multinational business enterprise. Management International Review. 2019;**59**(2):203-228. DOI: 10.1007/s11575-018-0373-z

[74] Zaefarian R, Eng T-Y, Tasavori M. An exploratory study of international opportunity identification among family firms. International Business Review. 2016;**25**(1):333-345. DOI: 10.1016/j.ibusrev.2015.06.002

[75] Lindstrand A, Hånell SM. International and market-specific social capital effects on international opportunity exploitation in the internationalization process. Journal of World Business. 2017;**52**(5):653-663. DOI: 10.1016/J.JWB.2017.05.002

[76] Mejri K, Umemoto K. Small- and medium-sized enterprise internationalization: Towards the knowledge-based model. Journal of International Entrepreneurship. 2010;**8**(2):156-167. DOI: 10.1007/s10843-010-0058-6

[77] Hilmersson M, Papaioannou S. SME international opportunity scouting—empirical insights on its determinants and outcomes. Journal of International Entrepreneurship. 2015;**13**(3):186-211. DOI: 10.1007/s10843-015-0155-7

[78] Miocevic D, Morgan RE. Operational capabilities and entrepreneurial opportunities in emerging market firms. International Marketing Review. 2018;**35**(2):320-341. DOI: 10.1108/IMR-12-2015-0270

[79] Faroque AR. Strategic orientations and international opportunity recognition and development in emerging country born globals: the moderating role of environmental dynamism. International Journal of Entrepreneurship and Small Business. 2015;**24**(2):163. DOI: 10.1504/IJESB.2015.067258

[80] Blankenburg Holm D, Johanson M, Kao PT. From outsider to insider: Opportunity development in foreign market networks. Journal of International Entrepreneurship. 2015;**13**(3):337-359. DOI: 10.1007/s10843-015-0154-8

[81] Fiedler A, Fath BP, Whittaker DH. Overcoming the liability of outsidership in institutional voids: Trust, emerging goals, and learning about opportunities. International Small Business Journal. 2017;**35**(3):262-284. DOI: 10.1177/0266242616662510

[82] Fang H, Kotlar J, Memili E, Chrisman JJ, De Massis A. The pursuit of international opportunities in family firms: Generational differences and the role of knowledge-based resources. Global Strategy Journal. 2018;**8**(1):136-157. DOI: 10.1002/gsj.1197

[83] Gabrielsson P, Gabrielsson M. A dynamic model of growth phases and survival in international business-to-business new ventures: The moderating effect of decision-making logic. Industrial Marketing Management. 2013;**42**(8):1357-1373. DOI: 10.1016/J.INDMARMAN.2013.07.011

[84] Oparaocha GO. SMEs and international entrepreneurship: An institutional network perspective. International Business Review. 2015;**24**(5):861-873. DOI: 10.1016/J.IBUSREV.2015.03.007

[85] Santangelo GD, Meyer KE. Extending the internationalization process model: Increases and decreases of MNE commitment in emerging economies. Journal of International Business Studies. 2011;**42**(7):894-909. DOI: 10.1057/jibs.2011.25

[86] Tian Y (Anna), Nicholson JD, Eklinder-Frick J, Johanson M. The interplay between social capital and international opportunities: A processual study of international

'take-off' episodes in Chinese SMEs. Industrial Marketing Management. 2018;**70**:180-192. DOI: 10.1016/J. INDMARMAN.2017.07.006

[87] Autio E, Sapienza HJ, Almeida JG. Effects of age at entry, knowledge intensity, and imitability on international growth. Academy of Management Journal. 2000;**43**(5): 909-924. DOI: 10.2307/1556419

[88] Chetty S, Ojala A, Leppäaho T. Effectuation and foreign market entry of entrepreneurial firms. European Journal of Marketing. 2015;**49**(9/10):1436-1459. DOI: 10.1108/ EJM-11-2013-0630

[89] Bingham CB. Oscillating improvisation: How entrepreneurial firms create success in foreign market entries over time. Strategic Entrepreneurship Journal. 2009;**3**(4):321-345. DOI: 10.1002/sej.77

[90] Crick D, Spence M. The internationalisation of 'high performing' UK high-tech SMEs: A study of planned and unplanned strategies. International Business Review. 2005;**14**(2):167-185. DOI: 10.1016/J.IBUSREV.2004.04.007

[91] Mainela T, Puhakka V. Organising new business in a turbulent context: Opportunity discovery and effectuation for IJV development in transition markets. Journal of International Entrepreneurship. 2009;**7**(2):111-134. DOI: 10.1007/s10843-008-0034-6

[92] Sarasvathy S, Kumar K, York JG, Bhagavatula S. An effectual approach to international entrepreneurship: Overlaps, challenges, and provocative possibilities. Entrepreneurship Theory and Practice. 2014;**38**(1):71-93. DOI: 10.1111/etap.12088

[93] Bai W, Johanson M. International opportunity networks. Industrial Marketing Management. 2017;**70**:167-179. DOI: 10.1016/J. INDMARMAN.2017.07.004

[94] Mort G, Weerawardena J. Networking capability and international entrepreneurship. International Marketing Review. 2006;**23**(5):549-572. DOI: 10.1108/02651330610703445

[95] Zahra SA, Rawhouser HN, Bhawe N, Neubaum DO, Hayton JC. Globalization of social entrepreneurship opportunities. Strategic Entrepreneurship Journal. 2008;**2**(2):117-131. DOI: 10.1002/sej.43

[96] McDougall P, Shane S, Oviatt BM. Explaining the formation of international new ventures: The limits of theories from international business research. Journal of Business Venturing. 1994;**9**(6):469-487. DOI: 10.1016/0883-9026(94)90017-5

[97] Reuber AR, Fischer E. International entrepreneurship in internet-enabled markets. Journal of Business Venturing. 2011;**26**(6):660-679. DOI: 10.1016/J. JBUSVENT.2011.05.002

[98] Lundberg H, Rehnfors A. Transnational entrepreneurship: Opportunity identification and venture creation. Journal of International Entrepreneurship. 2018;**16**(2):150-175. DOI: 10.1007/s10843-018-0228-5

[99] Young SL, Welter C, Conger M. Stability vs. flexibility: The effect of regulatory institutions on opportunity type. Journal of International Business Studies. 2018;**49**(4):407-441. DOI: 10.1057/s41267-017-0095-7

[100] Baker T, Gedajlovic E, Lubatkin M. A framework for comparing entrepreneurship processes across nations. Journal of International Business Studies. 2005;**36**(5):492-504. DOI: 10.1057/palgrave.jibs.8400153

[101] Webb JW, Kistruck GM, Ireland RD, Ketchen DJ Jr. The

entrepreneurship process in base of the pyramid markets: The case of Multinational Enterprise/ Nongovernment Organization Alliances. Entrepreneurship Theory and Practice. 2010;**34**(3):555-581. DOI: 10.1111/j.1540-6520.2009.00349.x

[102] Mainela T, Puhakka V, Sipola S. International entrepreneurship beyond individuals and firms: On the systemic nature of international opportunities. Journal of Business Venturing. 2018;**33**(4):534-550. DOI: 10.1016/J.JBUSVENT.2018.04.002

[103] Haaja E. Why do some SMEs engage in joint internationalisation and others do not? Exploring the role of mental images in collective international opportunity recognition. Journal of International Entrepreneurship. 2020;**18**:15-43. DOI: 10.1007/s10843-019-00253-4

[104] Williams DW, Wood MS. Rule-based reasoning for understanding opportunity evaluation. Academy of Management Perspectives. 2015;**29**(2):218-236. DOI: 10.5465/amp.2013.0017

[105] Lorenz MP, Ramsey JR, Richey RG. Expatriates' international opportunity recognition and innovativeness: The role of metacognitive and cognitive cultural intelligence. Journal of World Business. 2018;**53**(2):222-236. DOI: 10.1016/J.JWB.2017.11.004

[106] Chen J, Saarenketo S, Puumalainen K. Internationalization and value orientation of entrepreneurial ventures—a Latin American perspective. Journal of International Entrepreneurship. 2016;**14**(1):32-51. DOI: 10.1007/s10843-016-0169-9

[107] Short JC, Ketchen DJ, Shook CL, Ireland RD. The concept of "Opportunity" in entrepreneurship research: Past accomplishments and future challenges. Journal of Management. 2010;**36**(1):40-65. DOI: 10.1177/0149206309342746

[108] Vaghely I, Julien P-A. Are opportunities recognized or constructed? An information perspective on entrepreneurial opportunity identification. Journal of Business Venturing. 2010;**25**(1):73-86. Available at: http://econpapers.repec.org/article/eeejbvent/v_3a25_3ay_3a2010_3ai_3a1_3ap_3a73-86.htm

[109] Venkataraman S, Sarasvathy SD, Dew N, Forster WR. Reflections on the 2010 AMR decade award: Whither the promise? Moving forward with entrepreneurship as a science of the artificial. Academy of Management Review. 2012;**37**(1):21-33. DOI: 10.5465/amr.2011.0079

[110] Zahra SA. The virtuous cycle of discovery and creation of entrepreneurial opportunities. Strategic Entrepreneurship Journal. 2008;**2**(3):243-257. DOI: 10.1002/sej.47

[111] Chiasson M, Saunders C. Reconciling diverse approaches to opportunity research using the structuration theory. Journal of Business Venturing. 2005;**20**(6):747-767. DOI: 10.1016/j.jbusvent.2004.07.004

[112] Chetty S, Karami M, Martín OM. Opportunity discovery and creation as a duality: Evidence from small firms' foreign market entries. Journal of International Marketing. 2018;**26**(3): 70-93. DOI: 10.1509/jim.17.0005

[113] Ciravegna L, Lopez LE, Kundu SK. Country of origin and network effects on internationalization: A comparative study of SMEs from an emerging and developed economy. Journal of Business Research. 2014a;**67**(5):916-923. DOI: 10.1016/J.JBUSRES.2013.07.011

[114] Ciravegna L, Majano SB, Zhan G. The inception of internationalization of small and medium enterprises: The role of activeness and networks. Journal of Business Research. 2014b;**67**(6):1081-1089. DOI: 10.1016/j.jbusres.2013.06.002

[115] Chandra Y. A time-based process model of international entrepreneurial opportunity evaluation. Journal of International Business Studies. 2017;**48**(4):423-451. DOI: 10.1057/s41267-017-0068-x

[116] Spence M, Crick D. A comparative investigation into the internationalisation of Canadian and UK high-tech SMEs. International Marketing Review. 2006;**23**(5):524-548. DOI: 10.1108/02651330610703436

[117] Kontinen T, Ojala A. International opportunity recognition among small and medium-sized family firms. Journal of Small Business Management. 2011a;**49**(3):490-514. DOI: 10.1111/j.1540-627X.2011.00326.x

[118] Hannibal M, Evers N, Servais P. Opportunity recognition and international new venture creation in university spin-offs—Cases from Denmark and Ireland. Journal of International Entrepreneurship. 2016;**14**(3):345-372. DOI: 10.1007/s10843-016-0181-0

[119] Kalinic I, Sarasvathy S, Forza C. 'Expect the unexpected': Implications of effectual logic on the internationalization process. International Business Review. 2014;**23**(3):635-647. DOI: 10.1016/J.IBUSREV.2013.11.004

[120] Lee SH, Williams C. Dispersed entrepreneurship within multinational corporations: A community perspective. Journal of World Business. 2007;**42**(4):505-519. DOI: 10.1016/J.JWB.2007.08.001

[121] Johanson J, Vahlne J-E. Commitment and opportunity development in the internationalization process: A note on the Uppsala internationalization process model. Management International Review. 2006;**46**(2):165-178. DOI: 10.1007/s11575-006-0043-4

[122] Zhou L, Wu W-P, Luo X. Internationalization and the performance of born-global SMEs: The mediating role of social networks. Journal of International Business Studies. 2007;**38**:673-690. DOI: 10.1057/palgrave.jibs.8400282

[123] Prashantham S. New venture internationalization as strategic renewal. European Management Journal. 2008;**26**(6):378-387. DOI: 10.1016/J.EMJ.2008.09.005

[124] Birkinshaw J. Entrepreneurship in multinational corporations: The characteristics of subsidiary initiatives. Strategic Management Journal. 1997;**18**(3):207-229. DOI: 10.1002/(SICI)1097-0266(199703)18:3<207::AID-SMJ864>3.0.CO;2-Q

[125] Ahsan M, Fernhaber SA. Multinational enterprises: Leveraging a corporate international entrepreneurship lens for new insights into subsidiary initiatives. Journal of International Management. 2019;**25**(1):51-65. DOI: 10.1016/J.INTMAN.2018.07.002

[126] Dimitratos P, Plakoyiannaki E, Thanos IC, Förbom YK. The overlooked distinction of multinational enterprise subsidiary learning: Its managerial and entrepreneurial learning modes. International Business Review. 2014;**23**(1):102-114. DOI: 10.1016/J.IBUSREV.2013.08.003

[127] McGaughey SL. Hidden ties in international new venturing: The case of portfolio entrepreneurship. Journal of World Business. 2007;**42**(3):307-321. DOI: 10.1016/J.JWB.2007.04.011

[128] Mostafiz MI, Sambasivan M, Goh SK. Impacts of dynamic managerial capability and international opportunity identification on firm performance. Multinational Business Review. 2019;**27**(4):339-363. DOI: 10.1108/MBR-09-2018-0061

[129] Weerawardena J, Mort GS, Liesch PW. Capabilities development and deployment activities in born global B-to-B firms for early entry into international markets. Industrial Marketing Management. 2019;**78**:122-136. DOI: 10.1016/J.INDMARMAN.2017.06.004

[130] Schwens C, Kabst R. Internationalization of young technology firms: A complementary perspective on antecedents of foreign market familiarity. International Business Review. 2011;**20**(1):60-74. DOI: 10.1016/J.IBUSREV.2010.06.003

[131] Styles C, Genua T. The rapid internationalization of high technology firms created through the commercialization of academic research. Journal of World Business. 2008;**43**(2):146-157. DOI: 10.1016/J.JWB.2007.11.011

[132] Hohenthal J, Johanson J, Johanson M. Market discovery and the international expansion of the firm. International Business Review. 2003;**12**(6):659-672. DOI: 10.1016/J.IBUSREV.2003.06.001

[133] Styles C, Gray S. Advancing research in international entrepreneurship. International Marketing Review. 2006;**23**(5):467-485. DOI: 10.1108/imr.2006.03623eaa.001

Chapter 7

Halal Entrepreneurship: Concept and Business Opportunities

Moha Asri Abdullah and Md. Siddique E Azam

Abstract

The concept of entrepreneurship is not something new in Islam as it can be observed from the history as a noble profession practiced by the Prophet (PBUH) and His companions. However, in recent times, scholars of the Islamic economy have introduced a new term, "Halal entrepreneurship" or "*Halalpreneurship*" to define and differentiate entrepreneurs in the Halal industry from the conventional entrepreneurs. The integration of Islamic values reshapes the entrepreneurs in the Halal industry through certain features that justify using the term Halalpreneurs and *Halalpreneurship*. However, a limited number of research papers have attempted to define *Halalpreneurship*. In this context, this chapter aims to achieve two main objectives. Firstly, to provide a comprehensive overview of Halal entrepreneurship (*Halalpreneurship*) by identifying its salient features that differentiates from entrepreneurs. Such understanding and knowledge will help someone to identify his/her role as *Halalpreneur* in the Halal industry. Secondly, to explore the business opportunities in different sectors of the global halal industry for the *Halalpreneurs* to tap. To achieve the objectives, the chapter adopts the methodology of content analysis by reviewing research papers, books, journals, and articles from different secondary sources.

Keywords: *Halalpreneurship*, *Halalpreneurs*, halal industry, business opportunities

1. Introduction

The economic development of both developed and developing countries is now largely enhanced by entrepreneurship development. The term is often used as the synonym of job creation, and innovation that contributes to societal improvement. The established entrepreneurs are classified as Micro, Small, and Medium Enterprises (MSMEs). These MSMEs constitute more than 95% of the total establishment of an economy globally. The entrepreneurs are engaged in different industries of the global economy. The Halal industry, which represents the global Islamic economy, is one of the fastest-growing markets in the world. The key contributors to this global Halal industry are the Halal entrepreneurs (Halalpreneurs). Entrepreneurship has been defined by many scholars, researchers, industry players, and academicians globally. The definition has been acknowledged and adopted in more or less similar ways by most of the economies globally.

However, the concept of "entrepreneurship" in the Islamic economy is not exactly the same as the conventional economy. Although the nature of activities and literal definition is similar, the concept in Islam becomes different in some certain ways and is perceived as "*Halalpreneurship*." The term has been used in the

Halal industry implying to entrepreneurship by Global Islamic Economy (GIE) report-2018 by Thompson Reuters' and Dinar Standard. However, the industry is lacking a proper definition of the term. Simultaneously, numerous scholars in the Islamic economy have introduced entrepreneurs in Islam in their studies. For example, the activities, responsibilities, and objectives of Muslim entrepreneurs in the Islamic economy have been discussed by Ramdani et al. in their study [1]. Alternatively, entrepreneurs in Islam have been termed as Islamic entrepreneurs negating the assumption that Islam is intrinsically anti-modernization and anti-development [2]. Similarly, the same term, Islamic entrepreneurship, was justified to explain entrepreneurship in Islam [3]. Moreover, entrepreneurs in the halal food industry have been investigated as halal food entrepreneurs [4]. Finally, the term *Halalpreneurship* has been used to define halal-minded entrepreneurship to realize the motivation of the small and medium entrepreneurs (SMEs) to become *Halalpreneurs* [5]. However, none of these studies have defined or clarified the term *Halalpreneurs* or *Halalpreneurship*. Moreover, it has been identified as one of the significant gaps that the halal industry is lacking a universally accepted definition and proper understanding of *Halalpreneurship* [5].

Research questions: The research questions addressed by the current chapter are: (1) What is the concept of *Halalpreneurship?* (2) What is the definition of *Halalpreneurship?* (3) Who are the *Halalpreneurs?* (4) How *Halalpreneurs* are different from entrepreneurs? and (5) what business opportunities are there in the global halal industry for *Halalpreneurs*?

Objectives: Entrepreneurs in the Halal industry must have a proper understanding of the concept from Maqasid-al-Sharia'h perspective which is needed to justify the term "*Halalpreneurship*" and to differentiate *Halalpreneurs* from entrepreneurs. In this regard, the main objective of this chapter is to define and provide a comprehensive understanding of *Halalpreneurship* from *maqasid-al-shari'ah* perspective. Additionally, the chapter attempts to realize the underlying business opportunities for *Halalpreneurs* in different segments of the halal industry.

Methodology: To achieve the objectives stated above, an extensive review of literature from previous researches has been carried out. Simultaneously, to justify the Islamic point of view, analogies and explanations of relevant *hadith* and Quranic verses were studied. Moreover, recent reports, news articles, and web articles on the halal industry and global Islamic economy were critically analyzed.

Organization of the chapter: This chapter starts with defining the concept of entrepreneurship and *Halalpreneurship* following an overview of Maqasid-al-Sharia'h to justify the definition of Halalpreneurs (Section 2). Then, the chapter explores different aspects of *Halalpreneurs* that differentiate them from entrepreneurs (Section 3). Finally, in Section 4, the chapter identifies potential opportunities for *Halalpreneurs* in different sectors of the halal industry.

2. Concept and definition

2.1 Concept of entrepreneurship

The term entrepreneurship stems from the French word *entreprendre* that suggests "to accomplish something" or "to embrace". It is an imaginative activity that relies upon the ability to make and set up something from about nothing. Kuratko explained business entrepreneurship as facing challenges, responding to circumstances, bearing vulnerability and creating a balance between demand and supply in the market [6]. At the same time, as per Peter Drucker, entrepreneurship is ascribed as an efficient headway, which grasps in the purposeful and arranged outlook for changes, and it is the coherent perception of the open opportunities where such changes add to financial and social advancement. A comparative definition was given by Shane and Venkataraman [7]. Rindova et al. have characterized entrepreneurship as the business foundations that are coordinated to accomplish a few objectives towards social, cultural, monetary, and institutional through the activities of an individual or a group of individuals [8]. Additionally, Lumpkin and Dess [9], Low and MacMillan [10] and Gartner [11] characterized entrepreneurship as the arrangement of new pursuits or associations. Entrepreneurship may likewise infer looking for advantages of chances by the creative use of assets in manners which make a significant impact on the market.

2.2 Concept of *Halalpreneurship*

2.2.1 Understanding halal

The word "*Halal*" is an Arabic or Quranic word related to the Islamic lifestyle where the literal meaning of the word is permissible or lawful. That means the implication of the term is applicable to every conduct of human life whether it is a social, personal, economic, cultural, or political matter. When it comes to an economic perspective, the term has been used to denote the Islamic economy as the Halal industry. The Malaysian Standard (MS) provides an elaborated definition with all the requirements to be adopted in the halal industry [12]. Additionally, the application of the concept of halal adopts the concept "*Toyyib*" as well [13]. This is because in several places of the Quran, human beings are instructed to consume what is *halal* and *toyyib*. The meaning of *toyyib* can be translated as good, quality, healthy, sustainable and others. Hence, the association of the *toyyiban* aspect broadens the meaning and implication of halal in the economy [14]. Therefore, when we say halal, it means what is permissible or lawful in Islam, at the same time what is good and sustainable.

The opposite of *halal* is *haram* which means prohibited. In the Quran, Allah (SWT) has also prescribed what is prohibited and what to avoid in consumption as well as human conduct of Muslims and whole *ummah*. For example, consuming alcohol and pork is prohibited in Islam. Simultaneously, gambling, pornography, *riba* (usury), hoarding goods, deceiving customers, etc. are also prohibited. The gist is, to define *Halalpreneurship*, one must consider all the three concepts, i.e. *halal, toyyib*, and *haram*.

2.2.2 Understanding Halalpreneurship

Entrepreneurship is an important aspect of life which is also inseparable from Islam where it is perceived as *Halalpreneurship*. The scope of *Halalpreneurship* is within the *Shari'ah* ("*Aqidah, Fiqh, Akhlaq*") which ensures that its activities do not deviate from the guidelines of Islam. In Islam, *Halalpreneurship* is perceived as the role of *Khalifah* (Caliph) on the earth. The mission of *Khalifah* is to worship Allah *Subhanahu Wa Taala* (SWT) and to develop and prosper the world. Such a role implies the actions of entrepreneurship contributing to the good and prosperity of society, the world and humanity.

The term *Halalpreneurship* is recently being used in the fields of the global Halal industry that connects halal advancement with business practices through halalpreneurial activities. This includes the capacity and capability, exercises, and activities seeking opportunities and developing business establishment. The procedure of creativity and innovation in *Halalpreneurship* is complex. However, this phenomenon is significantly important to be understood for halalpreneurial development.

The concept of *Halalpreneurship* is based on *Maqasid-al-Shari'ah* (objectives of Islamic law). *Maqasid* means objective and *Shari'ah* implies to Islamic law. The five objectives of *Shari'ah* (**Figure 1**) are derived from the necessities (*dharuriyat*) of humankind. This is the first level of need in the human need model of *Shari'ah* which was proposed by Hamid-Al-Ghazali (d. 1111). Although the concept of Maqasid and the human need model in Islam dates back to 1399 C.E., the pioneering, and systematic study of the higher objectives of Islamic law was developed and introduced through the work on Maqasid-al-sharia'h by Muhammad al-Tahir ibn Ashur in 1946 [15]. *Halalpreneurship* management adopts the human need model (**Figure 2**) by Ghazali that implies the fundamental factors of motivation for *Halalpreneurs*.

In *Halalpreneurship,* it is the responsibility of *Halalpreneurs* to understand the product priorities of the consumers as illustrated in **Figure 2**. To address the objectives of *Shari'ah, Halalpreneurs* should prioritize the products and services that are in the category of necessity in their production. They should serve what the Muslim *ummah* and humanity need. They should not focus on luxury (*Tahsiniyat*) products or services when there is a need for basic goods and services in a society. Therefore, the first priority is to meet the demand for necessities and then luxury and embellishments.

2.3 Definition of *Halalpreneurship* and *Halalpreneurs*

The term was used by Professor Moha Asri Abdullah, International Institute for Halal Research and Training (INHART), International Islamic University Malaysia (IIUM) in a talk on "*Halalpreneurs:* Realities and Opportunities". The institute has recently produced a book on this topic entitled "Halal Entrepreneurship", funded by the International Institute of Islamic Thought (IIIT), Malaysia. The book provides

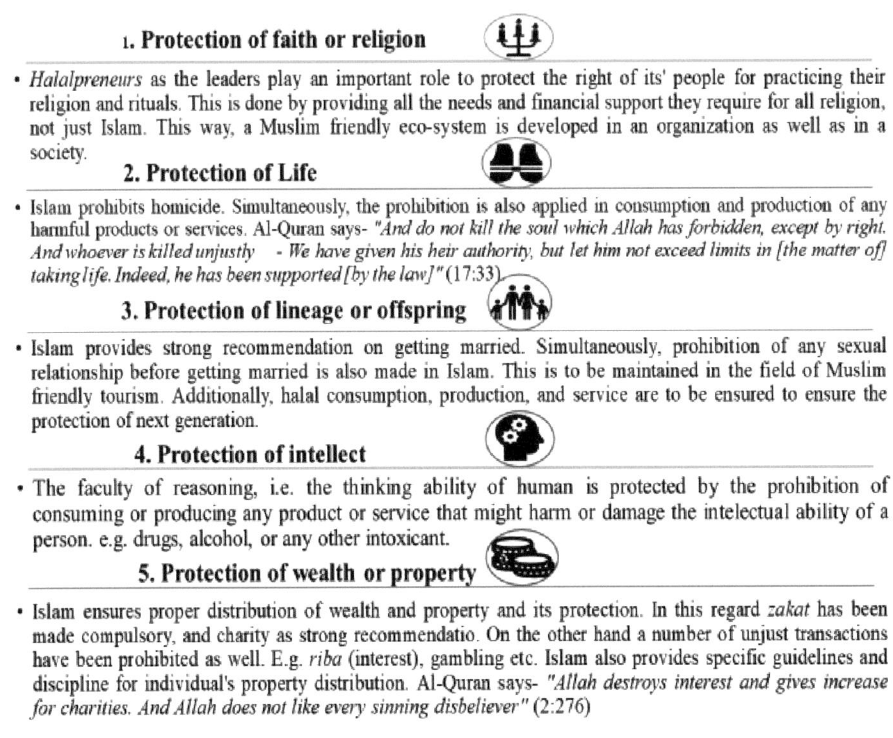

Figure 1.
Five objectives of Shari'ah. Source: *Author's generated.*

Figure 2.
Classification of human need in Shari'ah. Source: *[15], Figure author's generated.*

the concept and definition of *Halalpreneurship.* The term has also been used implying to entrepreneurship in the Halal industry by Global Islamic Economy (GIE) report-2018.

Any Muslim individual conducting entrepreneurial business in the global halal industry with the objective of producing only halal products and services and maintains his/her business conduct in a *Shari'ah*-compliant way is called an *Halalpreneur* [16]. However, according to Islamic scholars, non-Muslims can also be involved in the fields of the halal industry and become *Halalpreneurs* given the condition that they comply with *Maqasid-al-Shari'ah.* Non-Muslims are allowed to be *Halalpreneurs* based on the *maslaha* (public interest) for the benefit of *ummah* and mankind. It is to mention that, anyone who wants to conduct business providing halal products and services, must obtain a halal certificate for the particular product or service. Given that, to obtain a halal certificate he/she must comply to halal standard for respective products and services required by the authorizing bodies in respective countries. And, all the halal standards are developed complying with *Maqasid-al-Shari'ah.* Therefore, in this chapter, the term *Halalpreneurship* refers to Halal entrepreneurship i.e. entrepreneurship in the halal industry that complies with *Maqasid-al-Shari'ah.*

3. *Halalpreneurship* vs. entrepreneurship

In conventional economy unlimited wants and limited resources create scarcity which gives rise to the fundamental questions that are, what to produce, for whom to produce, and how to produce [17]? However, *Halalpreneurs* believe that there are always enough resources. If there is any scarcity, it is due to a lack of skill and knowledge, and inefficient use and distribution of the resources. Hence, the answers to the fundamental questions in *Halalpreneurship* are different from entrepreneurship. **Figure 3** shows the differences between *Halalpreneurship* and entrepreneurship regarding the fundamental questions of economics and some other salient points of *Halalpreneurship.*

Additionally, *Halalpreneurs* exhibit some unique characteristics that distinguish them from conventional entrepreneurs. The characteristics enlisted below, are based on *Maqasid-al-Shari'ah.*

a. ***Takwa***: It is the fear of Allah (SWT) that makes *Halalpreneurs* always conscious about all their deeds, whether it is bad or good, believing that they are

HALALPRENEURSHIP	VS Salient points	ENTREPRENEURSHIP
❑ The concept is based on *Maqasid Shari'ah*.	Concept	❑ The concept is based on country law/profit
❑ Goods/services based on product priorities such as necessities, comfort, luxury, not harmful and permissible (Halal) by *shari'ah*	What?	❑ What people want and makes profit
❑ Efficiency and productivity + profit + Halal process	How?	❑ Efficiency and productivity + desire to maximise profit + any approach
❑ Muslim *Ummah* and humanity	For whom?	❑ Solely based on market demand
❑ Islamic & Business Knowledge. Non-Muslims can also be *Halalpreneur* based on the public interest (Maslahah).	Knowledge	❑ Scope of knowledge is limited to business knowledge only.
❑ Profit + '*al-falah*' in this world and in the hereafter	Motivation	❑ Profit
❑ Customers, workers, suppliers, manufacturers, financiers, owners, community, Ummah (under the preview of Allah (SWT))	Stakeholder	❑ Customers, workers, suppliers, manufacturers, financiers, owners, community and people

Figure 3.
Salient features: Halalpreneurship *vs. entrepreneurship.* Source: *Author's generated.*

being watched by Allah (SWT), the Al-Aleem (all-knowing), even if the deed is done by their heart or thoughts only. Such, attribute of *Halalpreneurs* never allows them to involve with any activity which is not permissible (Haram) in Islam. As Allah recommends consuming halal (Quran 5:88) as well as to earn from halal only (Quran 2:168).

b. **Prioritizing *Solat* (prayer)**: Entrepreneurship is encouraged in Islam. The Prophet (PBUH) himself was a merchant and successful *Halalpreneur*. However, any worldly affairs including business conduct in *Halalpreneurship* come after *solat* (Al-Quran 62:10; 15:67). The obligatory prayers become first priority for *Halalpreneurs* [18].

c. **Truthfulness**: *Halalpreneurs* should be trustworthy regarding their social and business conduct. Truthful and trustworthy merchants are said to be with the Prophet (PBUH) together with the martyrs on the day of judgment (Al-Tirmidhi, Book 14: #1213).

d. **Philanthropist**: Islam permits us to make benefits by making business in society. Simultaneously, *Halalpreneurs* are recommended to give back to the same society they are being benefitted from. Giving charity in the form of *Zakat* is one of the five obligations for Muslims (Al-Quran 2:3,43,83,177; 7:156; 19:31; 19:55; 21:73; 22:35,41,78; 23:4; 27:3; 30:39; 31:4; 41:7 and more). Therefore, *Halalpreneurs* find themselves as philanthropists in their business venture and contribute to the uplifting of social well-being.

e. ***Shari'ah* knowledge:** Another important characteristic of *Halalpreneurs* is to have the basic knowledge and understanding of *Maqasid-al-Shari'ah*, the concept of *halalan toyyiban*, and Islamic guidelines. This knowledge is crucial for all as the non-Muslim can also become *Halalpreneur.* For example, the halal and *toyyib* concept is to be implemented in the procurement process, logistics, production, packaging, storage and others. Hence, any *Halalpreneur* should learn on the implementation of *Shari'ah* and halal standards in all the aspects of entrepreneurship under the condition of *Maslaha* (public interest).

4. Business opportunities for *Halalpreneurs*

Halalpreneurs is the source of creativity and innovation that postulates the Islamic economy in many ways. Unlike entrepreneurs, *Halalpreneurs* are driven towards *Al-Falalh* (success in this world and the world hereafter) with the motivation of pleasing Allah (SWT) and serving humanity. In this regard, *Halalpreneurs* thrive for business opportunities with knowledge and wisdom and having faith in Allah (SWT). Simultaneously, they tap the opportunities and conduct their business activities following the guidelines of the Quran, and the advice and practice of the Prophet (PBUH). Most importantly, they believe that opportunities are created by Allah (SWT). Such a conceptual model of *Halalpreneurship* was illustrated by Ramdani [19] as shown in **Figure 4**.

The business opportunities for *Halalpreneurs* in the global halal industry can be realized by looking into the current market status of the different fields of the halal industry. Therefore, this section explores different components of the halal industry (**Figure 5**) where market opportunities can be tapped by *Halalpreneurs.*

The current market value of the global halal industry is estimated to be US$4.7 trillion in 2018 including Islamic finance. This value is projected to be US$6.9 trillion by 2024 with a CAGR growth of 6.2% [21]. **Figure 6** exhibits the current market shares of different fields of the halal industry and their projection by 2024. It shows that after Islamic finance, the biggest sector of the halal industry is the halal food and beverage industry followed by modest fashion, media and recreation, Muslim friendly tourism, halal pharmaceuticals, and halal cosmetics.

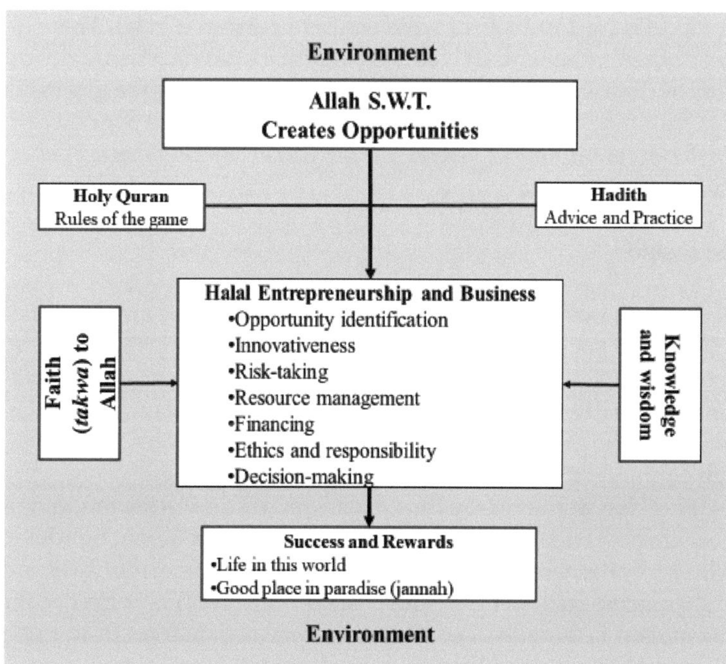

Figure 4.
Model of Halalpreneurship. *Source: [19].*

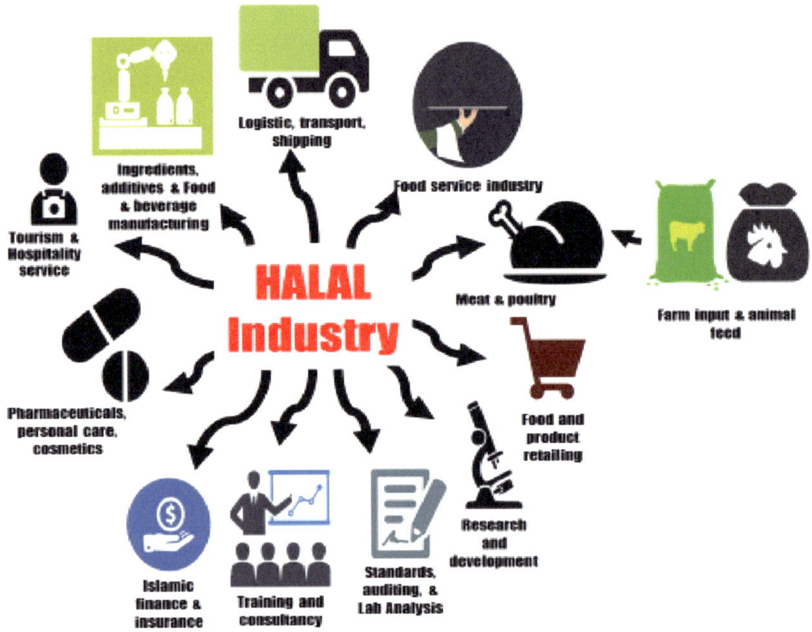

Figure 5.
Components of global halal industry. Source: *[20]*.

4.1 Halal food

The Global Islamic Economy (GIE) report 2019/2020 reveals that the Muslim spending for halal food and beverage (F&B) in 2018 was US$1.3 billion which has been projected to reach US$1.9 billion by 2024. The hot growth sectors of the F&B market are halal ingredients, and meat-based meals and snacks. The production of gelatine is 450,000 tons globally of which only 10 percent is halal. There is a gap in the supply of other ingredients as well. *Halalpreneurs* can tap the opportunities in these sectors by their innovative halal products and exploring the gap in demand and supply chain. The opportunity is further spread over halal organic and healthy foods, baby foods, emerging exporters, online restaurant booking, retail commerce, social media marketing, etc.

4.2 Modest fashion

The Muslim millennials are the target consumer in this sector of the halal industry. The market of modest fashion was estimated to be US$283 billion in 2018 and projected to reach US$402 billion by 2024 (**Figure 6**). Innovative *Halalpreneurs* have the opportunity to offer products and services in this market in terms of modest luxury wears, modest sportswear, fashionwear for teens and tween, role modeling, blogging, etc.

"Follow This" is a web series by BuzzFeed which is one of the most popular websites for information on different topics like culture, religion, politics, technology, etc. This show has recently started streaming on Netflix from 2018 and covered an episode on modest fashion titles "Covered-up Culture." The writer of the episode reveals how modest fashion has become a $billion worth market from a religious niche [22]. Modest fashion as a lifestyle is becoming the mainstream among the millennials. For example, the release of a modest clothing range by H&M in 2018, launching of "modest fashion edit" in 2019 by the collaboration of ASOS and

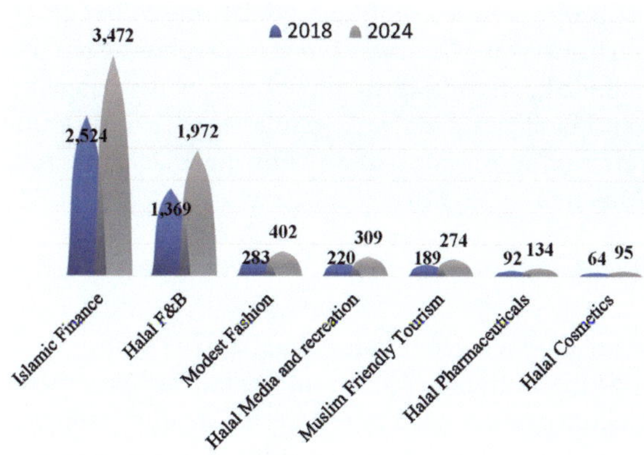

Figure 6.
*Market size of the global halal industry in 2018 and 2024 (**US$ billion**).* Source: *[20]*.

Verona collection. More success stories that are making headlines globally include Vogue Arabia, Harper's Bazaar Arabia, Harper's Bazaar Singapore [23]. In India, mubarakdeals.com is another example of success in the market of modest fashion [24]. Opportunities for *Halalpreneurs* in the field of modest fashion can be explored in terms of online shopping, fashion week or events, magazine publishers, styling services, influencer, designer and many more.

4.3 Media and recreation

Halal media and recreation refer to content targeting or suitable for Muslims. According to the GIE report 2019/2020, total Muslim spending in his sector was US$283 billion and projected to reach $US402 billion in 2024. Strong performance has been identified by the member countries of the Organization of Islamic Cooperation (OIC) in producing more Islamic themed content from the region. This sector of the halal industry targets the Muslim millennials, mainly. It has been forecasted that 54 percent of the Muslim population will be below 30 years old by 2030 (Thompson and Reuters, 2019). In Saudi Arabia, the ban on cinema has been lifted after 35 years in 2018. With the 2030-vision of achieving the goal of diversifying the Kingdom's economy and output, more than 300 screens in multiple theaters are scheduled to be open by 2020 [25]. This will create thousands of opportunities for *Halalpreneurs* in different roles that include journalist, editor, photographer, designer, researcher or producer, technical staff, copyrighter, presenters, content writer, graphics designer, and many more roles. The opportunities can be tapped in other OIC member countries as well, as the industry is growing significantly.

4.4 Muslim friendly tourism

Global Muslim spending on travel in 2018 was US$189 billion and projected to reach US$274 billion by 2024 (**Figure 6**). Simultaneously, global Muslim travelers are expected to grow 156 million in 2020 which was 121 million in 2017 [26]. Opportunities in this sector of the halal industry can be realized by realizing both the demand-supply side of the market. The demand for Muslim travelers comprises in terms of leisure, business, healthcare, and religious travel. On the other side, the supply side encompasses transport (bus, train, flights, etc.), accommodation (hotels, villas, resorts, apartments, homestays, etc.), F&B, travel agents, attractions and activities, Muslim friendly tour guides, and others related to travel and tourism.

Such demand and supply are based on Muslim faith-based needs. *Halalpreneurs* have potential opportunities in the market of the travel industry to meet the faith-based needs that include halal food, prayer facilities, water usage friendly toilets, Ramadan services and facilities, halal spa, gender-segregated swimming pool and gymnasium, assurance of elimination of any non-halal activity, recreational activities with privacy, Muslim friendly tour guide, etc.

4.5 Halal pharmaceuticals

The industry of halal pharmaceuticals valued US$92 billion in 2018 and expected to grow US$134 billion by 2024, and the market expansion may even be greater as the target consumer is not limited to the Muslim population only. The demand for halal pharmaceuticals among Muslim consumers is increasing due to the *Toyyiban* concept that assures efficacy, quality, safety, halal, and hygiene factors. Additionally, it has gained acceptance among non-Muslim consumers as well because of the ethical aspect and the requirements to comply with the halal standard that include good manufacturing practices (GMP) as a prerequisite before meeting other requirements of halal certification. Such quality assurance sets a high benchmark in the market which enables "*Halal*" to become a recognized value in the pharmaceutical industry globally. A number of pharmaceutical companies in Malaysia are leading the industry, as Malaysia is the first country to come up with a strong and comprehensive halal standard for the pharmaceutical industry [27].

4.6 Halal cosmetics

Halal cosmetics and personal care is another booming market in the global halal industry. As of 2018, the Muslim spending on halal cosmetics was US$64 billion which is expected to grow US$95 billion by 2024. The product base of this industry is expanded to personal care products, color cosmetics (face, eyes, lips, nails), and fragrance products. Additionally, these product lines are applied for hair care, face care, skincare, and beauty care. *Halalpreneurs* can feasibly tap the opportunities and generate revenues in this market. Some hot sectors of this industry for growth in 2020 are halal nail polish, lipstick, halal face cream, scents, and perfumes. The potential growth has been identified through e-commerce [21]. The cosmetics and personal care products are even demanded by men as they are conscious about their appearance as well. The halal certification, i.e. the halal logo gives a competitive advantage to the *Halalpreneurs* over competitors who do not have halal certification.

4.7 Potential markets

The GIE report (**Figure 7**) of 2019 shows the top 15 countries in the halal industry globally based on the global Islamic economy indicator (GIEI). Overall, Malaysia is leading the Islamic economy securing the number one position for Islamic finance and Muslim friendly travel. However, UAE is leading the other sectors of the halal industry securing the rank of number one. The figure also shows the top 10 potential markets in halal food, Muslim friendly tourism, modest fashion, media and recreation, and cosmetics and pharmaceuticals industry. Interestingly, some non-Muslim majority countries have also made their position in the list of top 10 GIE countries. Similarly, [28] categorized the global potential market by region which is, North America (U.S., Canada, Mexico), Europe (Germany, France, UK, Italy, Spain), Asia-Pacific (Indonesia, Malaysia, India, Rest of Asia Pacific), and Latin America, Middle East, Africa (LAMEA).

Figure 7.
Top 15 markets of the global halal industry according to GIEI 2019/2020. Source: [21].

5. Conclusions

The chapter introduces and explains a new term, "*Halalpreneurship*," similar to entrepreneurship. To understand and define *Halalpreneurship,* one must understand and consider what is *halal, toyyib,* and *haram. Halalpreneurship* refers to halal entrepreneurship which revolves around the Islamic economy and the individuals in *Halalpreneurship* are called *Halalpreneurs*, whereas entrepreneurship is a concept that is used in the conventional economy. Both *Halalpreneurs* and entrepreneurs imply business individuals who offer innovative products and services to the consumers, take risks, look for opportunities by the creative use of assets in manners that make a significant impact on the market. However, the concept of *Halalpreneurship* differs from entrepreneurship in certain aspects which comprise mainly the implication of ethical and religious (Islamic) values and guidelines in all kinds of activities in an economy that are related to entrepreneurship. The concept of *Halalpreneurship* is based on *Maqasid-al-Shari'ah* (five objectives of Islamic law). Any Muslim individual conducting entrepreneurial business in the global halal industry with the objective of producing only halal products and services and maintains his/her business conduct in a *Shari'ah*-compliant way is called a *Halalpreneur*. Non-Muslims are also allowed to be *Halalpreneurs* based on the *maslaha* (public interest) for the benefit of *ummah* and mankind.

A number of salient points differentiate *Halalpreneurship* from entrepreneurship. The points are concept, what to produce, how to produce, for whom to produce, the scope of knowledge, motivational factors, and stakeholders. Additionally, there are certain characteristics of *Halalpreneurs* that make them unique and differentiated from conventional entrepreneurs. Some of these characteristics include fear of Allah, the nature of prioritizing prayer, truthfulness, philanthropist, and knowledge of Islamic law.

Halalpreneurs is the source of creativity and innovation that postulates the Islamic economy in many ways. Halalpreneurs thrives for business opportunities with knowledge and wisdom and having faith in Allah (SWT). Simultaneously, they tap the opportunities and conduct their business activities following the guidelines of the Quran, and the advice and practice of the Prophet (PBUH). Business opportunities of Halalpreneurs are spread over the entire global halal industry that had a market value of US$4.7 trillion in 2018 including Islamic finance. The opportunities can be explored in different potential sectors of the halal industry that include Halal F&B, modest fashion industry, Halal media and recreation, Muslim friendly tourism, Halal pharmaceuticals, and Halal cosmetics. Furthermore, the emerging markets to explore opportunities are Halal logistic and supply chain, Halal technology, and Halal talent and skills (Human resources) development.

The potential markets for *Halalpreneurs* are the top 15 countries in the GIE where Malaysia is leading with maximum GIEI score followed by UAE in the second position. The other markets in the list include Bahrain, Saudi Arabia, Indonesia, Oman, Jordan, Pakistan, Kuwait, Qatar, Brunei, Sudan, Turkey, Iran, and Bangladesh, respectively. Interestingly, Brazil has ranked the third position in the halal F&B industry. Additionally, some other non-Muslim countries have also made their positions in the top 10 list of the GIE report in 2018.

Limitations of the chapter: The general objective of this chapter was limited to elucidate and explain the concept of halal entrepreneurship, i.e. *Halalpreneurship*. As the concept is new, limited literature was available relevant to the topic specifically. Although, the chapter attempts to provide an overview of the underlying opportunities for *Halalpreneurs* in different fields of the halal industry, to carry out a research and field survey in every filed was beyond the scope of the current chapter.

Recommendations for future study: Future study should carry out an in-depth investigation of each field of the halal industry to explore the business opportunities of *Halalpreneurs* in detail. Simultaneously, the issues and challenges faced by the *Halalpreneurs* in the halal industry need to be identified and addressed. Additionally, the factors driving the growth of the halal industry need to be realized so that policymakers can emphasize those forces more to enhance the expansion of the halal industry globally.

Author details

Moha Asri Abdullah* and Md. Siddique E Azam
International Institute for Halal Research and Training (INHART), International Islamic University Malaysia (IIUM), Kuala Lumpur, Malaysia

*Address all correspondence to: mosri@iium.edu.my

References

[1] Ramadani V, Dana LP, Gërguri-Rashiti S, Ratten V. An introduction to entrepreneurship and management in an Islamic context. In: Entrepreneurship and Management in an Islamic Context. Cham: Springer; 2017. pp. 1-5

[2] Kayed RN, Hassan MK. Islamic entrepreneurship: A case study of Saudi Arabia. Journal of Developmental Entrepreneurship. 2010 Dec;**15**(04):379-413

[3] Ratten V, Ramadani V, Dana LP, Gerguri-Rashiti S. Islamic entrepreneurship and management: Culture, religion and society. In: Entrepreneurship and Management in an Islamic Context. Cham: Springer; 2017. pp. 7-17

[4] Rahman RA, Mohamed Z. Malaysian halal food entrepreneurs' perspective towards globalization–A conceptual framework. Society of Interdisciplinary Business Research (SIBR). 2011. Available at SSRN: https://ssrn.com/abstract=1869683 or Available from: http://dx.doi.org/10.2139/ssrn.1869683

[5] Soltanian M, Zailani S, Iranmanesh M, Aziz AA. Motivations of SME entrepreneurs to become halalpreneurs. Journal of Science and Technology Policy Management. Emerald Group Publishing Limited; 2016;**7**(2):173-189. DOI: 10.1108/JSTPM-07-2015-0023

[6] Kuratko DF. Entrepreneurship: Theory, Process, and Practice. Cengage Learning; 2016

[7] Shane S, Venkataraman S. The promise of entrepreneurship as a field of research. Academy of Management Review. 2000;**25**(1):217-226

[8] Rindova V, Barry D, Ketchen DJ Jr. Entrepreneuring as emancipation. Academy of Management Review. 2009;**34**(3):477-491

[9] Lumpkin GT, Dess GG. Clarifying the entrepreneurial orientation construct and linking it to performance. Academy of Management Review. 1996;**21**(1):135-172

[10] Low MB, MacMillan IC. Entrepreneurship: Past research and future challenges. Journal of Management. 1988;**14**(2):139-161

[11] Gartner WB. "Who is an entrepreneur?" is the wrong question. American journal of small business. 1988;**12**(4):11-32

[12] Zakaria Z. Tapping into the world halal market: Some discussions on Malaysian laws and standards. Journal Syariah. 2008;**16**(3):603-616

[13] Holy Quran 2:168, 172-173; 23:51; 5:1,3,4. Translated by Ali MM. Ahmadiyya Anjuman Ishaat Islam Lahore USA; 2011

[14] Omar EN, Jaafar HS, Osman MR. Halalan toyyiban supply chain of the food industry. Journal of Emerging Economies and Islamic Research. 2013;**1**(3):23-33

[15] Khan MF, Ghifari NM. Shatibi's Objectives of Shariah and some Implications for Consumer Theory. Kuala Lumpur, Quill: Readings in Islamic Economic Thought: Selected Readings; 1992. pp. 176-202

[16] Abdullah MA, Azam MS. Halal entrepreneurship from Maqasid-al-Sharia'h perspective: Inseparable concept for Halalpreneurs. Food Research. 2020;**4**(1):34-42

[17] Menger C. Carl Menger and His Legacy in Economics. Durham, North Carolina, United States: Duke University Press; 1990

[18] Faizal PR, Ridhwan AA, Kalsom AW. The entrepreneurs' characteristic from al-Quran and al-Hadis. International Journal of Trade, Economics and Finance. 2013;**4**(4):191

[19] Ramadani V, Dana LP, Ratten V, Tahiri S. The context of Islamic entrepreneurship and business: Concept, principles, and perspectives. International Journal of Business and Globalisation. 2015;**15**(3):244-261

[20] Malaysia JK. Manual procedure for Malaysia halal certification (Third revision) 2014. In: Jabatan Kemajuan Islam Malaysia. Putrajaya: Jabatan Kemajuan Islam Malaysia (JAKIM); 2015

[21] Reuters T, Standard D. State of the Global Islamic Economy Report 2019/20. Dubai International Financial Centre. 2019:1-174. Available from: https://haladinar.io/hdn/doc/report2018.pdf

[22] Chamberlayne C. Harper's Bazaar Arabia [Online]. Available from: https://www.harpersbazaararabia.com/lifestyle/entertain/netflix-follow-this-series-features-a-modest-fashion-episode [Accessed: 03 August 2020]

[23] Cook S. Startup Empowering UK startups since 2000 [Online]. Available from: https://startups.co.uk/business-ideas/modest-fashion/ [Accessed: 03 August 2020]

[24] Kader SA. Salam Gateway [Online]. Available from: https://www.salaamgateway.com/story/mubarakdealscom-sees-opportunity-in-online-to-offline-modest-fashion-business-model-in-india [Accessed: 03 August 2020]

[25] Akeel M. Arab News [Online]. Available from: https://www.arabnews.com/node/1443446 [Accessed: 03 August 2020]

[26] Mastercard and CrescentRating. Global Muslim Travel Index [Online]. 2018. Available from: https://www.crescentrating.com/download/thankyou.html?file=X7UrOM8Y_GMITI-Report-2018-web-version%281%29.pdf

[27] Man SA, Pauzi N. The implication of differences in halal Standard of Malaysia, Indonesia, Brunei, and Singapore. The Journal of Muamalat and Islamic Finance Research. 2017;**204**(5775):1-4

[28] Ray A. Allied Market Research [Online]. Available from: https://www.alliedmarketresearch.com/halal-cosmetics-market [Accessed: 03 August 2020]

Section 3

Entrepreneurial Finance

Chapter 8

Does Financial Institution Proximity Affect the Development of Entrepreneurship?

Francesco Fasano, Maurizio La Rocca, Tiziana La Rocca and Veronica Marozzo

Abstract

The present contribution joins the stream of research investigating the relationship between local financial development, economic growth, and entrepreneurship. Relevant contributions highlighted that the probability of an individual to start a new business is higher when he/she moves from the least financially developed region to the most financially developed one. Indeed, higher levels of local financial development allow for easier access to external funds, which are crucial for the growth of new businesses. In this entrepreneurial context, the need of financial resources is especially relevant for research spin-offs (ROSs), which require significant resources to transfer to the market their innovative technologies. This chapter deepens the role of local financial development on entrepreneurship and, in particular, on research spin-offs. Empirical evidence highlight that at the time of ROSs' incubation, local financial development does not affect the performance of spin-offs, as they mainly rely on Universities and public contributions. Vice versa, when the RSOs enter the market, they are more in need of funds from the financial system, for which local financial development interestingly becomes strongly relevant to them, affecting corporate performance. Consequently, despite the internationalization of financial markets, policymakers should carefully encourage entrepreneurship through the development of local financial systems.

Keywords: financial system, local financial development, local context, entrepreneurship, research spin-off

1. Introduction

The firm's success typically depends on a number of internal drivers and external opportunities that can be exploited. In particular, the potential use of external financial resources and the eventual difficulty to access to these resources represent the greatest challenges that a firm must overcome nowadays. Manzocchi et al. [1] state that "External drivers encompass various aspects of the environmental context in which a firm operates, such as the standard and efficiency of the public administration, national or regional credit conditions, physical infrastructures and intangible capital. Most of these external factors may affect the productivity performance of rather similar firms if they are located in different areas of the same country".

Therefore, the characteristics of the local environment in which firms operate are at the core of the potential success of a firm. Among the variety of features related to the environment, the role of the financial system is noteworthy in affecting the competitiveness of a firm. With this regard, a large empirical literature, which begins with the work of King and Levine [2], shows that the development of the financial system is important for the overall economic growth at the country level and also directly for firms' performance [2–4]. As suggested by Guiso et al. [5], the local financial context is considered as a priority by small and medium-sized firms (SMEs), which means that the success of a firm depends on the possibility to exploit the opportunities provided by the external environment. The degree of development of the local financial system (i.e. a specific financial system in a definite geographic area, smaller than the national context) strongly shapes business activities [5] and is especially important for "financially constrained" firms. Such firms have difficult access to the financial market because they face asymmetric information problems [6]. In particular, the access to external financial resources, the amount of credit available and the conditions provided by the banks can differently affect firms' startup, survivorship and corporate performance, according to the area where the firm is located. Local areas with higher levels of financial development can better support firms' growth processes. Entrepreneurial venture and, in general, SMEs, that are typical informational opaque firms, are supposed to grow faster in economies characterized by relevant financial development. With this regard, local financial development has a key role on entrepreneurship. Noteworthy contributions argue that the opportunity to start-up a new entrepreneurial activity, where informational opacity is a very relevant driver, is higher in those contexts where the access to external financial market is higher [5], especially when bank competition is strong [7].

Accounting for these stylized facts, this chapter intents to examine the potential effect of local financial development on entrepreneurship, with a particular focus on new high-tech firms, such as research spin-off (RSOs). RSOs are very special start-up firms that are founded with the aim to exploit technological knowledge that originated within a University or a Research institute setting, in order to develop products or services. Considering that innovation is the root of the economic success and the development of a country, it is important an effective way to transfer technology from University and Research Center into the market, for which the role of RSOs is crucial. Thus, understanding how the local financial context affects the performance of RSOs is useful to provide practical implications to sustain corporate development and, in general, the economic growth of nations.

While some papers studying the impact of academic spin-offs at the local level did not take into account direct measure of local context [8], others investigating the factors that foster the creation of academic spin-off directly examined the role of the local context [9]. However, there is a gap in the literature due to the fact that until recently nobody scrutinized the role of the local financial context on RSOs. From one side, it could be argued that the degree of the development of the financial system does not affect RSOs business because this kind of firm works under the University arms' length, which is a sort of protected environment where financial resources mainly come from public contributions and research projects. However, on the other side, this could be true in the early stage of the RSOs or until the time of entrance into the product market. At this time, for many reasons (the need to have a wider production plane to deal with commercialization, having the need to financially support the payments to suppliers and customers with different time horizon, etc.) the degree of financial development in the local area where a firm is based on could become very relevant. In this context, in local settings with efficient financial markets, financial intermediaries should be able to provide better assess for the feasibility of RSOs' initiatives. Consequently, a key implication for managers is that RSOs should try to look for external financial resources in well-developed local financial areas. Indeed, in such contexts RSOs have fewer difficulties in obtaining outside funding and, as a result, they can easily finance their current activities and growth opportunities.

This contribution has also implications for policy makers by showing that despite the internalization of financial markets, the local financial context is still relevant for entrepreneurship. Indeed, the growth of RSOs depends on their ability to catch investment opportunities. The presence of developed financial systems increases the availability of funding in a specific geographic area and should be therefore encouraged. Moreover, policymakers could develop new instruments, such as online lending or the figure of financial promoters, which allow RSOs to access external debt. Such instruments could increase local financial development and help RSOs in their negotiations with banks or bring alternative sources of financing, especially in those provinces where the local banking system is poor.

The chapter is structured as follows. We describe the role of the financial system on economic growth in Paragraph 2. Paragraph 3 studies how local financial development could help corporate activities. Paragraph 4 moves one step further and investigates the role of the local financial development on entrepreneurship, while paragraph 5 specifically studies the impact of local financial development on research spin-offs. Finally, paragraph 6 provides some conclusions and implications.

2. Financial system and economic growth

The relationship between the financial system and economic development is based on the key role of the services that the financial system provides to the companies [2]. The presence of information asymmetries and significant transaction costs highlights the fundamental role of the financial systems [4][1] as they guarantee[2]:

- efficient allocation of resources among alternative projects;
- intertemporal reallocation of consumption[3];
- efficient risk-sharing in each period (risk-sharing in market-based systems and risk-taking in bank-based systems)[4].

[1] Classical economic models, based on the concept of market equilibrium, Pareto efficiency and the application of theorems, such Fisher's separation Theorem (1930), show that economic operators face little consistency with the economic reality. Only recently analyses are studying market frictions, such as the role of information asymmetries, agency and transaction costs. Particularly interesting also are the market microstructure studies that try to determine the weight of transaction costs on the markets and why the markets are more or less liquid.

[2] For a deep analysis on the functions of the financial system, see [10, 11].

[3] The concaveness of utility curves creates a mismatching between income and consumption flows. Economic agents prefer to have uniform consumption flows over time, while income streams have fluctuating patterns. The financial system allows to lend and borrow in such a way as to ensure uniform flows. This function is critical regardless of the presence of risk in the system.

[4] For example, if there was no stock market, all the risk would fall on the owner and few entrepreneurs would undertake innovative but very risky projects.

Studies on the relationship between the financial system and economic growth move from the work of Schumpeter [12], who highlighted the positive contribution of a developed financial system to the growth of the entire economy. According to his idea of "destructive creativity", an efficient financial system would be able to sustain radical innovations in the product market. This sustain consists in supporting the creativity and innovation of new companies that are in need of external financial resources and that cannot provide collateral activities.

Although someone observed that the role of the financial system and institutions has been overestimated [13], in general, the extant literature seems to empirically reveal the importance of the relationship between the financial system and economic growth [4]. This is a line of research that subsequently extended the analysis to the relationship between the development of the financial system and the growth of specific industrial sectors and, later, it focused on the impact of the activities of individual companies [14–16]. In particular, the extant literature [15] showed that companies operating in sectors where the availability of high external financial resources is crucial grow faster in the presence of a developed financial system, both if it's a bank-based or a market-based context[5]. Some international analyses compared the relationship between the financial system and economic development in bank-based countries and market-based countries. The controversial empirical evidence could not attribute the preeminence of one over the other economy [17].

From another perspective, the financial system has its own identity, that is different although related to the legal and enforcement system. Such identity is able to offer a range of essential services in supporting firms' growth [17]. With this regard, the services offered by a financial system play a key influence on a country's industrial growth[6].

Therefore, the literature suggests that the quality and efficiency of the financial system are fundamental to supporting both existing and new entrepreneurial activities.

3. Which role for local financial development to sustain business activities?

The integration and internationalization of the financial markets could limit the relevance of local financial development on firms' growth [5]. The consequence of such integration is that the financial markets tend to converge toward only one single great market. According to this perspective, companies with growth opportunities, a competitive advantage, and managerial capabilities should be able to overcome the obstacles associated with an inefficient local financial system by moving on the international market. On the contrary, the vast majority of small entrepreneurs could look for funds in the local financial system, as personal point of refecences at the first place, without a minimal idea about the chances to move in the international markets.

Relatively recent literature [5] suggests that the different levels of development and efficiency of the financial system within a single country make those geographical areas with a higher level of development and efficiency better able to assess the feasibility of new initiatives and, by funding them, support their growth.

5 For a review see [17, 18].

6 The literature documents the presence of a relevant cause-and-effect relationship between types and quality of services offered by the financial system and economic development, underying the need for further empirical research on this issue [17].

In light of this, the level of development and efficiency of the local financial system influences the economic growth of companies.

With this regard, a growing literature found that the "proximity" between financial intermediaries and firms plays a significant role in lending decisions [5]. Banks lend to firms operating in the same area, as it is easier to control the reliability, profitability and future potential projects of their customers [19].

Moreover, local financial development is especially important for SMEs and the startup of new business initiatives, as large companies should be able to easily enter the financial market, overcoming the local difficulties of an under-developed and inefficient financial system.

Companies with profitable growth capabilities could overcome the obstacles associated with an inefficient local financial system by relying on the international market. For example, in some countries, the activation and maintenance of a national financial market could be considered not relevant given the possibility of companies to be listed in foreign markets (such as Nasdaq) [5]. However, this phenomenon presents distortions and inefficiencies. Indeed, large enterprises enter the international financial markets, overcoming the local difficulties of an undeveloped and inefficient financial system, while small and medium-sized enterprises are more in need of local financial support. The inability of the financial system to appreciate, at the local level, the quality of companies' investment projects hampers development opportunities, limiting the growth of companies.

The different level of development of the financial system among local areas influences the intensity of business growth, limiting the economic convenience of venture capitals. This could limit corporate financial decisions, constraining firms and generating credit rationing problems. In other words, firms grow faster when they are located in regions where access to credit is easier, and financial intermediaries appreciate the quality of investment projects [5]. Besides, in such regions, there are more businesses per capita and the rate of new business creation is higher.

Main studies on this topic [5, 20] are based on the Italian context because it represents an ideal setting to study the role of local financial development on RSOs. In a country unified for almost 160 years where the same law applies there is a large persistence of differences in financial development across Italian provinces that make Italy a very suitable environment to investigate the effects of local financial development. A similar context can be found in Spain, a country that, likewise Italy, is bank-based and civil low. For these reasons, some other contributions investigate the effects of local financial development in Spain [21–23]. Empirical evidences also show that within the United States there is a relevant role on business activities among different development in local areas/States [24].

4. Local financial development and entrepreneurship

Recent literature suggests that entrepreneurship and, in general, the starting of new firms, is affected by the quality of the financial system. The improved access to external funds (credit availability) provided by financial development increases the opportunities to become an entrepreneur. Firm creation is higher in local markets with more bank competition [7] and is influenced by the development in the local financial market [5]. According to the work of Guiso et al. [5], the probability that a person becomes self-employed is indeed higher in more financially developed areas (5.6 percentage points). This result is consistent with the findings found based on US firms [25]. Similar results are obtained using as dependent variable the number of new firms in an area scaled by the total number of inhabitants. Moving from the least financially developed region to the most financially developed one, it is possible to observe an increase of the ratio of new firms to the population by 25 percent, roughly one firm for every 400 inhabitants. Also, this latter result is consistent with the findings based on the US [26].

The results based on the Italian context are robust to many controls. First, the level of per capita GDP as a measure of economic development of the area. Moreover, the efficiency of the local courts to account for differences in the enforcement system at the local level. In addition, the local level of "social capital" à la Putnam. Finally, they use instrumental variables in order to avoid any possibility of endogeneity related to the connection between the measure of financial development with some unobserved determinants of entrepreneurship.

Additionally, better access to funds allows people to become entrepreneurs at a younger age (earlier, on average, five years). Hence, in more financially developed regions the average age of existing entrepreneurs should be lower.

Therefore, even in a world of international integration of financial markets, where funds can freely flow cross-country, the quality of the local financial system continues to matter even to promote firm creation and entrepreneurship.

Although local financial development increases the entrepreneurship rate, there are still just a few papers investigating how local financial development affects business activities of new firms. For instance, a recent work studied the financial decisions of start-ups shaped by local financial development [27]. This contribution specifically investigates the effects of local banking development on the debt financing of new firms using a large sample of Italian firms [27]. Controlling for potential endogeneity issues, results show that new firms are more likely to use bank debt and have higher leverage in provinces with higher financial development. While traditional literature [28] suggests that new firms are mainly financed by equity capital, this study provides new and nuanced evidence on the role of local banking development for the debt financing of new firms.

5. Local financial development and research spin-off

The importance of research spin-offs in supporting economic and technological growth is crucial, as they transfer technology and innovation to the market [29]. Considering their relevance, it is of great interest the way to boost RSOs creation, as a way to promote competitiveness among countries. In this interesting line of research, it is interesting to scrutinize the relationship between local financial development and RSOs. As reported in literature, the startup of a company by a research organization is an important way to commercialize the results of a public research [30], and contributes to economic and social welfare by influencing the entire regional development [31, 32]. In fact, the generation and application of new ideas, technologies and scientific knowledge are widely recognized as a prerequisite for economic development, job creation and the formation of a competitive industrial structure [33].

A spin-off is a new legal and economic entity, created through the "separation" of a resource from an existing entity (parent organization) to carry out a new task, or reorganizing a task previously carried out in the entity of origin. When it comes to RSOs, it can be referred to those entities created through the separation from a resource (typically a new technology derived from academic research result), transferred to a new company through a voluntary process supported by the University [34]. RSO is a new firm in which two elements can be found: 1) the initiative must involve people employed by Universities or Research Institutes (typically researchers); 2) the new entity must acquire a technology developed within the University itself and, after the phase of development, it transfers this technology to the market [35]. Once defined the spinoffs and clarified their role, it is important to underlying that these legal entities are important because: 1) they contribute to the local economic development; 2) they make easier the commercialization of new technologies; 3) they provide support to main activities of research; 4) they have above-average performance; 5) they generate, if compared to licensing, more revenues for universities [36].

The literature about spinoffs is extensive. In particular, an interesting work [37] carried out a comparative investigation between 12 Italian and Swedish spin-offs, observing that an increase in productivity, in terms of public research results, due to the activity of spinoffs. More in general, the success of spin-offs depends from several factors [38]. Among those factors, many studies have highlighted the role played by the financial system. It is well known that the ability of companies to access external financial resources with positive effects is determined also by the presence of a well-developed financial system [39]. Access to external financial resources can be crucial for success in the long run of spin-offs as well as for other low-tech new firms [40, 41].

The extant literature found a positive relationship between the level of local financial development and the number of new spinoffs [42]. However, Agarwal and Bayus [43] showed, "it takes on average 14 years before a technology patented at a research institute reaches 2% of its peak sales at market maturity". Typically research spinoffs face a long incubation period before the commercialization of the product. Although the different phases of spinoff's life cycle vary a lot across the different industries, there is, in general, a considerable timescale between the first phase of their life cycle and the sales takeoff. Spinoff's life cycle can be summed up as follows [44]. A research phase, from an idea into a prototype, a second phase characterized by an intense activity of fundraising, that can be called the opportunity framing phase [45], or alternatively the gestation [46] or pre-start-up phase. A third phase characterized by an intense activity for developing the prototype in order to understand if it can have an effective commercial use. Once the spinoff has productively commercialized its product, established contracts with customers and its sales take off, then it enters in a new phase which may be labeled the post-start-up [47] or maturity phase [46].

During the first three-phase spinoffs are usually located inside dedicated areas that Universities make available (also known as "incubators"), where spinoffs exploit all the academic assets (laboratories, staff, etcetera). In this phase, sales are mainly equal to zero.

There is a typical structure break at the type RSOs move from an incubator stage with no sales and only revenues in terms of government contributions and/or research projects, to a stage where the RSO is financially autonomous, taking off on the product market, commercializing its products/services and having selling revenues.

Considering this cycle in the RSO, La Rocca et al. [48] argue that spin-off works on the prototype, preparing the event of the product launch entering into the market and figuring out how to set up the equipment for a production under steady conditions. The incubation period can be assessed considering that spinoffs are fully dependent from Universities and public contributions. Financial resources availability from financial institutions or public markets play a subordinate role at this stage of the spinoff. Until this stage, the role of the external financial context is meaningless and negligible.

It is at the time of the entrance in the product market, facing directly costumers, competitors and different financial issues, that the way of doing business for RSOs is going to change. RSOs start to become independent from Universities and public contributions. At this time, local financial development positively influences RSO performance [48]. The presence of a higher degree of local financial development and access to external sources of financing should better support spin-offs' funding decisions. In this context, financial institutions and public markets will be able to provide the financial support that best fit RSOs' financial needs. The potential support that the financial markets provide to spinoffs shows its benefits once the product is commercialized. Such support resulted evident both in the short-run, to deal with all the economic transactions raised into the market, and also in the long-run, providing the right financial tools to support the acquisition of an industrial building, machines and equipment. In this case, the degree of development of a financial system represents a resource that gives the possibility to spin-offs to commercialize innovations. It is worth noting that in a matching sample of high-tech startups (not-RSOs) the impact of local financial development is always positive, meaning that the nature of the RSOs significantly affects the role of external finance [48].

At the time a RSO is incubated inside the University or Research Institute and its survival is totally and uniquely dependent from non-operational earnings, the ROS is *de facto* a "proto-company" still *in nuce*, but not really operative at this stage. As long as the survival of RSOs depends on collecting money from public contributions and start-up competition awards more than on their own sales, the degree of financial system development does not influence the performance of spinoffs.

Therefore, the kind of revenues a RSO is based on the degree of financial independence from Universities and public contributions that specifies the stage in the life-cycle of academic spin-offs. At the time of RSO incubation, when sales are equal to zero, local financial development does not matter for spin-off performance. Vice versa, at the time the RSO has to take-off in the product market, finding financial resources outside can be hampered by the condition of opacity information caused by information asymmetries that typically affect RSO. Development of local financial market influences positively spinoffs, originally created within universities and Public Research institutes, at a greater extent when RSOs become fully independent and completely free from public contributions, namely, when the RSO takes-off in the product market and it is not anymore incubated inside the University sites.

This chapter also has limitations, as it does not discuss the operating nature of RSOs and, more in general, the qualitative aspects of RSOs that could explain the relationship between local financial development and corporate performance.

Moreover, the extant literature did not studied how local financial development could affect corporate performance. However, it could be interesting for future research to investigate how this institutional factor shapes the growth of the firm and its value.

6. Conclusion

Local financial development has a crucial role for the economic growth [2]. Such relevance is due to the fact that higher levels of local financial development ease access to external financial sources, spurring firms' investments and, consequently, business success. The extant literature interestingly demonstrated that easier access to financial markets encourages entrepreneurship, because it facilitates the startup of new businesses in search of external funding, which is important to catch growth opportunities. One of the most important entrepreneurial businesses is represented by RSOs. Such companies play a key role on the global economy, as they transfer technology and innovation from University and Research Center into the market. RSOs are always in need to catch investing opportunities, as innovation is expensive and requires efficient financial systems. Indeed, in the absence of funding, productivity is constrained and RSOs difficultly get growth opportunities. In this context, some interesting contributions highlighted that in countries where there is greater financial development, companies are more likely to innovate [49] and innovation is higher in firms that have access to external resources [50]. Hence, well-developed financial systems have a positive effect on entrepreneurship, corporate growth and, as a result, the company's performance.

Considering the relevance of local financial development for RSOs, the present chapter deepens the relationships between local financial development and the performance of entrepreneurial firms, with a focus on RSOs. Due to the intrinsic nature of these firms, La Rocca et al. [48] show that RSOs need a long period (incubation period) during which their research requires to be refined and engineered before being commercialized. During this period the main revenues and financial sources of spinoffs are made up of public contributions and prizes obtained from participation in startup competitions. At this early stage, the use of debt or other financial resources is limited and the role of local financial development is absent. Differently, at the end of the incubation period, the impact of local financial development on spinoffs' performance interestingly turns from negative to positive.

In the light of the above, this chapter provides important implications for firms, which should carefully take into account the institutional setting in which they are embedded, and for policymakers, who should undertake important initiatives aimed at increasing local financial development. The key evidence of this chapter is that local financial development represents a strong tool in order to transfer new innovative technologies into the market.

Author details

Francesco Fasano[1]*, Maurizio La Rocca[1], Tiziana La Rocca[2] and Veronica Marozzo[2]

1 University of Calabria, Rende, Italy

2 University of Messina, Messina, Italy

*Address all correspondence to: francesco.fasano@unical.it

References

[1] Manzocchi S, Quintieri B, Santoni G. Internal vs. external firm productivity drivers. A study of the Italian counties. LLEE Luiss; 2014.

[2] King RG, Levine R. Finance and growth: Schumpeter might be right. Q J Econ 1993;108:717-37. https://doi.org/10.2307/2118406.

[3] Rajan RG, Zingales L. Banks and Markets: the Changing Character of European Finance. vol. Working Pa. 2003. https://doi.org/10.3386/w9595.

[4] Levine R. Financial development and economic growth: views and agenda. The World Bank; 1999.

[5] Guiso L, Sapienza P, Zingales L. Does local financial development matter? Q J Econ 2004;119:929-69. https://doi.org/10.1162/0033553041502162.

[6] Love I. Financial development and financing constraints: International evidence from the structural investment model. Rev Financ Stud 2003;16:765-91. https://doi.org/10.1093/rfs/hhg013.

[7] Di Patti EB, Dell'Ariccia G. Bank competition and firm creation. International Monetary Fund; 2001.

[8] Iacobucci D, Micozzi A. How to evaluate the impact of academic spin-offs on local development: an empirical analysis of the Italian case. J Technol Transf 2015;40:434-52. https://doi.org/10.1007/s10961-014-9357-8.

[9] Fini R, Grimaldi R, Sobrero M. Factors fostering academics to start up new ventures: an assessment of Italian founders' incentives. J Technol Transf 2009;34:380-402. https://doi.org/10.1007/s10961-008-9093-z.

[10] Allen F, Gale D. Comparing financial systems. MIT press; 2000.

[11] Forestieri G, Mottura P. Il sistema finanziario. Egea; 2013.

[12] Schumpeter AJ. A Theory of Economic Development. Cambridge, MA, Harvard University Press.; 1911.

[13] Lucas Jr RE. On the mechanics of economic development. J Monet Econ 1988;22:3-42. https://doi.org/10.1016/0304-3932(88)90168-7.

[14] Levine R, Zervos S. Stock markets, banks, and economic growth. Am Econ Rev 1998:537-58.

[15] Rajan R, Zingales L. Financial development and growth. Am Econ Rev 1998;88:559-86.

[16] Demirgüç-Kunt A, Maksimovic V. Law, finance, and firm growth. J Finance 1998;53:2107-37. https://doi.org/10.1111/0022-1082.00084.

[17] Rajan RG, Zingales L. Financial systems, industrial structure, and growth. Oxford Rev Econ Policy 2001;17:467-82. https://doi.org/10.1093/oxrep/17.4.467.

[18] Demirgüç-Kunt A, Levine R. Bank-based and market-based financial systems: Cross-country comparisons. In: (A. Demirgüç-Kunt and R. Levine E., editor., in Financial Structure and Economic Growth: A Cross-Country Comparison of Banks, Markets, and Development, MIT Press, Cambridge, MA.; 2001.

[19] Petersen MA, Rajan RG. Does distance still matter? The information revolution in small business lending. J Finance 2002;57:2533-70. https://doi.org/10.1111/1540-6261.00505.

[20] Deloof M, La Rocca M. Local financial development and the trade credit policy of Italian SMEs.

Small Bus Econ 2015;44:905-24. https://doi.org/10.1007/s11187-014-9617-x.

[21] Palacín-Sánchez M-J, Di Pietro F. The role of the regional financial sector in the capital structure of small and medium-sized enterprises (SMEs). Reg Stud 2016;50:1232-47. https://doi.org/10.1080/00343404.2014.1000290.

[22] Utrero-González N. Banking regulation, institutional framework and capital structure: International evidence from industry data. Q Rev Econ Financ 2007;47:481-506. https://doi.org/10.1016/j.qref.2006.02.006.

[23] González VM, González F. Influence of bank concentration and institutions on capital structure: New international evidence. J Corp Financ 2008;14:363-75. https://doi.org/10.1016/j.jcorpfin.2008.03.010.

[24] Jayaratne J, Strahan PE. The finance-growth nexus: Evidence from bank branch deregulation. Q J Econ 1996;111:639-70.

[25] Black SE, Strahan PE. Entrepreneurship and bank credit availability. J Finance 2002;57:2807-33. https://doi.org/10.1111/1540-6261.00513.

[26] Evans DS, Jovanovic B. An estimated model of entrepreneurial choice under liquidity constraints. J Polit Econ 1989;97:808-27. https://doi.org/10.1086/261629.

[27] Deloof M, La Rocca M, Vanacker T. Local Banking Development and the Use of Debt Financing by Start-ups (Summary). Front Entrep Res 2016;36:6.

[28] Berger AN, Udell GF. The economics of small business finance: The roles of private equity and debt markets in the financial growth cycle. J Bank Financ 1998;22:613-73. https://doi.org/10.1016/S0378-4266(98)00038-7.

[29] Chiesa V, Piccaluga A. Exploitation and diffusion of public research: the case of academic spin-off companies in Italy. R&D Manag 2000;30:329-40. https://doi.org/10.1111/1467-9310.00187.

[30] Czarnitzki D, Rammer C, Toole AA. University spin-offs and the "performance premium." Small Bus Econ 2014;43:309-26. https://doi.org/10.1007/s11187-013-9538-0.

[31] Bellini N, Ferrucci L. Ricerca universitaria e processi di innovazione: le piccole e medie imprese nel Progetto Link. vol. 188. FrancoAngeli; 2002.

[32] Pleschak F. Entwicklungstendenzen des Technologietransfers und Anforderungen an seine Ausgestaltung., In: Pleschak F (ed) Technologietransfer, Anforderungen und Entwicklungstendenzen, Karlsruhe; 2003, p. 1-16.

[33] Atasu A, Van Wassenhove LN, Sarvary M. Efficient take-back legislation. Prod Oper Manag 2009;18:243-58. https://doi.org/10.3401/poms.1080.01004.

[34] Palumbo R. Dall'Università al mercato. Governance e performance degli spinoff universitari in Italia: Governance e performance degli spinoff universitari in Italia. FrancoAngeli; 2010.

[35] Carayannis EG, Rogers EM, Kurihara K, Allbritton MM. High-technology spin-offs from government R&D laboratories and research universities. Technovation 1998;18:1-11. https://doi.org/10.1016/S0166-4972(97)00101-6.

[36] Shane SA. Academic entrepreneurship: University spinoffs and wealth creation. Edward Elgar Publishing; 2004.

[37] Bellini E, Capaldo G, Edström A, Kaulio M, Raffa M, Ricciardi M ZG. The role of academic spin-offs in connecting technological local assets in regional contexts: A comparative analysis of Italian and Swedish cases., In 44th ICSB Conference; 1999.

[38] Smilor R, Matthews J. University venturing: technology transfer and commercialisation in higher education. Int J Technol Transf Commer 2004;3:111-28. https://doi.org/10.1504/IJTTC.2004.003519.

[39] Christopoulos DK, Tsionas EG. Financial development and economic growth: evidence from panel unit root and cointegration tests. J Dev Econ 2004;73:55-74. https://doi.org/10.1016/j.jdeveco.2003.03.002.

[40] Ortìn P, Salas V, Trujillo M, Vendrell F. El Spin-off Universitario en España como modelo de creación de empresas intensivas en tecnología. 2007.

[41] Patzelt, H Shepherd D. Strategic entrepreneurship at universities: Academic entrepreneurs' assessment of policy programs. Entrep Theory Pract 2009;33:319-40. https://doi.org/10.1111/j.1540-6520.2008.00291.x.

[42] Fini R, Grimaldi R, Santoni S, Sobrero M. Complements or substitutes? The role of universities and local context in supporting the creation of academic spin-offs. Res Policy 2011;40:1113-27.

[43] Agarwal R, Bayus BL. The market evolution and sales takeoff of product innovations. Manage Sci 2002;48: 1024-41. https://doi.org/10.1287/mnsc.48.8.1024.167.

[44] Rasmussen E. Understanding academic entrepreneurship: Exploring the emergence of university spin-off ventures using process theories. Int Small Bus J 2011;29:448-71. https://doi.org/10.1177/0266242610385395.

[45] Vohora A, Wright M, Lockett A. Critical junctures in the development of university high-tech spinout companies. Res Policy 2004;33:147-75. https://doi.org/10.1016/S0048-7333(03)00107-0.

[46] Vanaelst I, Clarysse B, Wright M, Lockett A, Moray N, S'Jegers R. Entrepreneurial team development in academic spinouts: An examination of team heterogeneity. Entrep Theory Pract 2006;30:249-71. https://doi.org/10.1111/j.1540-6520.2006.00120.x.

[47] Clarysse B, Moray N. A process study of entrepreneurial team formation: The case of a research-based spin-off. J Bus Ventur 2004;19:55-79. https://doi.org/10.1016/S0883-9026(02)00113-1.

[48] La Rocca M, La Rocca T, Fasano F, Vecellio P. Does local financial development affect the survival of RSO?, University of Calabria, Working Paper. 2020.

[49] Sharma S. Financial development and innovation in small firms. The World Bank; 2007.

[50] Ayyagari M, Beck T, Demirgüç-Kunt A. Small and medium enterprises across the globe. Small Bus Econ 2007;29:415-34. https://doi.org/10.1007/s11187-006-9002-5.

Chapter 9

Financial Fragility and Corporate Bond Funding of SMEs: An Analysis of the Italian Case

Emanuele Rossi and Simone Boccaletti

Abstract

The chapter analyzes the financial policy of corporate bond issuers in the new Italian junior bond market specifically dedicated to unlisted firms and SMEs, using a proprietary firm-level dataset on 127 first-time mini-bond issuers across 2013–2017 years jointly with a control sample of around 5200 Italian private firms that have not issued corporate bonds across the same years. Since SME access to the debt capital market is largely considered a valuable source of debt funding diversification, especially for growth firms with a prominent exposure on bank debt, we test using OLS regressions whether bond issuers are able to reduce their financial vulnerability in comparison with similar nonissuers firms. The aim is to assess the extent to which the financial choices of SMEs regarding nonequity external funding can become a key factor in facing real and financial shocks like those triggered by the current pandemic Covid-19 outbreak. Our findings suggest that the access to the junior bond market is beneficial for the Italian unlisted companies in terms of a pronounced improvement in our financial fragility indicators.

Keywords: small business finance, bond financing, SMEs, financial fragility, mini-bonds
JEL classification: G12, G23, G24, G32

1. Introduction

The pandemic Covid-19 outbreak has severely disrupted the economic systems across European countries during the 2020 first semester. Widespread lockdowns have brought to a halt for a few months the firms' production and services delivering in many countries and major concerns have arisen on the capacity of many firms to survive the real and financial shocks induced by the current pandemic. Despite all governments and public authorities vast subsidizing programs deployed to help economy recovery, still small and medium sized enterprises (SMEs) remain particularly exposed to the negative consequences of the current Covid-19 outbreak due to their higher perceived financial vulnerability.

Among European countries, Italy has been the first country to be harshly hit by the coronavirus outbreak and one of the more exposed to negative economic consequences of the pandemic. Moreover, its economic system is very much reliant on SMEs on the economy supply side. Anecdotal evidence points out that many small businesses are struggling to re-open and resume their activities after the slow easing up of the government lockdown measures.

Under these circumstances, the present study aims to test the financial policies that Italian SMEs have developed across the years starting from the aftermath of the 2008 financial crisis and the ensuing 2011 Greek sovereign debt crisis, up to recent years. There are many ways to deal with this issue and its many specifics. We opt to focus on how SMEs in Italy have chosen to diversify their debt funding away from bank lending through corporate bonds funding, since SME access to the debt capital market is largely considered a valuable source of debt funding diversification, especially for growth firms with a prominent exposure on bank debt [1–5]. Beyond that, one of the main goals of a firm's sound financial policy, particularly in the case of SMEs, should be to devise financial choices that may help reducing the financial vulnerability to potential unexpected financial shocks [6, 7].

There are several reasons for our research focus. First, it is well documented that SMEs tend to be over-reliant on bank debt, especially short-term lending [8]. Second, the last global financial crisis heightened in southern European countries by the spillover of Greek sovereign debt crisis in 2011 has produced a lasting credit crunch propelled by risk aversion from banks and their concerns on borrowers default risk, which it has been particularly severe for SMEs [9, 10]. Third, in order to counter the negative effect of this credit crunch on SMEs, the Italian government has promoted in June 2012 a raft of reforms in order to facilitate the SMEs and unlisted firms' access to bond financing[1] [3]. A new junior bond market for mini-bonds, named *ExtraMot-Pro*, within the domestic *Borsa Italiana* stock exchange, has been launched in February 2013, with a set of soft requisites for SMEs issuers. In brief, the new junior bond market is characterized by minimal regulations and simplified admission requirements in comparison with those set up for the senior corporate bond market.

More in particular, we analyze in this chapter whether mini-bond issuers have improved their financial resilience thanks to this market-based financial choice across the years between the two major recent crises (i.e., the 2011 Greek sovereign crisis and the 2020 pandemic-induced crisis). By focusing on this topic, our study may contribute to shed new light on the emerging debate on how small businesses can recover from the current crisis triggered by the Covid-19 pandemic.

Our empirical analysis is performed using regression models based on a proprietary hand-collected dataset of 127 mini-bonds issued by nonfinancial firms across 2013–2017 years jointly with a sample of nearly 5200 Italian private firms that have not issued corporate bonds across the same years. The dataset combines evidence on mini-bonds issuers, collected from *Borsa Italiana* website and admission prospectuses, with detailed financial statements data from Bureau Van Dijk' Amadeus/Aida dataset.

The chapter is organized as follows. Section 2 discusses our research question and the testable hypothesis. Section 3 describes our dataset and provides sample description. Section 4 illustrates the research design and the empirical methodology. Section 5 sets out the empirical results and discusses the main implications of the study. Section 5 concludes the paper.

---

[1] The regulatory framework for mini-bonds in Italy has been established by "Decreto Sviluppo" (D.L. n. 83, June 22, 2012), "Decreto Sviluppo Bis" (D.L. n. 179, October 18, 2012), "Piano Destinazione Italia" (D.L. n. 145, December 23, 2013), "Decreto competitività" (D.L. n. 91, June 24, 2014). For further detail, see the Borsa Italiana website: https://www.borsaitaliana.it/prolink/extramotpro/ilcontestonormativo/ilcontestonormativo.en.htm

2. The financial fragility of SMEs: does corporate bond financing make SMEs more resilient to potential crisis?

In our research setting, we are interested in testing one of the key ingredients that normally shapes the firms' financial policy [11, 12]: how firms' external funding choices could make them less financial fragile when facing potential unforeseen real or financial shocks like those induced by the current coronavirus pandemic. The basic idea, here, is the more the firm is less dependent from a unique or very few sources of external funding (for instance, bank lending), the better for the firm from a financial vulnerability point of view. We reckon that this topic is nowadays extremely important in particular for SMEs, which are the firm size-class clearly more at risk of survival in the current economic climate at least in those countries most affected by the pandemic.

In order to tackle this issue we ask ourselves whether the choice of debt diversification away from bank lending can improve or not the firms' financial fragility and, thus makes them, at least on paper, more resilient to potential external financial shocks or crises.

Prior literature on SME access to debt capital market have focused on the benefits that corporate bonds offers in terms of: positive management culture change linked to the firm financial life-cycle when approaching market-based finance [13]; enhanced market visibility on prospective investors [14–17]; acclimatization function and progressive step toward other more complex forms (even equity) of capital market funding [18]; and, even, reduced financial costs on subsequent bank lending thanks to heightened bargaining power in the firm-bank relationships [19]. On the contrary, there is still less evidence on the role that corporate bond financing may play on addressing the SMEs financial fragility issue. It is true that, at least on paper, any opportunity of debt diversification may help small businesses achieve a better and more balanced financial policy, but it is important also to verify whether this goal is somehow supported by the empirical data as we cannot take for granted that smaller firms are in practice able to improve their financial resilience through this channel of funding since there can be the suspicion that firms are replacing one form of debt (bank lending) with another one (debt securities). This is a quite relevant question in the current economic climate dominated by the pandemic crisis.

Ideally, to develop a comprehensive study on this research topic we should need a large dataset across years of firms' financial data around the crisis (in this case the pandemic) both before and after the event. Since we can only source data before the coronavirus outbreak, we are obliged to use firm-level data in the years before the 2020 pandemic crisis. We, thus, consider the firm's choice of corporate bond funding as the major external debt diversification solution molding the firm financial policy.

Under these circumstances, we formulate the following main research question. Does corporate bond financing make SMEs more resilient to potential crisis? To answer this research question we opt to create a firm-level financial fragility indicator using core financial reports data both before and after the time of mini-bonds funding for issuer firms and compute the variation reported by this indicator across the years. The basic idea is that the difference between ex-post (after the bond issuance) score and the ex-ante score (before the mini-bond funding) of our financial fragility indicator should give us a good proxy of the impact of the treatment (the corporate bond funding) on the firm financial fragility and, thus, on the ability of the firms' financial policy to reach its desired outcome in terms of improved (less) financial fragility.

Even if financial vulnerability can be measured along many dimensions, and there is not always a wide consensus on how measure it, we are confident that our metric that include five different financial ratios commonly used by scholars and practitioners in assessing firms' financial health is reasonable robust. We then use this indicator as our dependent variable in our regressions as depicted later in our Section 4. Among the explanatory variables, together with other control variables, we employ a mini-bond financing dummy which is equal to one in case of SME funding through this channel and zero otherwise.

In this way, we can empirically test our main hypothesis on whether Italian SMEs mini-bond issuers are able to reduce ex-post their financial vulnerability as a consequence of this debt diversification choice in comparison with similar and comparable nonissuer firms. In sum our hypothesis is the following:

H.: Italian SME mini-bond issuers that diversify their debt funding through the access to the debt capital-market become ex-post less financial fragile.

If the above hypothesis is positively confirmed by our tests, we can claim that corporate bond funding may prove to be a key ingredient of a firm's sound financial policy aiming to improve its financial resilience to potential unexpected financial shocks, particularly in the case of SMEs.

3. Dataset and sample description

3.1 Dataset on Italian companies

Since we cannot test the counterfactual assumption of our hypothesis, i.e. what could happen to the financial vulnerability of those issuers firms if they have not chosen to access the debt capital market, we have to rely on a matched control group of private firms that have not issued corporate bonds across the same years under investigation. This control group is created from a large sample of around 6000 Italian firms extracted from Bureau Van Dijk' Amadeus/Aida dataset (hereafter Amadeus).

Therefore, in order to analyze the role of corporate bond funding in changing SMEs financial fragility, we have sourced data for two different samples. First, the listed mini-bonds sample (i.e. issuers firms) and, second, the matched control group sample formed by comparable private firms that have not issued mini-bonds (nonissuers firms).

For the first sample, we source data on mini-bonds listed on the junior bond market ExtraMot Pro, from its starting date in 2013 up to the end of December 2017. We obtained from the *Borsa Italiana* website the raw information on listed bonds and its issuers on the 15th January 2020. The total number of bonds net of delisting is 241, from 160 different firms. We consider only first time issuers, so we eliminate subsequent bond offerings from the same firm, since the decision to access the capital market could be persistent across time, following the standard approach used in the going public literature, dating back to the seminal work of Pagano et al. [20]. Then, we match the obtained dataset with accounting information about the issuers, collected from the Amadeus database. Due to a lack of complete accounting information for some issuers, the dataset comprises 127 mini-bonds issued by nonfinancial companies. We consider only nonfinancial firm issuers because financial statements information for financial and nonfinancial companies are not easily comparable.

As regards our control group, we source from the same Amadeus database a subset of nearly 40,000 private Italian nonfinancial firms with a number of employees between 1 and 2000 units, total asset between 0.3 and 1500 €/million, and with at least 5 years of available accounting data across the years where we have corporate bonds offerings. From this large dataset, we randomly draw 1200 nonissuing firms' observation, with a comparable size of the issuers' firms, for each year of mini-bond issuance (from 2013 up to 2017). In this way, we are able to match issuers in a given year with a control group randomly drawn for the same year. Hence, the final raw control group is composed by 6000 firms. However, due to lack of some relevant accounting information, our final sample consists of 5319 firms (127 issuers and 5192 from the control group).

For what concerns firm-level accounting data for constructing our dependent and independent variables, we collect for the two firms' samples not only ex-ante data, (i.e. before the time of bond funding for issuers and the same year for the matched control group) but also data of 2 years after. For example, for mini-bond issuers that first-time entered the debt capital market during the 2017, we have collected financial statements data for the years 2016 and 2019. For a firm in the control group, the procedure is the same: if the firm is drawn in the 2017 sub-sample, we collected data for the years 2016 and 2019. In this way, we have homogeneous data between the issuers sample and the control group.

3.2 Sample descriptive characteristics

Our corporate bond issuers sample, which is composed by 127 offerings, is depicted in **Table 1** which illustrates the distribution of issuers by size (in terms of sales) using the firms' financial reports from the most recent year prior to the issuance date. In accordance with the standard EU Commission definition, we define a SME as a firm with fewer than 250 employees, total assets lower than €43 million, or sales lower than €50 million. A small firm is defined as a firm with fewer than 50 employees, total assets lower than €10 million, or sales lower than €10 million.

Table 1 distribution highlights that SMEs cover around 49% of our sample (i.e. first two size classes). **Table 2** shows the distributions of issuer firms by industry. The majority of these bonds were issued by manufacturing firms, followed by the retail sector. The positive correlation between issuers' size and mini-bond capital raised is confirmed in **Table 3**. As a matter of fact, larger bonds are issued by unlisted firms with more than 50 €/million sales. For SMEs with sales under the 50 €/million threshold, the average capital raised remains quite low. **Table 4** displays the issuance motivations as declared in the bonds prospectuses, and highlights that the main use of proceeds of the mini-bond funding is to exploit growth opportunities but still debt restructuring and diversification of funding are acknowledged by a high percentage (around 23%) of issuers, behind supporting firms' growth target. **Table 5** divides our sample into four groups according to the issuer-size in order to

Size class	# of observation	frequency
<10 million	12	9.45%
Between 10 and 50 million	50	39.37%
Between 50 and 100 million	18	14.17%
>100 million	47	37.01%
Total	127	100.00%

The sample is split accordingly to four different size classes based on sales in €/million. The table shows the number of the observations and the percentage with respect to the total for each category. Our elaboration on proprietary dataset.

Table 1.
Issuers distribution by size class.

Sector	# of observation	Frequency
Accommodation and catering	2	1.57%
Agriculture, silviculture and fishing	2	1.57%
Arts, sports and entertainment	2	1.57%
Buildings and constructions	7	5.51%
Energy	5	3.94%
Health and social care	2	1.57%
ICT	7	5.51%
Manufacturing	54	42.52%
Professional and scientific activities	8	6.30%
Real estate	2	1.57%
Rental and travels	6	4.72%
Retail activities	16	12.60%
Transports and storing	3	2.36%
Water, sewer and waste	11	8.66%
Total	*127*	*100.00%*

The number of firms and the frequencies are displayed. Our elaboration on proprietary dataset.

Table 2.
Issuer distribution across sectors, using the ATECO 2007 classifications.

Size class	Average issue	Total volume	Total volume (%)
<10 million	11.80	141.58	3.17%
Between 10 and 50 million	6.17	308.33	6.90%
Between 50 and 100 million	14.89	267.45	5.98%
>100 million	79.88	3754.16	83.96%
Total	35.21	4471.52	100%

Principal capital raised, by issuers size class. The table depicts the average capital raised and the total volume of principal capital for the four issuers size classes. Values are displayed in €/million. Our elaboration on proprietary dataset.

Table 3.
Issues' volume (€/millions), by issuers' size classes.

provide a more detailed examination of the issuers' characteristics through selected financial ratios. It is useful to highlight that smaller issuers are more leveraged, but, interestingly, have a higher interest coverage ratio (the ratio between EBITDA and interest expenses) and EBITDA over sales with respect to larger firms, while asset tangibility (as measured as tangible fixed asset over total assets) is, as expected, lower. Lastly, **Table 6** exhibits the differences in key financial ratios between the control group and minibond-issuers. The two samples present strong similarities in terms of size and profitability (i.e. ROI), which can guarantee us a good fit of our control group. On the other hand, issuers are overall more indebted, and in particular to banks. This evidence confirms that the use of mini-bond funding is aimed to exploit growth opportunities when bank lending is particularly costly and/or rationed, or to diversify the funding sources.

Motivation	# of observation	Frequency
Support working capital	20	10.10%
Growth	84	42.42%
Exploit merge/acquisition opportunity	13	6.57%
Internationalization	22	11.11%
Debt restructuring/diversification of funding	45	22.73%
Not declared/unavailable	14	7.07%
Total	198	100%

Motivations declared by issuers in the bond prospectuses. This table shows the motivations reported in the bond prospectus, divided into 5 main categories: Supporting the working capital, growth, exploit M&A opportunity, internationalization, debt restructuring or diversification of funding. The number of declared use of proceeds exceeds the number of issuers due to the fact that some issuers have declared more than one use of proceeds.

Table 4.
Use of proceeds.

Category	D/E Ratio	Bank debt exposure	Interest coverage	Short-term bank debt ratio	Current ratio	ROI	*EBITDA/ Sales*	*Tangible ratio*
<10 million	2.61	34.82%	17.85	16.85%	1.15	6.6	23.03%	21.00%
	4.73	*29.28%*	*37.07*	*17.53%*	*0.42*	*10.16*	*34.92%*	*27.51%*
Between 10 and 50 million	2.53	50.39%	7.91	26.78%	1.22	8.13	14.56%	27.28%
	2.52	*18.30%*	*13.20*	*13.50%*	*0.51*	*6.78*	*10.13%*	*24.53%*
Between 50 and 100 million	2.18	45.16%	6.06	26.58%	1.06	10.19	12.79%	20.33%
	1.4	*15.06%*	*9.14*	*14.77%*	*0.17*	*8.81*	*9.40%*	*19.75%*
>100 million	1.58	43.49%	5.96	25.04%	1.17	8.77	12.36%	25.45%
	2.21	*18.25%*	*4.70*	*15.86%*	*0.44*	*7.53*	*8.45%*	*18.81%*
Total	2.14	45.62%	*7.71*	25.16%	*1.17*	8.55	14.30%	25.02%
	2.58	*19.47%*	*14.08*	*15.06%*	*0.44*	*7.64*	*13.90%*	*22.11%*

Issuers' descriptive statistics. The table reports selected financial ratios for issuers, divided into four size classes (in terms of sales). Means and standard deviations (in italics) are reported. D/E Ratio is the issuer's debt to equity ratio; Bank debt exposure is the ratio between the bank debt to total debt. The interest coverage ratio is the ratio between the issuer's EBITDA and its interest expenses. The short-term bank debt ratio is the ratio between bank short term debt and total debt. The current ratio is the ratio between issuer's current assets and current liabilities. Tangible asset ratio is the ratio between tangible fixed assets and total assets. Our elaboration on proprietary dataset.

Table 5.
Selected financial ratios by issuers' size class.

4. Research design and methodology

4.1 Empirical method

In order to study whether the access to the mini-bond market reduces firms' financial fragility, we perform a set of OLS regression models using the pooled sample of issuers and nonissuers of mini-bonds across the years analyzed

Variable	Issuers	Control sample
Sales (Natural logarithm)	17.69	18.05
	1.68	*1.06*
D/E Ratio	2.14	1.46
	2.58	*3.53*
Bank debt exposure	45.62%	29.72%
	19.47%	*23.81%*
Interest coverage	7.71	24.77
	14.08	*46.68*
Short-term bank debt ratio	25,17%	20.31%
	15.06%	*19.42%*
Current ratio	1.17	1.42
	0.44	*0.75*
ROI	*8.55*	8.65
	7.64	*7.81*
EBITDA/Sales	14.30%	7.37%
	13.90%	*8.45%*
Tangible ratio	25.02%	19.22%
	22.11%	*17.79%*
# of observation	127	5192

Difference between the issuers' sample and the control group. Standard deviations are reported in italics. Size is measured by the natural logarithm of sales. D/E Ratio is the issuer's debt to equity ratio; Bank debt exposure is the ratio between the bank debt to total debt. The interest coverage ratio is the ratio between the issuer's EBITDA and its interest expenses. The short-term bank debt ratio is the ratio between bank short term debt and total debt. The current ratio is the ratio between issuer's current assets and current liabilities. Tangible ratio is the ratio between tangible fixed assets and total assets.

Table 6.
Differences between the two samples (issuers and nonissuers).

(2013–2017). This methodology has often been employed in the prior going public literature, starting from the Pagano et al. study [20], on IPOs equity markets.

We choose as the dependent variable a measure of financial fragility (or vulnerability) using an equally weighted basket of financial ratios that aims to capture the exposure of the firm to the negative consequences of potential real and financial shocks.

In the OLS regressions, we estimate beta coefficients using a proxy of financial fragility as the dependent variable and combinations of the explanatory variables for different specifications, as depicted in the next section. More in detail, we compute the variation in the score of our financial fragility indicator for each firm between 2 years after the event (the corporate bond issuance) and the year before the same event. When the difference is positive, it means that our proposed financial fragility metric has worsened (becoming higher), the opposite if the difference is negative.

The basic structure of our regressions is as follows:

$$\Delta FinFragility = \alpha + \beta_1 (Minibond)_{i,t} + \sum\nolimits_k \gamma_k FirmControls_{i,t-1} + \epsilon, \quad (1)$$

where $Minibond_{i,t}$ is a dummy variable equal to 1 in case of mini-bond funding of firm i at time t and zero otherwise, and $FirmControls_{i,t-1}$ is a vector of firm-specific control variables about the issuers and nonissuers characteristics using the last available accounting information at the date of the bond offering. We control for sector and time fixed effects.

4.2 Dependent and explanatory variables

As indicated previously, our dependent variable is the change in firms' financial fragility, and it portrays the exposure of the firms to the negative consequences to potential financial shocks. We build a measure of financial fragility (or vulnerability) using an equally weighted scoring indicator of five financial ratios that capture the most significant dimensions of firms' financial health. They are the following: interest coverage financial ratio; current ratio; short-term bank debt over total debt; financial leverage (i.e. debt to equity ratio), bank debt exposure (bank debt over total debt). The procedure is the ensuing: for each year and for each five financial ratio we create a ranking system starting from a score of 1 (lowest financial fragility) up to 5 (highest financial fragility) based on a quintile classification of the financial ratio (we used also different ranking criteria, but our empirical results remain robust and are not affected significantly). For example, for year 2016 we have a starting sample of 28 mini-bond issuers and 1200 firms in the control group. Then, for each financial ratio we compute the score for all firms. Then, we compute the financial fragility indicator for all firms by computing the average of all 5 scores (with equal weights).

Next, we calculate the difference of the score of the financial fragility indicator between $t + 2$ and $t - 1$, relative to the reference year. We think that a two-year time span after the event is a good compromise in order to assess the effect of the firms' financial policy choices on the desired outcomes in terms of better financial resilience. Longer event windows (up to 3 year after the event or more) have undesired features such as: the loss of a significant number of observations in our issuers sample since for mini-bond issued during 2017 we do not have a 3 year ex-post track record of financial reports; and the longer the time horizon the more the effects on our financial fragility indicator can be influenced by other factors than merely the financial policy choice under scrutiny. **Table 7** shows the differences in the average financial fragility indicator score for the two sub-samples. As a matter of fact, mini-bond issuers have a higher average score because they are more leveraged, more indebted to banks and have a lower interest coverage with respect to the control group.

Variable	Issuers	Control sample	Total
Before t0	3.91	3.2	3.21
	0.64	*0.98*	*0.98*
After t0	3.73	3.12	3.14
	0.62	*0.93*	*0.93*
Difference	−0.18***	−0.07***	−0.07***
	0.63	*0.58*	*0.58*
# of observation	*127*	*5192*	*5319*

*Financial fragility scores for the two samples before and after the bond issuance date. Standard deviations are reported in italics. T0 is the event year of bond issuance for both samples. Values are average scores of the financial fragility indicator that spans from a score of 1 (lowest financial fragility) to a score of 5 (highest financial fragility). Stars denote the standard level of p-value significance: *=10%, **=5%, ***=1%. Our elaboration on proprietary dataset.*

Table 7.
Differences in the financial fragility average score.

	Mean	Std. Dev.	Min	Max	obs
ΔFinFragility	−0.075	0.583	−3.4	2.6	5319
Minibond	0.024	0.152	0	1	5319
Tangible ratio	0.194	0.179	0.001	0.983	5319
EBITDA/Sales	7.55%	8.69%	−19.36%	99%	5319
Asset-liability mismatch	8.713	18.201	0.017	76	5319
Size	19.691	1.232	12.638	22.777	5319
SME	30.28%	49.86%	0	1	5319
Small	5.41%	22.61%	0	1	5319

Descriptive statistics of the pooled sample variables. ΔFinFragility is the difference in the financial fragility indicator between t + 2 and t − 1; Minibond is a dummy variable equal to 1 if the firm issued minibond at t0; Tangible ratio is the ratio between the tangible fixed assets and the total assets. EBITDA/Sales is the ratio between EBITDA and Sales; the asset liability mismatch variable is the book value of equity over fixed assets ratio; size is the natural logarithm of total assets; SME (Small) is a dummy variable equal to 1 if the firm is a SME (Small) as defined in appendix A.

Table 8.
Variables' descriptive statistics.

As far as concerned the explanatory variables, we introduce a mini-bond financial dummy variable (*MiniBond*) which is equal to one in case of mini-bond funding of firm i at time t and zero otherwise. Beyond that, we consider a selection of firm-specific control variables: firm size (as log of total asset), profitability (measured as the EBITDA on sales), tangibility (measured as tangible fixed assets over total assets), and book value of equity over fixed assets ratio as a measure of firms' asset-liability mismatch. We introduce also two size dummies, a *SME* and a *Small* dummy variable, that controls for the issuers' classification according to EU Commission standard definition as a SME (Small) or not. SMEs are naturally opaque firms and obtain funds almost exclusively through private equity and bank debt [13]. In general, the informational asymmetry issue may cause shortage of finance and credit rationing and may lead to a disparity in access to bond financing between SMEs and large firms [21, 22]. The dummy size variables aim to test whether is actually more difficult for private SMEs or smaller firm to improve their financial resilience. Appendix A summarizes and describes our firm-specific variables that we have used in the regressions, while **Tables 8** and **9**, report the descriptive statistics and correlation coefficients for the empirical variables, respectively.

5. Empirical results

Table 10 shows the outcomes of our regressions, in which the beta coefficients and standard errors (in italics) are displayed. The effect of the mini-bond financing dummy on the change reported in the score of the financial fragility indicator 2 years after the event is negative and highly statistically significant (at the 5 percent level). Thus, the access to the debt capital market is conducive for the Italian companies to a decrease in the financial fragility after the event relative to the same indicator value displayed before this relevant change in their financial policy previously adopted. Consequently, our research hypothesis is confirmed.

As regards the other firm-specific control variables, we note that the tangibility variable displays a statistically significant (at 1 percent level) negative beta

DOI: http://dx.doi.org/10.5772/intechopen.93701

	ΔFinFragility	Minibond	Tangible ratio	EBITDA/Sales	Asset-liability mismatch	Size	SME	Small
ΔFinFragility	1.00							
Minibond	−0.0284	1.00						
Tangible ratio	−0.0871	0.0493	1.00					
EBITDA/Sales	0.0029	0.1210	0.3055	1.00				
Asset-liability mismatch	0.0428	−0.0223	−0.4125	−0.0223	1.00			
Size	−0.0945	0.0622	0.3201	0.3528	−0.1249	1.00		
SME	0.0404	−0.0606	−0.2672	−0.2907	0.1182	−0.7613	1.00	
Small	0.0555	−0.0156	−0.1413	−0.0990	0.0811	−0.4259	0.2583	1.00

Correlation coefficients of the variables used in the OLS regressions. ΔFinFragility is the difference in the financial fragility indicator between $t + 2$ and $t - 1$; Minibond is a dummy variable equal to 1 if the firm issued minibond at t0; Tangible ratio is the ratio between the tangible fixed assets and the total assets. EBITDA/Sales is the ratio between EBITDA and Sales; the asset liability mismatch variable is the book value of equity over fixed assets ratio; size is the natural logarithm of total assets; SME (Small) is a dummy variable equal to 1 if the firm is a SME (Small) as defined in appendix A.

Table 9.
Correlation coefficients.

Dependent variabile: ΔFinFragility				
Specification:	1	2	3	4
Minibond	−0.115**	−0.117**	−0.118**	−0.118**
	0.056	*0.056*	*0.056*	*0.056*
Tangible ratio	−0.273***	−0.274***	−0.290***	−0.282***
	0.054	*0.054*	*0.054*	*0.054*
EBITDA/Sales	0.238	0.219	0.188	0.190
	0.137	*0.137*	*0.135*	*0.135*
Asset-liability mismatch	0,0003	0.0003	0.0003	0.0003
	0.0004	*0.0005*	*0.0005*	*0.0005*
Size	−0.028*	−0.017		
	0.013	*0.013*		
SME	−0.074***	−0.066**	−0.036*	−0.043**
	0.026	*0.026*	*0.019*	*0.019*
Small		0.095*		0.117**
		0.047		*0.045*
Constant	0.554	0.335	0.029	0.030
	0.367	*0.372*	*0.281*	*0.280*
Industry dummies	YES	YES	YES	YES
Year dummies	YES	YES	YES	YES
R squared	0.045	0.046	0.044	0.046
#obs	5319	5319	5319	5319

Outcome of the OLS Regressions with four different specification. The dependent variable is the difference of the financial fragility indicator between t + 2 and t − 1. Minibond is a dummy variable equal to 1 if the firm issued minibond at t0; Tangible ratio is the ratio between the tangible fixed assets and the total assets. EBITDA/Sales is the ratio between EBITDA and Sales; the asset liability mismatch variable is the book value of equity over fixed assets ratio; size is the natural logarithm of total assets; SME (Small) is a dummy variable equal to 1 if the firm is a SME (Small) as defined in appendix A. In all specifications industries dummies and year dummies are included. Beta coefficients and robust standard errors (in italics) are displayed. Stars denote the standard level of p-value significance.
*=10%.
**=5%.
***=1%.

Table 10.
OLS regressions on financial fragility.

coefficient implying that the firms that presents higher tangible asset at the event date are more able to reduce their financial vulnerability. Here, our results suggest that SMEs with more intangible assets tends to develop, ceteris paribus, a more fragile financial structure and this it is happened even before the current pandemic crisis. We reckon that this is an interesting result as it shows that the presence of consistent tangible assets not only offers a wider scope for pledging collateral to potential investors playing a mitigating role regarding the borrower default risk [23, 24] but it can also be helpful to reduce the financial fragility.

Size variables presents a mixed picture. On one hand, in the specification 1 in which size is measured as log of total asset, we have a statistically negative coefficient showing that size as expected matters: the larger the firm the better its financial resilience. On the other hand, when we consider more in detail the two size dummies (SME e Small), the former has a negative coefficient implying that, inside the small-medium size class, the larger firms are still less vulnerable from a financial point of view. On the contrary, the Small dummy in all regression specifications changes beta coefficient sign and becomes positive and statistically significant indicating that smaller firms (i.e. firms with sales lower that 10 million euro) tends to worsen across time their financial fragility score. This result is not totally unexpected as smaller firms are fundamentally less financial resilient as showed by substantial prior literature [5, 25] and by the anecdotal evidence. Other control variables such as, for instance, profitability are not statistically significant.

Even if our findings are quite robust, we must be aware that our study is limited to a firm-level dataset which is confined to the years up to the coronavirus outbreak and we cannot include in our tests the actual effects on firm financial data of the current global pandemic. Therefore, our results must be read with great caution as it is highly probable that the current crisis may display asymmetric effects across countries, geographical areas and industries that are not reflected in our dataset. Future researches based on new post-pandemic data can fully address this void.

6. Concluding remarks

The goal of our study is to contribute to shed new light on the emerging debate on how small businesses can recover from the current crisis triggered by the Covid-19 pandemic. Since SME access to the debt capital market is widely viewed as a valuable source of firm debt diversification, especially for growth firms with a prominent exposure on bank debt, we test whether SME bond issuers are able to reduce their financial vulnerability thanks to this financial policy. The aim is to assess the extent to which SMEs financial choices regarding nonequity external funding can become a key factor in facing real and financial shocks like those triggered by the current Covid-19 pandemic.

Our empirical analysis has been performed using OLS regression models based on a proprietary hand-collected dataset of 127 first-time mini-bonds issuers across 2013–2017 years jointly with a control sample of around 5200 Italian private firms that have not issued corporate bonds across the same years.

Based on our empirical analysis we find a robust evidence on the role that corporate bond financing can play on addressing the SMEs financial fragility issue. Debt diversification away from bank lending helps smaller firms to achieve a more balanced and sound financial policy and, thus in turn, firms are able to improve their financial resilience through this channel of funding. We think that this circumstance is becoming more and more relevant in the current economic climate dominated by the adverse effects on SMEs of the global pandemic crisis. Corporate bond funding offers benefits for SMEs that are not merely confined to what previous literature has already described such as: (a) hastening a more capital market-oriented management culture linked to the firm life-cycle; (b) enhanced market visibility on prospective investors; (c) providing an acclimatization function and a platform for progressive steps toward other more complex forms (even equity) of capital market funding; and (d) reduced costs on subsequent bank lending thanks to heightened bargaining power in the firm-bank relationships.

As a matter of fact, we offer empirical evidence that corporate bond financing has reduced the financial fragility of Italian SMEs. For these reasons, we can expect that even after the pandemic outbreak the mini-bond funding channel may still play a key, and maybe even enhanced, role in order to overcome the negative consequences of the current financial climate for SMEs where firms will be probably more and more indebted and more reliant on bank lending. Although our study is limited to the Italian unlisted firm context, we reckon that our findings can provides useful insights to other countries particularly considering that the economic effects of the current pandemic have been so pervasive.

Appendix A: variables' definitions

Variable name	Definition	Source	Notes
ΔFinFragility	Difference between the financial fragility indicator at t + 2 and the financial fragility indicator at t − 1	Self-constructed from financial ratios from Amadeus—Bureau van Dijk database	See section 4.2
Minibond	Minibond dummy variable	Borsa Italiana website	Equal to 1 if the firm issued mini-bond, zero otherwise
Tangible ratio	Tangible ratio is the ratio between the tangible fixed assets and the total assets	Amadeus—Bureau van Dijk database	
EBITDA/ Sales	The ratio between EBITDA and sales	Amadeus—Bureau van Dijk database	
Asset-liability mismatch	The book value of equity over fixed assets ratio	Amadeus—Bureau van Dijk database	A level below 1 of the ratio indicates a mismatch
Size	Natural log of Total Assets	Amadeus—Bureau van Dijk database	
SME	SME dummy variable	Self-constructed	Equal to 1 if the firm employees are less than 250 and total asset less than € 43 million and sales lower than € 50 million, zero otherwise
Small	Small dummy variable	Self-constructed	Equal to 1 if the firm employees are less than 50 and total asset and sales less than €10 million, zero otherwise

Author details

Emanuele Rossi* and Simone Boccaletti
Department of Business and Law, University of Milano-Bicocca, Milan, Italy

*Address all correspondence to: emanuele.rossi@unimib.it

References

[1] Holton S, Martina Lawless M, McCann F. Firm credit in the euro area: A tale of three crises. Applied Economics. 2014;**46**(2):190-211

[2] Lawless M, O'Connel B, O' Toole C. Financial structure and diversification of European firms. Applied Economics. 2015;**47**(23):2379-2398

[3] Altman EI, Esentato M, Sabato G. Assessing the creditworthiness of Italian SMEs and mini-bond issuers. Global Finance Journal. 2018. DOI: 10.1016/j.gfj.2018.09.003

[4] Andrieu G, Staglianò R, van der Zwan P. Bank debt and trade credit for SMEs in Europe: Firm-, industry-, and country-level determinants. Small Business Economics. 2018;**51**(1):245-264

[5] Masiak C, Block JH, Moritz A, Lang F, Kraemer-Eis H. How do micro firms differ in their financing patterns from larger SMEs? Venture Capital. 2019:1-25

[6] Ferrando A, Griesshaber N. Financing Obstacles among Euro Area Firms: Who Suffers the Most? Resource Document. European Central Bank. 2011. Available from: http://www.ecb.europa.eu/pub/pdf/scpwps/ecbwp1293.pdf [Accessed: 22 March 2020]

[7] Garagorri ISME. Vulnerability analysis: A tool for business continuity. In: North K, Varvakis G, editors. Competitive Strategies for Small and Medium Enterprises. Heidelberg: Springer; 2016

[8] European Central Bank. SME Access to Finance in the Euro Area: Barriers and Potential Policy Remedies. Monthly Bulletin, 79-97. Resource Document. European Central Bank. 2014. Available from: https://www.ecb.europa.eu/pub/pdf/other/art2_mb201407_pp79-97en.pdf [Accessed: 22 March 2020]

[9] Canton E, Grilo I, Monteagudo J, van der Zwan P. Perceived credit constraints in the European Union. Small Business Economics. 2013;**41**(3):701-715

[10] Casey E, O'Toole C. Bank lending constraints, trade credit and alternative financing during the financial crisis: Evidence from European SMEs. Journal of Corporate Finance. 2014;**27**:173-193

[11] Beck T, Demirgüç-Kunt ASLI, Maksimovic V. Financing patterns around the world: Are small firms different? Journal of Financial Economics. 2008;**89**(3):467-487

[12] Moritz A, Block JH, Heinz A. Financing patterns of European SMEs—An empirical taxonomy. Venture Capital. 2016;**18**(2):115-148

[13] Berger A, Udell GF. The economics of small business finance: The roles of private equity and debt markets in the financial growth cycle. Journal of Banking and Finance. 1998;**22**(6–8):613-673

[14] Diamond D. Monitoring and reputation: The choice between bank loans and directly placed debt. Journal of Political Economy. 1991;**99**(4):689-721

[15] Chemmanur T, Fulghieri P. Reputation, renegotiation, and the choice between bank loans and publicly traded debt. Review of Financial Studies. 1994;**7**(3):475-506

[16] Denis DJ, Mihov VT. The choice among bank debt, non-bank private debt, and public debt: Evidence from new corporate borrowings. Journal of Financial Economics. 2003;**70**(1):3-28

[17] Hale G, Santos JA. The decision to first enter the public bond market: The role of firm reputation, funding choices, and bank relationships. Journal of

Banking and Finance. 2008;**32**(9): 1928-1940

[18] Eisele A, Nowak E. Market innovations for (non-bank) financing of SMEs in the light of the crisis and new regulation: A policy perspective. In: Mayer C et al., editors. Finance and Investment. The European Case. Vol. 12. UK: Oxford University Press; 2018. pp. 221-238

[19] Ongena S, Pinoli S, Rossi P, Scopelliti AD. Bank credit and market-based finance for corporations: The effects of minibond issuances in Italy. In: Working Paper Presented at Conference "Securities Markets. Trends, Risks and Policies". Milan, Italy: Bocconi University; 2019

[20] Pagano M, Panetta F, Zingales L. Why do companies go public? An empirical analysis. Journal of Finance. 1998;**53**(1):27-64

[21] Berger AN, Udell GF. A more complete conceptual framework for SME finance. Journal of Banking and Finance. 2006;**30**(11):2945-2966

[22] Ang JS, Cole RA, Lin JW. Agency costs and ownership structure. Journal of Finance. 2000;**55**(1):81-106

[23] Hall G, Hutchinson P, Michaelas N. Determinants of the capital structure of European SMEs. Journal of Business Finance and Accounting. 2004;**31**(5–6): 711-728

[24] De Jong A, Kabir R, Nguyen T. Capital structure around the world: The roles of firm- and country-specific determinants. Journal of Banking and Finance. 2008;**32**(9):1954-1969

[25] Mol-Gomez-Vasquez A, Hernández-Cánovas G, Koëter-Kant J. Bank market power and the intensity of borrower discouragement: Analysis of SMEs across developed and developing European countries. Small Business Economics. 2019;**53**(1):211-225

Section 4

Entrepreneurial Dynamics and Innovation

Chapter 10

Entrepreneurship at Any Age

William (Marty) Martin

Abstract

Entrepreneurship represents a mindset and set of behaviors which can occur at many ages across the developmental continuum from early childhood to late adulthood. In this selective review of the literature, a narrative analysis illuminates insight to inform academics and practitioners regarding the intersection of age and entrepreneurship. These insights are first built upon a conceptual foundation grounded in a developmental perspective and then organized into opportunities and challenges facing entrepreneurs at various ages along the developmental continuum. Entrepreneurs of all share many commonalities yet they are also face unique opportunities and challenges. Many of these opportunities and challenges are age based. These commonalities and challenges must be understood by all those stakeholders in the entrepreneurship ecosystem to enhance the success of entrepreneurs of all ages.

Keywords: ages, developmental, generational, bias, stereotype

1. Introduction

Entrepreneurship as an academic field and societal trend appears to be growing. The field of entrepreneurship is defined as "...the study of sources of opportunities; the processes of discovery, evaluation, and exploitation of opportunities [1]." Entrepreneurs are "...individuals who discover, evaluate, and exploit them [opportunities] ([1], p. 217)." Entrepreneurs may be of nearly any age from school age children to older adults.

Despite the reality that there are entrepreneurs of all ages, far too many of us automatically imagine that the entrepreneur is an adult in their early 20s to mid-30s, college educated, and has launched a technological venture. One study found that the mean age for launching a company is in the late 30s to early 40s [2]. The Kaufmann Foundation [3] found that the most frequent ages of entrepreneurs in descending order in 2019 were the following: 20–34 (27.2%); 55–64 (25.1%); 45–54 (24.8%); and 35–44 (22.9%). This age breakdown reflects a change from 1996 during which it was found that as age increased, the rate of new entrepreneurs decreased. The Kaufmann Foundation is missing two age cohorts: entrepreneurs under the age of 20 and entrepreneurs 65 and older. This chapter will focus on entrepreneurs along the age continuum.

Regardless of the age of the entrepreneur, there are both common challenges and unique challenges. Furthermore, there are also common and unique opportunities. This chapter will first frame entrepreneurship from a developmental theoretical frame and then review the literature on the relationship between age and entrepreneurship. This literature review will not be exhaustive due to space limitations. After theorizing about entrepreneurship and reviewing the pertinent literature,

IntechOpen

the challenges and opportunities experienced by entrepreneurs at different ages will be described. These challenges and opportunities will be discussed not just from the lens of the entrepreneur but entrepreneurial ecosystems. Toward the end of this chapter, recommendations will be presented for entrepreneurs of specific age groups and entrepreneurship support organizations (ESOs). Next, a research agenda with specific hypotheses will also be presented for academics to include age as a key variable in research. Finally, recommendations will be formulated for entrepreneurship educators in formal and informal educational settings.

2. Theoretical frame: developmental perspective

The theoretical frame in this chapter is grounded in a developmental perspective drawing upon Amartya Sen's capability approach. Sen equates human development with the enlargement of positive freedoms [4]. A related concept of Sen's capability approach is agency. Agency is "a person's ability to pursue and realize the goals that he or she values...the opposite of a person with agency is someone who is forced, oppressed, or passive ([4], p. 3)." Moreover, human agency is a central concept among motivation theories [5].

This capability approach is reinforced with a lifespan developmental approach drawing upon Baltes [6]. According to Baltes [6], "Lifespan developmental psychology involves the study of constancy and change in behavior throughout the life course (ontogenesis), from conception to death (p. 611)." The behavior of focus in this chapter is entrepreneurial activity. A team of researchers [7] assert citing the body of research, "Individuals' orientation toward entrepreneurial activities differs depending on where they stand in their lifespans (p. 1)." Our lifespans are typically measured by age and occasionally by developmental periods such as adolescence.

Yet, age is a more commonly used marker of human development. There are two categories of age: chronological and subjective. Chronological age is marked by date of birth or the number of years alive. Varying patterns of entrepreneurship have been documented regarding chronological age [8]. In contrast to chronological age, subjective age is how young or old an individual experience themselves to be [9]. Beyond chronological age, age-related factors such as a future time perspective account for changes in motivation [10]. Hence, age is objective and subjective as well as static and dynamic.

Age is not the only marker of the development of human development and entrepreneurship. It was empirically found that entrepreneurial activity varies by age, yet this relationship is mediated by perceived opportunities and perceived skills [11]. As it relates to opportunities, it was found that entrepreneurial intent among high school students was positively influenced by parents first, peers second, and the neighbors third [12]. Hence, entrepreneurs are embedded in a social context. The impact of context on the development of entrepreneurial behavior is well established [13]. Furthermore, in one study, it was empirically demonstrated that entrepreneurs embedded in a supportive social context are more likely to translate their entrepreneurial intent into an actual startup [14].

Any discussion of development circles back to the nature/nurture debate. The nature/nurture debate will not be resolved here. Yet, the evidence is clear that the chances of a child becoming an entrepreneur is increased by 60% if one of the parents is an entrepreneur [15]. This finding does not address the degree to which entrepreneurship is influenced by genetics. Obschonka [16] writes, "Recent research in behavioral genetics suggests that entrepreneurship has a substantial genetic component (p. 196)." Regardless of the relative contributions of nature or nurture, Obschonka [16] concludes that, "...adolescence is a crucial developmental phase in entrepreneurial development (p. 200)." Another period of an increase in entrepreneurial activity is job loss of individuals over the age of 50 as described by Moulton and Scott [17]: "We find that job loss shows a strong association into self-employment, particularly less desirable forms of self-employment (p. 1539)." This finding is important because it demonstrates that entrepreneurship or self-employment is not inherently desirable.

Returning to the nature/nurture debate, entrepreneurship educators assume that entrepreneurship can be learned [18]. As such, this assumption suggests that entrepreneurship can be nurtured along the age continuum. One such entrepreneurship education program targeting primary/elementary school children described the effects of such education as follows:

> *"The implementation of this EE model from September 2009 to June 2014 allowed us to conclude that children can be entrepreneurs and can open, operate, and close a small enterprise in the short term, thanks to the experience transmitted by the tutors and advisers ([19], p. 303)."*

However, there is a dearth of literature on entrepreneurship education targeting older adults over the age of 50. Moreover, most of these programs target younger entrepreneurs [20]. Hantman and Gimmon [21] describe an entrepreneurship incubator in which 70% of the 22 participants, all of whom were 55 or older, launched a new venture over the 12-meeting training program.

3. Brief literature review: age and entrepreneurship

It is beyond the scope here to review the body of literature on the relationship between age and entrepreneurship. The research to date is mixed regarding the relationship between age and entrepreneurship. The UK (United Kingdom) government [22] defines older entrepreneurship as any entrepreneur 50 and older.

Past research has shown an inverted U-shaped relationship between age and entrepreneurship [7]. It has also been argued that there is a negative relationship between age and engaging in entrepreneurship [11, 23]. In an empirical study examining high-growth companies, it was found that founders under the age of 25 are strongly disadvantaged at creating high growth companies with a surge in creating such companies after the age of 35 and another surge after the age of 46 until plateauing at age 60 [24]. As for business ownership, individuals over the age of 55 represent one-third of all firms although this same age cohort launches 15 percent of new firms [25].

The type of business launched also vary by age. Personal services, retail and restaurants are more likely launched by entrepreneurs in the 35–53 age cohort [25]. In contrast, entrepreneurs 55 and older are more likely to launch high-tech manufacturing, real estate, metal & machinery, and health care services [25]. Entrepreneurial ventures can be categorized into four segments: financed growth; organic growth; stable small employer; and stable micro [25]. Financed growth firms were defined as those with at least $400,000 in financing cash inflows and organic growth firms were defined as those with less than $400,000 in financing cash inflows [25]. The other segments are the following: stable small employer and stable micro. The difference is that the stable small employer is defined as having over $500,000 in expenses primarily payroll and the stable micro has no or very few employees with less than $500,000 in expenses [25]. It was found that younger entrepreneurs 35 and under were less likely to own financed growth and stable small employer ventures [25]. Yet, the 35–54 age cohort were overall overrepresented across all firms based upon a population comparison. Among the older entrepreneurs 55 and older, they were more likely to be in the stable small employer and micro segment [25].

As for exits, it was found that "a founder at age 50 is approximately twice as likely to experience a successful exit compared to a founder at age 30 ([24], p. 74)." Yet, founders 55 and older are the least likely to employ others although the most likely to survive [25].

Another finding emerging from the growing body of literature on age and entrepreneurship is that entrepreneurs of different ages manifest different goals related to what it means to be an entrepreneur [7]. To this point, younger and older entrepreneurs are more likely to launch ventures which are more socially oriented than middle age entrepreneurs [7]. These types of ventures fall under the category of social entrepreneurship.

4. Challenges/opportunities

There is a wide array of reasons why ventures fail to launch, why ventures fail to generate a profit, why ventures fail to survive, and why ventures fail to exit. One of the more common challenges has to do with managing the finances of entrepreneurial ventures regardless of the age of the entrepreneur. Competence in accounting practices has been found to be a challenge for entrepreneurs between the ages of 18 to 59 and a predictor of small business failure [26]. Working capital has always represented a challenge for small businesses [26]. Lack of liquidity has become even more of a challenge given the impact of COVID-19 [27]. Although this is not the only challenge, this challenge is more than likely related to the survival of the entrepreneurial venture.

A common challenge may revolve around stereotype bias and entrepreneurs especially those who are under the age of 18 and even over the age of 50. This type of bias may present roadblocks to those seeking to become entrepreneurs because they do not fit the "mental model" of the appropriate age of an entrepreneur. Related to both age groups is an increasing degree of interdependence among others. Specifically, for those entrepreneurs under the age of 18, it is likely that parental involvement will be higher. For those over the age of 50, it is likely that involvement with children and even aging parents will be higher. In fact, empirical evidence is emerging about the U-shaped curve of age discrimination in the workplace [28]. This empirical work has to be extended to entrepreneurial settings until researchers being to investigate bias and stereotyping in entrepreneurship using age as a variable in addition to the numerous studies investigating gender.

Younger and older entrepreneurs may benefit from a different set of resources. Regarding entrepreneurship, it was found that a focus on opportunity seeking is central to venture growth among entrepreneurs from 24 to 74 [29]. Of all the generations, the millennial generation is more interested in digital entrepreneurship than previous generations [33].

Regarding specific opportunity sets for entrepreneurs, it is conceivable that younger entrepreneurs have greater physical resources such as enhanced cognitive function and are also less encumbered with family and other responsibilities [24]. As for older entrepreneurs, it is conceivable that they have greater access to capital of all types including financial, social, and human [24]. Mental health is a key moderator between the age of the entrepreneur and a focus on opportunities [29]. Intergenerational entrepreneurship represents another opportunity for entrepreneurs of all ages. This ranges from launching firms together to intergenerational entrepreneurship education [30].

5. Recommendations: from entrepreneur to entrepreneurship ecosystem

The role of formal and informal organizations in shaping and supporting entrepreneurship is critical [31]. Yet, the type of support may vary given the heterogeneity of entrepreneurs. Bohlmann et al. [11] found that entrepreneurs of different ages need different types of support. Furthermore, the current entrepreneurship ecosystem has been critiqued by Bohlmann et al. [11] "These programs do not accurately take the needs and motivation of different ages into account (p. 8)."

Brieger et al. [7] recommend that high quality entrepreneurship support organizations offer services appropriate for specific life phases.

As an example, Gielnik et al. [29] based upon their study on the role of mental health for maintaining a high level focus on opportunities suggest that policy makers should invest in maintaining or improving mental health and invest in increasing learning & development opportunities targeting older entrepreneurs.

6. Future research agenda: age and entrepreneurship

Entrepreneurship research is increasingly taking a development approach. Even further, research is increasingly investigating older entrepreneurs who are 55 and older [21]. Future research ideally will draw upon a range of theories including developmental theories. Yet, researchers have eleven theoretical perspectives from which to frame future research beyond developmental theories. Eleven perspectives include the following: negative relationship personal health; rigidity; time allocation; risk propensity; discrimination; positive relationship human capital; social capital; financial capital; emotion; family obligation; and gender stereotype.

Beyond the theoretical base of future research, different research designs are recommended including cross-sectional and longitudinal designs. Given the focus on age and entrepreneurship, cohort based, and panel research designs are also worth pursuing among future researchers. The challenge for researchers may be to collaborate with researchers from other disciplines such as developmental psychology, family systems, sociology, and gerontology [32].

This line of research should go beyond age and also examine cohort effects by generation. To this point, the call for such research has been made, "It is critical that scholars of international entrepreneurship explore millennial entrepreneurs and contrast them across generations and countries ([33], p. 9)." Given the social context of younger and older entrepreneurs in particular, intersectionality as a construct is warranted [34].

This research should be grounded in qualitative, quantitative, mixed methods and even deploy big data analytic models. Much of the research should be hypothesis driven but not all of the research due to the nascent aspects of the nexus between age and entrepreneurship as well as generation and entrepreneurship. The following hypotheses represent a starting point to engage researchers in contributing to the dearth on aging and entrepreneurship. These hypotheses are by no means exhaustive.

H1: There are differences in entrepreneurial intent among entrepreneurs across the age continuum.

H2: There are differences in entrepreneurial motivation among entrepreneurs across the age continuum.

H3: There are differences in "push" and "pull" factors among entrepreneurs across the age continuum.

H4: There are differences in opportunities in entrepreneurial financing among entrepreneurs across the age continuum.

H5: There are differences in entrepreneurial exits among entrepreneurs across the age continuum.

7. Inclusive entrepreneurship education: all ages matter

It has previously been mentioned that the ideal entrepreneur and most entrepreneurship education program are not inclusive by age. In fact, they target younger entrepreneurs often under the age of 30. Following this trend, there appears to be a lot of focus on weaving entrepreneurship education into primary/elementary school and secondary/high school not to mention colleges/universities. These efforts should continue but ought to be expanded to include other age groups over the age of 30 up to retirement age or older.

If indeed entrepreneurship educators offer targeted entrepreneurship curricula that is age appropriate, then this education ought to also embrace an inter-generational element rather than "segregating" the target audiences by age cohorts. Yet, the case can be made for exclusive entrepreneurship education targeting specific age cohorts given the unique challenges and opportunities facing entrepreneurs at different ages and developmental periods.

The case for targeting specific age cohorts and even generational cohorts can be further subdivided into types of entrepreneurs within a given age cohort and generational cohort. As an illustration, it was found that there are eight types of entrepreneurs in the Baby Boom Generation (born between 1946 and 1964) [35]. This typology categorizes entrepreneurs into these categories or types: new versus existing, new opportunity versus new necessity, full-time versus part-time, and incorporated versus unincorporated entrepreneurs [35]. The author of this study argues "Understanding baby boomer entrepreneurs better and assisting them to develop entrepreneurship could be an effective strategy for our aging population ([35], p. 70)."

8. Recommendations

The recommendations set forth for entrepreneurs are presented from the lens of offering tailor made recommendations for different age groups across the developmental continuum.

8.1 School age entrepreneurs

School age entrepreneurs are deeply embedded in a family context and increasingly a school context with a rise in entrepreneurship educational programs targeting school age entrepreneurs. The degree to which these ventures are actually family firms is subject to further discovery, but the role of parents, other relatives and others is critical to the success of school age entrepreneurs. The current legal and regulatory system not to mention societal norms may impose unique barriers for school age entrepreneurs because they have not achieved the age of majority. Hence, stakeholders in the entrepreneurship ecosystem should continue to design and deliver tailored solutions for school age entrepreneurs while at the same time advocating to relax some legal and regulatory barriers.

8.2 College age entrepreneurs

College age entrepreneurs are increasingly warmly embraced by colleges and universities which offer degree and certificate programs in entrepreneurship. These efforts should continue along with the hackathons and business plan competitions. Likewise, research should continue involving college age entrepreneurs yet educational, programming and research investments need to be more inclusive of other age groups beyond the college age entrepreneurs. In most nations, college attendance and graduation are the exception not the rule. As such, attention should be paid to those who are college but decide not to attend college and start ventures in the skilled trades, retail, and food/beverages as well as gig workers.

8.3 Young adult entrepreneurs

Young adult entrepreneurs have decided to choose a particular path in life regarding their occupational identify and way to earn an income. At some point, during young adult, these entrepreneurs will make a commitment as a partner and even add the role of a parent. As such, greater attention is warranted to look at the varying roles for young adults and how they balance the tasks associated with these roles as well as the challenges of launching a new venture often without steady cash flow to ensure survival.

8.4 Middle age entrepreneurs

Middle age entrepreneurs are often ignored by the entrepreneurship ecosystem except to include them as mentors and financiers. These entrepreneurs often select entrepreneurship after some adverse life event ranging from a health event to a job loss event. Hence, programming ought to focus upon not just launching a venture but also managing grief and other emotions associated with a sudden loss of stability. Similar to young age entrepreneurs, these middle age entrepreneurs with aging parents may be part of the "sandwich generation" requiring different types of programming, support, and advocacy.

8.5 Older age entrepreneurs

Older age entrepreneurs are nearly invisible in the entrepreneurship ecosystem as participants. Proactive steps must be taken to include older entrepreneurs to counter the bias and stereotyping which occurs among older entrepreneurs. This step will require that leaders and decision makers in the entrepreneurship ecosystem look at their own biases and stereotypes and rid their organizations of such biases which become part of the culture, policies, and procedures.

Although these recommendations are presented as if they are separate, they are not. Leading organizations dedicated to enhancing entrepreneurship along the lifespan should seek to be "friendly" and "serve" entrepreneurs of all age or differentiate based upon serving entrepreneurs of a certain age group.

Furthermore, the designers, funders and evaluators of entrepreneurship programs targeting entrepreneurs at various ages must also consider the differences among the opportunity versus the necessity entrepreneurs. This categorization is similar to the push/pull framework [36]. This framework suggests that some entrepreneurs are pushed into entrepreneurship for such reasons as a lack of other career alternatives and others are pulled into entrepreneurship to pursue opportunities.

9. Conclusion

Entrepreneurship is all too often considered a more viable career option for those who are younger. Yet, as discussed above, the empirical evidence including a meta-analysis conclude that the opposite is true. Specifically, older entrepreneurs are more likely to succeed than younger entrepreneurs [37]. A central theme throughout this chapter is to challenge some assumptions that the general public, the media, academics and other stakeholders in the entrepreneurship ecosystem have about who is an entrepreneur, who seeks to be an entrepreneur out of necessity or opportunity seeking, and who should be served by entrepreneurship support organizations. The empirical evidence suggests a quite different picture that what is imagined in the eyes of most about the prototypical entrepreneur.

Fundamentally, entrepreneurship is a choice that individuals make at various stages of their life's journey. This choice sometimes arises out of identifying an opportunity, sometimes arises out of needing to earn income, and sometimes arises out of the existential need to "chart your own course." Regardless of the origins of the choice, entrepreneurship may occur at nearly any age from 10 to 100. The age and generational diversity of entrepreneurs is a reality that must be embraced by policy makers, entrepreneurship educators, entrepreneurship support organizations, and entrepreneurship researchers. Embracing the age and generational diversity of entrepreneurs begins with you and your beliefs about who aspires to and currently is an entrepreneur.

Conflict of interest

The authors declare no conflict of interest.

Author details

William (Marty) Martin
DePaul University, Chicago, USA

*Address all correspondence to: martym@depaul.edu

References

[1] Shane S, Venkataraman S. The promise of entrepreneurship as a field of research. Academy of Management Review. 2000;**25**(1):217-226

[2] Kautonen T, Down S, Minniti M. Ageing and entrepreneurial preferences. Small Business Economics. 2014;**42**(3):579-594

[3] Kaufmann Foundation. Who is the entrepreneur? Race and ethnicity age, and immigration trends among new entrepreneurs in the United States, 1996-2019. Trends in Entrepreneurship, No. 9. Available from: https://www.kauffman.org/wp-content/uploads/2020/07/Kauffman_Trends-in-Entrepreneurship-Who-is-the-Entrepreneur-9-Race-and-Ethnicity-Age-and-Immigration-Trends-Among-New-Entreprenurs-in-the-United-States_2020.pdf

[4] Sen A. Development as Freedom. New York: Anchor Books;

[5] Deci EL, Ryan RM. Intrinsic Motivation and Self-Determination in Human Behavior. New York: Plenum Press; 1985

[6] Baltes PB. Theoretical propositions of life-span developmental psychology: On the dynamics between growth and decline. Developmental Psychology. 1987;*23*(5):611-626. DOI: 10.1037/0012-1649.23.5.611

[7] Brieger SA, Bäro A, Criaco G, Terjesen SA. Entrepreneurs' age, institutions, and social value creation goals: A multi-country study. Small Business Economics. 2020 Jan 24:1-29. doi: 10.1007/s11187-020-00317-z

[8] Ainsworth S. Aging entrepreneurs and volunteers: Transition in late career. In: Bal PM, Kooij DT, Rousseau D, editors. Aging, Workers, and the Employee-Employer Relationship. Springer; 2015

[9] Montepare JM. Subjective age: Toward a guiding lifespan framework. International Journal of Behavioral Development. 2009;**33**(1):42-46. DOI: 10.1177/0165025408095551

[10] Henry H, Zacher H, Desmette D. Future time perspective in the work context: A systematic review of quantitative studies. Frontiers of Psychology. 2017;**28**:1-22. DOI: 10.3389/fpsyg.2017.00413

[11] Bohlmann C, Rauch A, Zacher H. A lifespan perspective on entrepreneurship: Perceived opportunities and skills explain the negative association between age and entrepreneurial activity. Frontiers in Psychology. 2017 Dec 1;**8**:2015. DOI: 10.3389/fpsyg.2017.02015

[12] Patuelli R, Santarelli E, Tubadji A. Entrepreneurial intention among high-school students: The importance of parents, peers, and neighbors. Eurasian Business Review. 2020 Apr 11;**10**(2):225-251

[13] Obschonka M, Silbereisen RK. Entrepreneurship from a developmental science perspective. International Journal of Developmental Science. 2012;**6**:107-115. DOI: 10.3233/DEV-2012-12105

[14] Meoli A, Fini R, Sobrero M, Wiklund J. How entrepreneurial intentions influence entrepreneurial career choices: The moderating influence of social context. Journal of Business Venturing. 2020 May 1;**35**(3):105982. DOI: 10.1016/j.jbusvent.2019.105982

[15] Lindquist MJ, Sol J, Van Praag M. Why do entrepreneurial parents have entrepreneurial children? Journal of Labor Economics. 2015 Apr 1;**33**(2):269-296. DOI: 10.1086/678493

[16] Obschonka M. Adolescent pathways to entrepreneurship. Child Development Perspectives. 2016 Sep;**10**(3):196-201. DOI: 10.1177%2F0266242619843234

[17] Moulton JG, Scott JC. Opportunity or necessity? Disaggregating self-employment and entry at older ages. Social Forces. 2016 Jun 1;**94**(4):1539-1566

[18] Sarasavathy SD, Venkataraman S. Entrepreneurship and method: Open questions for an entrepreneurial future. Entrepreneurship Theory and Practice. 2011;**35**(1):113-135. DOI: 10.1111%2Fj.1540-6520.2010.00425.x

[19] de Lourdes Cárcamo-Solís M, del Pilar Arroyo-López M, del Carmen Alvarez-Castañón L, García-López E. Developing entrepreneurship in primary schools. The Mexican experience of "My first enterprise: Entrepreneurship by playing". Teaching and Teacher Education. 2017 May 1;**64**:291-304. DOI: 10.1016/j.tate.2017.02.013

[20] Matricano D. Grey vs. young entrepreneurs: are they really that different in terms of entrepreneurial intentions? Empirical evidence from Italy. International Journal of Business and Management. 2018;**13**:76. DOI: 10.5539/ijbm.v13n2p76

[21] Hantman S, Gimmon E. Dare to dream: New venture incubator for older adults. Educational Gerontology. 2014;**40**(10):1-8. DOI: 10.1080/03601277.2014.893748

[22] U.K. Government. Help and support for older workers. Department for Work and Pensions. 2020. London. Available from: https://www.gov.uk/government/publications/help-and-support-for-older-workers/help-and-support-for-older-workers

[23] Levesque M, Minniti M. The effect of aging on entrepreneurial behavior. Journal of business venturing. 2006 Mar 1;**21**(2):177-194. DOI: 10.1016/j.jbusvent.2005.04.003

[24] Azoulay P, Jones BF, Kim JD, Miranda J. Age and high-growth entrepreneurship. AER: Insights. 2020;**2**(1):65-82. DOI: 10.1257/aeri.20180582

[25] JP Morgan Chase & Co. Gender, age, and small business financial outcomes. 2014. Available from: https://www.jpmorganchase.com/corporate/institute/document/institute-report-small-business-financial-outcomes.pdf

[26] Sibanda JJ, Manda DC. Symptoms of accounting practices that contribute to small business failures. Problems and perspectives in management. 2016(14, Iss. 4 (contin.)):194-202.

[27] Cowling M, Brown R, Rocha A. <? covid19?> Did you save some cash for a rainy COVID-19 day? The crisis and SMEs. International Small Business Journal. 2020 Aug 4: doi: 10.1177%2F0266242620945102

[28] Marchiondo LA, Gonzales E, Ran S. Development and validation of the workplace age discrimination scale. Journal of Business and Psychology. 2016 Dec 1;**31**(4):493-513. DOI: 10.1007/s10869-015-9425-6

[29] Gielnik, M.M., Zacher, H., & Frese, M. Focus on opportunities as a mediator of the relationship between business owners' age and venture growth. Journal of Business Venturing. 2012. 27: 127-142. doi:10.1016/j.jbusvent.2010.05.002

[30] Baschiera B, Santini S, Socci M. Intergenerational entrepreneurship education: Older entrepreneurs reducing youngsters' social and work disengagement. Problems of Education in the 21st Century. 2018;76(1):7.

[31] Lange GS, Johnston WJ. The value of business accelerators and incubators–an

entrepreneur's perspective. Journal of Business & Industrial Marketing. 2020 Apr 4. doi:10.1108/JBIM-01-2019-0024

[32] Zhao H, O'Connor G, Wu J, Lumpkin GT. Age and entrepreneurial career success: A review and meta-analysis. Journal of Business Venturing. 2020

[33] Liu J, Zhu Y, Serapio MG, Cavusgil ST. The new generation of millennial entrepreneurs: A review and call for research. International Business Review. 2019 Oct 1;**28**(5):101581. DOI: 10.1016/j.ibusrev.2019.05.001

[34] Dy A. Agwunobi AJ. International Journal of Entrepreneurial Behavior & Research: Intersectionality and mixed methods for social context in entrepreneurship; 2019 Nov 11

[35] Zhang T. Eight types of "baby boomer" entrepreneurs. Australian Journal of Career Development. 2019;**28**(1):61-72. DOI: 10.1177/1038416218810220

[36] Halvorsen CJ, Morrow-Howell N. A conceptual framework on self-employment in later life: Toward a research agenda. Work, Aging and Retirement. 2017;**2**:313-324. DOI: 10.1093/workar/waw031

[37] Maalaoui A, Tornikoski E, Partouche-Sebban J, Imen S. Why some third age individuals develop entrepreneurial intentions: Exploring the psychological effects of posterity. Journal of Small Business Management. 2020;**58**(3):447-473. DOI: 10.1080/00472778.2019.1659684

Chapter 11

Innovation Processes in Aquaculture: Comparing Companies in Norway and Chile

Knut Ingar Westeren

Abstract

In the last 20 years, aquaculture in general and harvested Atlantic salmon in particular has experienced very high growth rates compared to other food products, and at the same time, salmon production has evolved from semi-manual production techniques to the utilization of high-tech capital-intensive production equipment. This development has seriously challenged the environmental considerations and escalated fish health measures to combat existing and evolving problems. As an answer to these challenges and because of relatively high profit margins, aquaculture of harvested Atlantic salmon has also had a speedy innovation path. This chapter will give a theoretical background and an empirical analysis based on data collection at three companies, two in Norway and one in Chile. The focus is on how innovations take place in different stages of the production process, and how these are built into the production and managerial system. The results show, as expected, links between company operations and the actual innovations, but these links do not have the same structure in Norway and Chile. Factors like human and financial resources, technology, and company organization seem to explain most of the differences between how innovations take place in the companies.

Keywords: innovations, technology, knowledge, harvested salmon, Norway, Chile

1. Introduction

Driven by population growth, urbanization, and increasing wealth, aquaculture has grown by approximately 8 percent per annum over the past 20 years—faster than any other food sector. In 2018, world aquaculture production was 82.1 million tons live weight of which the marine production was 30.8 million tons and about 5 million tons came from salmonids [1]. The harvested salmon part of aquaculture has the possibility to continue this strong growth and thus makes a significant contribution to providing the global population with valuable proteins. Aquaculture is a resource-efficient method of producing protein-rich food. The companies in the study have a feed conversion rate of 1.05 to 1.09, which means that at best, the company uses 1.05 kg of feed to produce 1 kg of fish.

This ongoing growth, however, must not come at the cost of the environment or the climate. Aquaculture still requires amounts of wild fish which are processed into fishmeal and fish oil and used as feed, although the share of wild fish in aquaculture feed has been reduced in the last years and is now down below 20%. In some cases, aquaculture production is still not sustainable [2].

Facilities generate nutrient-rich effluent which is often channeled into coastal waters. The waters then become over-fertilized, causing algal bloom and oxygen-deprived zones. Innovative developments for reducing the food conversion rate do at the same time reduce emissions and improve profitability. For some time now, the industry has been testing products for their environmental compatibility, embracing all aspects from the extraction of the raw materials through to recycling [3]. The other fundamental challenge is fish health where the industry has spent hundreds of millions USD to develop medicines and procedures that substantively reduce the sea lice and other fish health problems. Given this background, it is easy to argue that the study of innovations will increase in importance in aquaculture. Innovation has been one of the most important subjects in any research and business agenda analysis in recent years, and also aquaculture has been analyzed from many viewpoints.

In the following sections, we will first give a theoretical background for the central concepts we use. Then we will present the empirical part and discuss the data collected and how these data relate to the central questions.

Research question 1: How do the companies in Norway and Chile handle different aspects of the innovation processes?

Research question 2: How can we explain differences in innovation creation and management between the companies in these two countries?

2. Central concepts: innovation perspectives

2.1 Innovation perspectives

Innovation plays a key role in the various phases of a company's development and has a decisive influence on the speed of business growth. The knowledge about transfer of technology in particular plays a key role in promoting innovative activity. Innovation is also an important source of stimulating competitive advantage, independent of the situation of the global economy. There are numerous definitions of innovation often starting with Schumpeter [4] and ending with the Oslo Manual [5]. Most definitions contain these key elements: (1) product, (2) process, (3) implementing a new resource, (4) a new market or a new sales formula, and (5) a new type of organizational system. We also have to consider Schumpeter's criteria that an innovation has to add value. How this shall be understood and measured is debated thoroughly, see [6]. Another reasonably agreed viewpoint is to look at innovations as a process which can be divided into three stages—(1) the creative/idea-generating phase, (2) the actual implementation of the innovation, and (3) innovation management, see [7].

Innovations have also been analyzed by looking at how models have evolved through different time periods. This began in the 1950s–60s with the linear model which looked at the three stages above as a linear process. Then came the interactive models, from 1970 to 1990, that posited that innovations had different types of loops and feed-back effects and the interactive models also introduced networking as a part of innovation analysis.

Starting in the 1990s, we have seen several developments in different directions:

- The division between radical and incremental innovations [8]
- Disruptive innovations [9]
- Innovation systems [10]

- The open innovation concept [11]
- Eco-innovations [12]

Another aspect of the innovation concept that has demonstrated importance is the link between knowledge and innovations. This question has been investigated since the concepts of the knowledge economy started to emerge in the late 1990s. More or less all studies end up concluding that there is a link between knowledge and innovations—the crucial question is what characterizes this link, see [7, 13]. Other discussions on delineation of the innovation concept is the private/public question. The private sector must innovate to survive in markets by developing competitiveness while the public sector needs to innovate to improve services to the public. The difference here is that the private sector normally can measure the income side as a part of production while valuating from a public sector perspective the quality/cost benefit is not all that easy. Another discussion centers around the differences in innovations in goods compared to services. The Oslo Manual [5] gives guidelines for how to handle this, but so far innovation in products and processes has gained more attention for goods than for services.

2.2 The innovation process and the creative/idea-generating phase and innovative behavior

One main contribution to analyze creativity and innovations comes from Amabile [14] where she takes as the point of departure the following keywords as the fundaments to develop creativity:

1. Expertise (knowledge)
2. Motivation (why we engage)
3. Creative thinking (challenge the status quo)

The three keywords from Amabile are discussed in all standard textbooks on innovation like [15], so there will only be a few comments here that are relevant for the focus of the chapter. The expertise keyword relates to knowledge which is one of the most discussed concepts in social science. The first aspect looked at is normally knowledge level, which indicates that you must have a knowledge platform to stand on to be creative. Then knowledge is linked to creative thinking and how the knowledge transfer process takes place. Here the division between explicit and tacit knowledge becomes important. There is a long, extensive and important debate on how tacit knowledge can be converted to explicit knowledge in companies, and how companies can create an environment that promotes creative knowledge transfers, see [16] for a more general presentation and [17] for a case study.

Amabile [14] discusses motivation as an important factor related to innovations. She finds that when people are intrinsically motivated, they engage in their innovative initiatives for the challenge and enjoyment of it. Amabile's work is paralleled by a number of emerging studies that started in the 1990s trying to explain what they called innovative behavior in organizations, see [18–20]. Based on [19, 21] Yuan and Woodman [22] have the following definition of the innovative behavior: "We define innovative behavior as an employee's intentional introduction or application of new ideas, products, processes, and procedures to his or her work role, work unit, or organization." [22], p. 324.

One fundamental assumption of this definition is that the behavior of all employees is intentional. This raises questions about how we can analyze innovative behavior and how we can explain why some employees are more innovative than others. Practitioners and scientific analysts agree that innovative behavior challenges organizations in one way or another. Studies like Janssen [23] looked at innovative behavior as a three-stage process in this order: idea generation, idea promotion, and idea realization.

When we analyze innovative behavior, it is important to be aware of which level in the organization we put focus on. Normally we divide into the individual level, the work group/team level, and the organizational level. There is interaction between levels, but as we will see from the data collection in project, production takes place in teams, which consist of individuals. Most studies consider that organizations like companies are divided into groups, and in each group, there is at least one person that has managerial responsibility, which in our case is the site manager. But also, of fundamental importance are the individual attributes for both the leader and the participants in the group. The outcome variable which is innovative behavior can be made operational by looking at six characteristics, see [20]. This was developed further by Janssen [23] using nine work behavior elements for innovative behavior: "(1) Creating new ideas for difficult issues (idea generation); (2) Searching out new working methods, techniques, or instruments (idea generation); (3) Generating original solutions for problems (idea generation); (4) Mobilizing support and trust for innovative ideas (idea promotion); (5) Acquiring approval for innovative ideas (idea promotion); (6) Making important organizational members enthusiastic for innovative ideas (idea promotion); (7) Transforming innovative ideas into useful applications (idea realization); (8) Introducing innovative ideas into the work environment in a systematic way (idea realization); (9) Evaluating the utility of innovative ideas (idea realization)" [23], p. 292.

Yuan and Woodman [22] also tried to explain innovative behavior and they used skill variables like education and organizational variables like (power) distance. One result from [22] was that the importance of the supervisor and his relationship to the rest of the group was fundamental. This corresponded with the results from the project reported in this study. Yuan and Woodman [22] also did more detailed statistical analysis trying to identify paths. This suggested several interesting results but most of them seemed to be quite context dependent.

2.3 Innovation management

2.3.1 Fundamentals of innovation management

There are numerous models and suggestions about how to manage innovations. We begin looking at the concepts of Tidd and Bessant [24] where they outlined how innovation can be analyzed as a core process within an organization. They use four keywords or key areas to look at this. The first is **searching** which means how the organization must look for opportunities for innovation. The next step is to **select** what the organization can and will do and why. The third step is about **implementation**, i.e. how the company will manage the process, so the innovation is working successfully in the company. For the fourth and final step, they use the word **capture**. This is the process by which the company will benefit from the innovation and implement the innovation into the general strategy of the company.

It is interesting to see how different studies and articles rely on the same factors when analyzing innovation management. In this respect, we will look at work like [25–27]. The article by Adams et al. [25] gives a literature review and summary of many studies which examined innovation management, so one can say that the results in [25] are the state of the art. The following list of indicators can be used to analyze the innovation process, adapted from [25]:

a. Inputs and resource situation: Manpower, capital, and financial resources

b. Knowledge management: Idea generation, knowledge repository, and information flows

c. The integration of innovation strategy and firm strategy

d. Organization and culture

e. Technology and technological collaboration

f. The use of IT-based solutions

g. Commercialization: market research, market testing, marketing, and sales

h. Complexity and risk

The question about innovation in low-tech industries compared to high-tech industries is relevant for aquaculture. Fagerberg et al. [7] discussed this theme in their "Handbook of Innovations" to determine if there are significant differences between innovation management and innovation processes in low-tech, medium-tech and high-tech companies. Thirty years ago, fish farming was a low-tech industry but a transition into use of high-tech equipment has rapidly taken place, fostering productivity, ecologic and sustainable development arguments. This has led to a demand of high-level knowledge for almost all aspects of innovation in aquaculture.

2.3.2 Some comments on the relationship between organizational structure and innovations

There is a sizeable amount of literature on development from hierarchical organizations to network based organizational models. The main achievement from the point of view of innovation is that creative ideas can be linked by different networks to different people and show different possibilities without everything going through one established hierarchical model. This argument again is linked to the knowledge management assumption that knowledge workers now have a greater demand for autonomy than earlier. An article by Jensen [28] describes how the autonomy pyramid is turned upside down with the introduction of what can be called the knowledge economy and knowledge organizations. One argument from Jensen is that several people at different levels in the organization may have more knowledge than the responsible manager. This knowledge contributes to innovativeness in such a way that it is counterproductive to have a hierarchal system. If the network organization is too loosely coupled so that core knowledge and competences are without managerial control, there could be negative consequences.

Another argument that has changed organizational thinking is what can be called the learning organization. Studies by Senge and Suzuki [29] and Lundvall and Borrás [30] suggested that organizations improved in flexibility and innovativeness when the organizational structure had learning processes on every level. Another argument for change in organizational structure that promotes innovativeness is the development of project-based organizations. Because of factors like managerial freedom, risk reduction, and possibilities for making contacts independently, we have seen many innovative processes taken out of the company and organized on a project basis.

2.4 Innovations in aquaculture

2.4.1 Background

Aquaculture is one of the fastest growing food producing segments the later years. Norway and Chile are the leading countries in the world for harvested salmon production and a total of more than 90% of the salmon production from the two countries is exported. With today's open cage technology there are only a limited number of places in the world where the natural conditions enable efficient production of salmon in the sea. In addition to Norway and Chile, the UK, Canada, the Faroe Islands, and Australia also contribute to worldwide production. **Table 1** shows global production which has shown an increase in production of about 66% from 2010 to 2018.

High profitability on the one hand and environmental challenges on the other are factors that have driven innovation and alternative manufacturing technologies in the aquaculture industry in recent years. Current trends in the development of innovations and new technology in aquaculture are proceeding in several directions:

- Developments in traditional open cage facilities
- Several facilities are being developed and tested for land-based farming
- Semi-closed facilities in the sea
- Submersible facilities and larger offshore installations

Since 2005 Norwegian producers have been obliged to monitor how emissions from the plants affect the area around the site in order to monitor whether the

	2005	2010	2015	2016	2017E	2018E
Norway	574	945	1234	1171	1208	1253
Chile	385	130	598	504	564	677
UK	120	143	166	157	177	153
Canada	108	122	135	146	139	145
Faroe Islands	17	42	76	78	80	72
Australia	18	33	54	51	61	61
United States	10	18	20	23	22	19
Ireland	12	18	16	16	17	14
Iceland	7	1	4	8	12	14
Others	1	4	16	8	14	9
Total	1252	1456	2319	2162	2294	2418

Production figures in 1000 tons.
Source: Ref. [31].

Table 1.
Global production of Atlantic salmon from 2005 to 2016 and estimates for 2017 and 2018.

environmental impact is at all times sound and sustainable both in the individual locality and in the region. This has given rise to several innovative initiatives.

Fish health and measures for combating fish diseases are serious issues in aquaculture production. The major problem with fish health in aquaculture is sea lice. There are different treatments for combating the sea lice and the use of antibiotics is being reduced to nearly zero. If there are disease challenges in individual locations or over larger areas, measures introduced by the authorities can have major consequences for production. Significant research and innovative activities are required to find measures that can improve fish health with impacting production as little as possible.

2.4.2 Innovations in aquaculture

On this background, it is easy to argue that the study of innovations will increase in importance in aquaculture. There have been several articles and projects dealing with innovations in aquaculture but still many gaps remain to be filled. Joffre et al. [32] compiled a literature review and they find that "*Lack of detailed analysis of the innovation process*" ([32], p. 139) is a field where new knowledge needs to be added, and this is our main concern.

Joffre et al. [32] have suggested to look at innovations in aquaculture by diving them into the following categories:

- Technology-driven
- Systemic
- Business and managerial

Our study of innovations in three companies shows that technology-based innovations play a major role. This relates to feeding systems, equipment for monitoring the fish in the cage, new procedures for delousing of the salmon, and measures for improving productivity of maintenance. The different technology-based innovations vary over a broad spectrum of technologies from incremental to radical innovations. On the radical side we have seen the introduction of solutions that combine hydroacoustic technology to monitor fish movement with advanced machine learning algorithms to observe fish behavior and objectively measure fish appetite. This enables the person responsible for feeding to optimize operations and reduce the feed conversion ratio while increasing growth rates. The use of equipment like this also demands new types of knowledge transfers, from the producer of the equipment to the site personnel and internally at the site.

The above example also shows us that innovations are linked together. The new technology demands new knowledge which means the management of the company must have a systemic approach to adopt a new knowledge structure. Whether this example can be called a systemic innovation is questionable but at some point, a new knowledge structure can be labeled innovative. Another technological example is a new mechanical water-based delousing system. Here the personnel at the site work together with the personnel on the delousing boat and there must be transfers of knowledge both ways. The delousing procedures also affect the business approaches because of the slaughtering logistics of the fish in the cage. We found several other examples that one innovation that originated in one part of the production system at the site had consequences for other parts. Often the chain of reactions started in the technology area and then spread to system and business parts.

3. Empirical part

The data collection that forms the empirical part of the project started in 2017 with support from the Regional Research Fund, Nord, Norway [33]. The project's main goal was to analyze innovations, competitiveness, and transfer of knowledge in salmon aquaculture production in two companies in Norway and one in Chile. In this chapter, we focus on the innovations part of the project. Data was collected from three companies:

Marine Harvest (now renamed Mowi), Chile: MH Chile

Marine Harvest (now renamed Mowi), Norway, Region North Norway: MH North

Midt-Norsk Havbruk, (Mid-Norwegian Aquaculture): MNH

Mowi is one of the largest aquaculture companies in the world (the main product is harvested Atlantic salmon) with total sales (in 2019) of more than 4.1 billion EUR, operations in 25 countries and about 15,000 employees [34]. Midt-Norsk Havbruk is a Norwegian company with sales of more than 100 million EUR. So, these are large and profitable companies.

We started the data collection at Marine Harvest's production sites in Chile in 2017. In Chile, Marine Harvest has operations in Region X and Region XI. We collected data from seven sites in Region X where Puerto Montt is the city where Marine Harvest has its headquarters. We have also collected data from three sites in Region XI outside the town of Aysen. We did data collection from Marine Harvest's sites in Region North in Norway at the beginning of 2018 and during the data collection we visited six sites. From Mid-Norwegian Aquaculture, MNH, we collected data from eight sites.

We used a structured questionnaire filled in by the research team when we were visiting the sites. We used three kinds of questions, with some being numeric about production, size etc. Then we had some questions where we asked for evaluation of statements using a Likert scale. Finally, we had some questions about innovation processes. The data collection process was quite resource intensive because we stayed at the sites for only 1 day, with boat transport to and from the site consuming up to 6 hours of that day. All formal information was checked against the databases of the companies.

Table 2 shows the data collection by company and by employee position. We have a total of 35 questionnaires collected from Marine Harvest Chile (MH Chile), 52 from Marine Harvest North (MH North) and 37 from Mid-Norwegian Aquaculture (MNH). The distribution of responses show that we have about as many responses from site managers as from operators in Chile, while in Norway we have a higher number of responses from operators than from site managers. Normally, there are 4–7 people in the work team at the site and the data shows that we have a reasonably

		Company			**Total**
		MH Chile	**MH North**	**MNH**	
Operator	N	18	43	26	87
	In %	51.4	82.7	70.3	70.2
Site manager	N	17	9	11	37
	In %	48.6	17.3	29.7	29.8
Total	N	35	52	37	124
	In %	100.0	100.0	100.0	100.0

N: number of answers—in all **Tables 2–17**, *N represents numbers of answers.*
Source: the source for all **Tables 2–17** *is data collection done as a part of the project [33].*

Table 2.
Distribution of respondents with respect to position and company.

representative distribution from the sites in Norway. The reason we have a relatively large share of site managers in Chile is because of transport and accessibility considerations.

Table 3 shows that the average group size for the sites in Chile is 6.14, at MH North 5.02 and for MNH 3.92. Another important difference lies in how the work is organized. At the sites in Chile, everyone lives at the site 24/7 and it is normally a week's shift. The sites in Norway organize work by traveling to the site in the morning and leaving in the evening - a working day that normally begins at 8 am and ends between 4 and 5 pm.

We also asked for information on how long the employees had worked at the site and in the company. **Table 3** shows very similar results in the sense that in both Norway and Chile, employees have an average of about 5 years at the site and between 10 and 11 years in the company.

Table 4 contains information about structural factors on how production takes place. In Chile, the cages used are based on rectangular steel structures where, in most cases, 14 to 16 cages are attached together. In Norway, the system is more flexible in the sense that the site can have from 6 to 14 circular cages made from high density polyethylene (like Isoflon PEHD 1000) floating 10–30 m from each other. The Chilean system has the advantage that the cages are easier to access, with walkways along the cage edges, while the Norwegian (European) system cages are only possible to access by boat.

Furthermore, we find in **Table 4** the volume in m^3 (cubic meters) of water that is inside the cages that were currently in operation. Here we see that the total volume of water is less in Norway than in Chile since the number of cages in Norway is smaller and the size in volume of the individual cages is relatively similar. We also have information of the number of fish at the site at the time of data collection, and the average weight was 3.36 kg in Chile and from 2 to 3 kg in Norway. The data collection shows that we have many observations of fish that are relatively early in the growth cycle. This applies to the relevant sites in both Chile and Norway. The same trend is also found in the data showing how many months are left before the fish are to be processed.

Maintaining and developing routines is essential for production in companies and other organizations where stability is needed in production. On the other hand, the ability to change routines is seen as an indicator of the extent to which a company has a potential for the development of competitiveness and stimulate innovation. We examined how routines could change in the companies and important indicators were type and frequency of changes in routines and the extent to which the changes were implemented and followed up. In **Table 5** we see the main results

		Number of years employed in same job	Number of years employed in the company	Number of people in the workgroup
MH Chile	N	35	35	35
	Average	5.60	10.37	6.14
MH North	N	52	52	52
	Average	5.67	11.79	5.02
MNH	N	37	37	37
	Average	5.11	11.03	3.92
Total	N	124	124	124
	Average	5.48	11.16	5.16

Table 3.
Number of years of experience and group size.

		Number of cages	Cage volume in m³	Number of fish in cage*	Average weight of fish*	Months before slaughter*
MH Chile	N	35	35	35	35	35
	Average	14.46	286,149	769,957	3.36	5.66
MH North	N	52	52	52	52	52
	Average	10.90	260,915	1,281,154	3.10	7.83
MNH	N	37	37	37	37	37
	Average	8.03	240,810	1,298,648	2.14	7.08
Total	N	124	124	124	124	124
	Average	11.25	262,038	1,142,084	2.89	6.99

**At data collection point of time.*

Table 4.
Information on production structure, average figures.

		Changes in routines	Formal changes in routines
MH Chile	N	35	35
	Average	3.86	1.34
MH North	N	52	52
	Average	3.65	3.25
MNH	N	37	37
	Average	4.11	3.84
Total	N	124	124
	Average	3.85	2.89

Table 5.
Changes in routines.

from the questions asked about changes routines. We asked site manager and operators at the site asked if there have been proposals for changes in procedures within the respondent's area of responsibility:

1. never

2. previously you can remember

3. the last 3 months

4. last month

5. last week

We also asked if the suggestion was followed up and the criterion here was if the suggestion has been written down. Furthermore, it is asked what type of proposal it was, whether the change was linked to the product, the manufacturing processes, the organization, or logistics.

Table 5 shows that the average score for the company in Chile was 3.86, while for the sites in Norway it was 3.65 and 4.11, which gives the same average score for Chile and Norway. Since higher numbers show greater frequency the results show major differences in the process of formalizing proposed changes in routines at sites in Chile compared to Norway, which shows clearly higher implementation capacity in Norway.

The extent to which the proposals have been followed up also show a relatively large difference between Norway and Chile in the sense that around 94% answer yes to follow-up in Norway while the corresponding figure is 62.9% in Chile, see **Table 6**. The results here also show that innovative behavior contributes stronger through the process of changing routines in Norway compared to Chile. This may be related to managerial/organizational factors, culture, and that resources for changes are more easily accessible in Norway than in Chile. This will be commented in detail in the next section.

In this project, we did a thorough data collection on innovation using a structured questionnaire, but we also made notes from comments of the interviewed persons. As stated in the theoretical part of this chapter, innovation is currently one of the most discussed topics influencing company developments, see Westeren et al. [13]. Aquaculture has changed fundamentally from utilizing manual methods of production to be a capital high-tech and innovative intensive production. With a few exceptions, aquaculture has also earned high profits, which has enabled a rapid pace for innovative actions, see [33].

It is not easy to interview employees of companies about innovations because it is necessary to distinguish between innovations and changes in production more generally. We used the well-known criteria for innovation from the Oslo Manual [5], where the central criteria states that innovations must have something new or improved that differs significantly for the company and relates to a product, process or the organization. The theoretical part of this chapter gives a thorough discussion of this. The interviews took place after we had first explained the innovation criteria to the respondent.

Table 7 shows that some respondents had never initiated any proposals for innovation, and these are taken out of the percentage calculations. The product from aquaculture companies is salmon delivered to the wellboat. There are weight and quality classifications, but the product is generally a standard commodity. Therefore, the majority of the proposals for innovations are linked to the production process at the site. The span of the proposals here is very wide, ranging from major changes in feeding systems to smaller proposals for new ways of carrying out maintenance and other smaller technical tasks.

Table 8 shows the results of the question regarding the origin of the ideas for the innovations. Here there is a difference in the structure of the answers in the

		Is the proposal for a change in routines followed up		Total
		Yes	No	
MH Chile	N	22	13	35
	In %	62.9	37.1	100.0
MH North	N	49	3	52
	In %	94.2	5.8	100.0
MNH	N	35	2	37
	In %	94.6	5.4	100.0
	N	106	18	124
	In %	85.5	14.5	100.0

Table 6.
Follow-up of suggestions for changes in routines.

		Types of innovative proposals			Number of valid answers	Unanswered
		Product	Production process	Organization		
MH Chile	N	6	20	4	30	5
	In %	20.0	66.7	13.3	100.0	
MH North	N	8	38	3	49	3
	In %	16.3	77.6	6.1	100.0	
MNH	N	0	32	2	34	3
	In %	0.0	94.1	5.9	100.0	
Total	N	14	90	9	113	11
	In %	12.4	79.6	8.0	100.0	

Table 7.
Types of innovative proposals.

		Origin of the innovation				Number of valid answers	Unanswered
		Completely self-generated	From the site collectively	From the company	Outside the company		
MH Chile	N	14	16	0	0	30	5
	In %	46.7	53.3	0.0	0.0	100.0	
MH North	N	8	34	4	3	49	3
	In %	16.3	69.4	8.2	6.1	100.0	
MNH	N	7	19	8	0	34	3
	In %	20.6	55.9	23.5	0.0	100.0	
Total	N	29	69	12	3	113	11
	In %	25.7	61.1	10.6	2.7	100.0	

Table 8.
Origin of the innovation.

sense that Chile has a predominance of innovations stemming from self-generated proposals, while in Norway the innovation ideas to a greater extent are generated from a cooperative process at the site.

Table 9 provides information on the length of time between when the idea of innovation was proposed until it was actually tested or put into practice. Here it is interesting to see that what one might call the maturation time of the idea varies both in Norway and in Chile, but on the average, the time to process the idea through the system was longer in Chile than in Norway.

We also have information as to whether the innovative idea was an answer to an acute or persistent problem. The results indicate that innovativeness essentially was a response to a persistent problem.

We have also asked respondents to estimate the cost of implementing the innovative idea and the results are stated in **Table 10**. The cost figure for Chile is in Chilean pesos (CLP) and for Norway in Norwegian kroner (NOK). Taking into account that 1 NOK is about 75 CLP, the average cost in Norwegian NOK for the innovative ideas in Chile is approximately 100,000 NOK, and for the Norwegian projects, it is about 200,000 NOK. This means that the Norwegian projects are on

		Time it took from the idea was generated until it was put forward in the company				Number of valid answers	Unanswered
		1 month	6 months	12 months	More than 1 year		
MH Chile	N	12	8	4	6	30	5
	In %	40.0	26.7	13.3	20.0	100.0	
MH North	N	17	29	3	0	49	3
	In %	34.7	59.2	6.1	0.0	100.0	
MNH	N	18	12	3	1	34	3
	In %	52.9	35.3	8.8	2.9	100.0	
Total	N	47	49	10	7	113	11
	In %	41.6	43.4	8.8	6.2	100.0	

Table 9.
The time it took from the idea was generated until it was put forward in the company.

		Cost of producing the innovation in CLP and NOK	The number of days it took to produce the innovation.
MH Chile	N	30	30
	Average	CLP 7,501,000 (= approx. NOK 100,000)	12.6
MH North	N	49	49
	Average	NOK 201,673	19.82
MHH	N	33	33
	Average	NOK 200,303	26.91

Table 10.
Cost of producing and the time it took for the innovative projects.

average twice as costly as in Chile. **Table 10** also shows the calculation of the average number of days it took to produce the innovation after the decision was made. The result here is 12.60 days in Chile, 19.82 days for MH North, and 26.91 for MNH in Norway which seems likely since the Norwegian projects are clearly greater than the Chilean ones, both in cost and scope.

Table 11 shows the results of where the decision to implement the innovation was actually made. The table shows a structural difference between Chile and Norway in the sense that more decisions are made at the company level in Chile, while in Norway, the majority of decisions are made on the site. The message here is that in Chile the decision has been moved further up the company hierarchy even though the projects in Chile are clearly smaller than the projects in the Norway.

Table 12 shows the distribution of answers after asking if the innovations need new knowledge to be implemented. Here the results show a clear necessity for new knowledge with larger needs for new knowledge in Norway since the Norwegian innovations are larger and more comprehensive. Westeren [33] show that the majority of innovations required new ways to exchange knowledge and this tendency was higher in Norway than in Chile.

We also asked if the innovations affected the corporate culture. **Table 13** shows the results that Chile clearly sees no influence, while Norway sees somewhat more influence on the organization, yet both countries remain negative on the average.

		At what level is the decision to implement innovation				Number of valid answers	Unanswered
		The company central	The company at the regional level	Production unit (site)	The person who made the proposal		
MH Chile	N	8	10	12	0	30	5
	In %	26.7	33.3	40.0	0.0	100.0	
MH North	N	0	17	29	3	49	3
	In %	0.0	34.7	59.2	6.1	100.0	
MNH	N	0	11	23	0	34	3
	In %	0.0	32.4	67.6	0.0	100.0	
Total	N	8	38	64	3	113	11
	In %	7.1	33.6	56.6	2.7	100.0	

Table 11.
At what level is the decision to initiate innovation?

		Does innovation need new knowledge to be implemented		Number of valid answers	Unanswered
		Yes	No		
MH Chile	N	18	12	30	5
	In %	60.0	40.0	100.0	
MH North	N	39	10	49	3
	In %	79.6	20.4	100.0	
MNH	N	30	4	34	3
	In %	88.2	11.8	100.0	
Total	N	87	26	113	11
	In %	77.0	23.0	100.0	

Table 12.
Does innovation need new knowledge to be implemented?

		Influencing the organizational culture of organization		Number of valid answers	Unanswered
		Yes	No		
MH Chile	N	4	26	30	5
	In %	13.3	86.7	100.0	
MH North	N	19	30	49	3
	In %	38.8	61.2	100.0	
MNH	N	16	18	34	3
	In %	47.1	52.9	100.0	
Total	N	39	74	113	11
	In %	34.5	65.5	100.0	

Table 13.
Does innovation affect the organizational culture?

Table 14 shows the results of the question of whether implementing the innovation requires stronger trust in the network between those who work at the site. The answer to this is a clear yes in Norway, while we get a clear no in Chile. One explanation for this in Chile is a two-level leadership structure at the sites. The site manager and the assistant site manager make the managerial decisions at the site in Chile. The operators are to a lesser extent involved, mainly when the innovative ideas come from the operator level. In Norway, the management of the site, including innovation decision making, is done under a much more collectivistic "atmosphere". Innovations will always be linked to changes, and those changes challenge the network of trust. Since knowledge is higher and more equally distributed in Norway, it is easier to build trust and confidence among all employees.

It is further asked in **Table 15** whether implementing the innovations will require changes in the IT-based systems at the site. The answer here gives a main emphasis on no in both countries which is somewhat surprising since digitalization has significantly advanced in both countries, especially in the use of advanced surveillance and feeding systems.

Table 16 provides the results regarding potential problems funding the innovation. Here we get a unanimous response that funding is not a problem for

		Does the idea require a stronger network of trust		**Number of valid answers**	**Unanswered**
		Yes	**No**		
MH Chile	N	10	20	30	5
	In %	33.3	66.7	100.0	
MH North	N	40	9	49	3
	In %	81.6	18.4	100.0	
MNH	N	25	9	34	3
	In %	73.5	26.5	100.0	
Total	N	75	38	113	11
	In %	66.4	33.6	100.0	

Table 14.
Does the idea require a stronger network of trust between the employees?

		Does innovation require changes in the IT-based systems		**Number of valid answers**	**Unanswered**
		Yes	**No**		
MH Chile	N	8	22	30	5
	In %	26.7	73.3	100.0	
MH North	N	13	36	49	3
	In %	26.5	73.5	100.0	
MNH	N	10	24	34	3
	In %	29.4	70.6	100.0	
Total	N	31	82	113	11
	In %	27.4	72.6	100.0	

Table 15.
Does innovation require changes in the IT-based systems?

		Problems funding innovation		Number of valid answers	Unanswered
		Yes	No		
MH Chile	N	16	14	30	5
	In %	53.3	46.7	100.0	
MH North	N	0	49	49	3
	In %	0.0	100.0	100.0	
MNH	N	0	34	34	3
	In %	0.0	100.0	100.0	
Total	N	16	97	113	11
	In %	14.2	85.8	100.0	

Table 16.
Problems funding the innovation.

		The innovation planned and/or implemented			Number of valid answers	Unanswered
		Only planned	Implemented	Partially implemented		
MH Chile	N	16	10	4	30	5
	In %	53.3	33.3	13.3	100.0	
MH North	N	1	48	0	49	3
	In %	2.0	98.0	0.0	100.0	
MNH	N	0	34	0	34	3
	In %	0.0	100.0	0.0	100.0	
Total	N	17	92	4	113	11
	In %	15.0	81.4	3.5	100.0	

Table 17.
The innovation planned and/or implemented.

innovations in Norway. This must be understood in the context that Norwegian innovations are normally funded as a part of the implementation process and the companies in Norway showed a positive attitude for doing innovations. The results are clearly different in Chile where about half of the projects have financing problems. This seems to illustrate the fact that he innovation process in Chile is much more bureaucratic and decoupled from the site.

Some of the same reality is set out in **Table 17** where it is asked to what extent the innovation is only planned or also implemented. For the projects in Norway, nearly all proposed innovations are completed or under implementation. We see a quite different degree of implementation in Chile in the sense that many proposed innovations may not have been implemented or only partially implemented.

4. Discussion and conclusions

The research questions are about how companies in Norway and Chile handle different aspects of the innovation process. The production equipment of the companies is quite comparable, with the Norwegian equipment being a little more technologically advanced than the Chilean. But the organizational set up differs in at least two ways. The site manager has more autonomy toward the executive level in Norway. And consequently, the most knowledge demanding processes - feeding and monitoring of the salmon in the cage - is a process that rotates between all members of the group at the site, while in Chile, this is the responsibility of the site manager and the assistant site manager. Other differences include a slightly higher education level in Norway, in addition to a more equally oriented labor culture in Norway than in Chile.

Looking back at the literature review, creativity is a central aspect. In the tables about change in routines, we see a quite high and equal drive to generate the initiatives to challenge routines as a start of an innovative process. But when we come to the crucial stage of formalization, the Chilean sites lose pace. We find a significant difference in what we might call implementation and completion ability. The flatter organizational structure and more collective attitude in Norway seem to be important elements to explain why the innovative behavior in order to change routines is stronger and more related to the site.

We were surprised by the results in **Table 7** where there is a quite considerable difference between product and process innovations among the Norwegian companies. One explanation is that at NH North they had initiated a program for improving the condition of the salmon in the process of transfer to the wellboat, and they classified this as a product innovation. At MH North they also implemented fish health measures to reduce mortality for the transfer of salmon from the cage to the wellboat also classified as a product innovation. This discussion reveals the fact that innovations often are linked together. To have one innovation that contributes to increase quality of the salmon into a higher quality class (a product innovation) it is often necessary to develop equipment which can represent a process innovation. But still, aquaculture will mainly have process innovations linking together activities since it has developed into a high-tech industry producing a quite standardized commodity. We saw emphasis of this integrated view on innovations more in Norway than in Chile, which is supported by the results in **Table 12**, where new knowledge and new ways to exchange knowledge are more emphasized in Norway. This is also an argument for the open innovation focus because a demand for more integrated innovations makes it favorable to have different kinds of input at an early stage.

The results from **Tables 10** and **11**, combined with our experience based on the visits to the sites, have revealed a view that innovations were more efficiently used as a tool to strengthen competitiveness in Norway as compared to Chile. The Norwegian innovation management was based on a different logic than the Chilean. This refers to the selection and implementation processes mentioned in the literature review. When an innovative idea was suggested and accepted in Norway, the financial resources were an integral part of the innovation management. That is why we find the large differences in **Tables 16** and **17** where there were no problems financing the innovation in Norway compared to nearly 50% of all projects in Chile encountering financing issues. This also explains the very high conduction rate in Norway compared to Chile.

All three companies had a reasonably good resource situation in that they enjoyed good profit margins, with Norway probably doing a little better. However, this does not explain the big differences in innovation management that we find. The first element as an explanation is better possibilities for taking decisions at the site level in Norway. In Chile, we find more of the pyramidal structure including a stronger belief in control from the central/regional company level.

In Chile, we also find a smaller willingness to include financial planning in the innovation process, even given that the projects are smaller and not so knowledge-demanding as in Norway. This indicates what we can recall from the theoretical considerations about innovative behavior—keywords like support, trust, and approval are important to explain the differences between Norway and Chile, see **Table 14**. This points back to the more fundamental discussion about trust in innovation processes. This theme is investigated by research by Sankowska [35], Panayides and Lun [36] and Ellonen et al. [37], and they all find a positive relation between trust and innovation. Sankowska [35] is using Structural Equation Modeling and finds that trust affects innovations both directly and through the processes of knowledge creation and transfer. The results from this project shed light on innovation processes in three large and resourceful companies and the results must be interpreted in this context. There is reason to believe that smaller aquaculture companies also try to develop innovation strategies but how this more in detail goes on needs to be investigated.

Concerning future research more in general, we refer to one of the latest books about innovation and knowledge creation, Bathelt et al. [38]. They give a thorough discussion on the most relevant perspectives of innovation, but they encourage further research on innovation because "we are still faced with many unanswered questions and new challenges in economic and social life that need new analytical perspectives as well as new answers and solutions" [38], p. 1.

Author details

Knut Ingar Westeren
Faculty of Social Sciences, Nord University, Levanger, Norway

*Address all correspondence to: knut.i.westeren@nord.no

References

[1] FAO. The State of World Fisheries and Aquaculture 2020: Sustainability in Action. Rome: FAO; 2020. Available from: http://www.fao.org/state-of-fisheries-aquaculture

[2] Diana JS, Egna HS, Chopin T, Peterson MS, Cao L, Pomeroy R. Responsible aquaculture in 2050: Valuing local conditions and human innovations will be key to success. Bioscience. 2013;**63**:255-262

[3] OECD. The Ocean Economy in 2030. Paris: OECD; 2016. p. 254

[4] Schumpeter JA. The Theory of Economic Development: An Inquiry into Profits, Capital, Credit, Interest, and the Business Cycle. New Brunswick: Transaction Publishers; 1982. p. 244

[5] OECD. Oslo Manual: Guidelines for Collecting and Interpreting Innovation Data. Paris: OECD; 2018. Available from: https://www.oecd.org/sti/inno/oslo-manual2018-info.pdf

[6] Battisti G, Stoneman P. Defining and Measuring the Innovativeness of Firms. Warwick: Economic Statistics Centre of Excellence (ESCoE); 2019. p. 54

[7] Fagerberg J, Mowery DC, Nelson RR. The Oxford Handbook of Innovation. Oxford: Oxford University Press; 2005

[8] Henderson RM, Clark KB. Architectural innovation: The reconfiguration of existing product technologies and the failure of established firms. Administrative Science Quarterly. 1990;**35**(1):9-30

[9] Christensen CM. The innovator's Dilemma: When New Technologies Cause Great Firms to Fail. Cambridge (MA): Harvard Business Review Press; 2013

[10] Lundvall B-Å. National Systems of Innovation: Toward a Theory of Innovation and Interactive Learning. London: Anthem Press; 2010

[11] Chesbrough H, Vanhaverbeke W, West J. Open Innovation: Researching a New Paradigm. Oxford: Oxford University Press; 2006

[12] OECD. Sustainable Manufacturing and Eco-Innovation. Paris: OECD; 2009. Available from: https://www.oecd.org/innovation/inno/43423689.pdf

[13] Westeren KI, Cader H, de Fátima Sales M, Similä JO, Staduto J. Competitiveness and Knowledge: An International Comparison of Traditional Firms. London: Routledge; 2018

[14] Amabile TM. How to Kill Creativity. Boston, MA: Harvard Business School Publishing; 1998

[15] Dawson P, Andriopoulos C. Managing Change, Creativity and Innovation. London: Sage; 2014. p. 638

[16] Nonaka I, Teece DJ. Managing Industrial Knowledge: Creation, Transfer and Utilization. London: Sage; 2001. DOI: 10.4135/9781446217573

[17] Westeren KI. Theoretical considerations of the innovation concept and case study - Innovation in a food producing firm. Informe Gepec. 2014;**18**(2):163-176

[18] Kanter RM. When a thousand flowers bloom: Structural, collective, and social conditions for innovation in organization. In: Staw BM, Cummings LL, editors. Research in Organizational Behavior. Greenwich, CT: JAI Press; 1988. pp. 169-211

[19] West MA, Farr JL. Innovation at work: Psychological perspectives. Social Behavior. 1989;**4**:15-30

[20] Scott SG, Bruce RA. Determinants of innovative behavior: A path model of

individual innovation in the workplace. Academy of Management Journal. 1994;**37**(3):580-607

[21] West MA, Farr JL. Innovation at work. In: West MA, Farr JL, editors. Innovation and Creativity at Work: Psychological and Organizational Strategies. Chichester: Wiley; 1990. pp. 3-13

[22] Yuan F, Woodman RW. Innovative behavior in the workplace: The role of performance and image outcome expectations. Academy of Management Journal. 2010;**53**(2):323-342

[23] Janssen O. Job demands, perceptions of effort - Reward fairness and innovative work behavior. Journal of Occupational and Organizational Psychology. 2000;**73**(3):287-302

[24] Tidd J, Bessant J. Managing Innovation, Integrating Technological, Market and Organizational Change. 5th ed. Chichester: Wiley; 2013. p. 680

[25] Adams R, Bessant J, Phelps R. Innovation management measurement: A review. International Journal of Management Reviews. 2006;**8**(1):21-47

[26] Dodgson M. The Management of Technological Innovation: An International and Strategic Approach. Oxford: Oxford University Press; 2000

[27] Hidalgo A, Albors J. Innovation management techniques and tools: A review from theory and practice. R&D Management. 2008;**38**(2):113-127

[28] Jensen HS. Management and learning in the knowledge society. Journal of Regional Analysis and Policy. 2008;**38**(2):130-137

[29] Senge PM, Suzuki J. The Fifth Discipline: The Art and Practice of the Learning Organization. New York: Doubleday; 1994

[30] Lundvall B-Å, Borrás S. The Globalising Learning Economy. Implications for Innovation Policy. Brussels: European Commission; 1997

[31] Finansdepartementet. NOU 2019:18 Skattlegging av havbruksvirksomhet. Oslo: Finansdepartementet; 2019

[32] Joffre OM, Klerkx L, Dickson M, Verdegem M. How is innovation in aquaculture conceptualized and managed? A systematic literature review and reflection framework to inform analysis and action. Aquaculture. 2017;**470**:129-148

[33] Westeren KI. Competitiveness, Competence Management and Transfer of Knowledge in Food Fish Production in Norwegian and International Context. Report to RFF Nord. Levanger: Nord University; 2019

[34] Mowi. Salmon Farming Industry Handbook 2020. Bergen: Mowi; 2020

[35] Sankowska A. Relationships between organizational trust, knowledge transfer, knowledge creation, and firm's innovativeness. The Learning Organization. 2013;**20**(1):85-100

[36] Panayides PM, Lun YV. The impact of trust on innovativeness and supply chain performance. International Journal of Production Economics. 2009;**122**(1):35-46

[37] Ellonen R, Blomqvist K, Puumalainen K. The role of trust in organisational innovativeness. European Journal of Innovation Management. 2008;**11**(2):160-181

[38] Bathelt H, Cohendet P, Henn S, Simon L, editors. The Elgar Companion to Innovation and Knowledge Creation. Cheltenham: Edward Elgar Publishing; 2017. p. 840

Chapter 12

Entrepreneurship in Urban Jungles through High-Tech Vertical Farming

Suaad Jassem and Mohammad Rezaur Razzak

Abstract

Demographic movements forecasted by the United Nations indicates that, over the next few decades greater portion of people will be concentrated in and around large cities of the world. Such population dynamics in parallel with emerging phenomena such as global pandemics and impact of climate change are posing threats to the supply chain of agricultural production. The reliance on traditional open-field cultivation and transportation of fresh products to distant urban locations are coming under threat. This has been further exposed by the current pandemic (Covid-19) that is impeding farm production along with movement of people and goods. A viable solution lies in vertical in-door farming driven by advanced technologies. The use of high-tech solutions to grow vegetables, fruits and flowers close to consumption centers has taken off successfully in many locations around the world. However, majority of such projects have been set up by investors; with access to substantial capital. In order to mitigate the possibilities of food shortages in densely populated cities, initiatives need to be undertaken to foster growth of large-scale entrepreneurship by individuals that can venture into this field on a smaller scale and with less capital outlay.

Keywords: vertical farming, indoor farming, high-tech farming

1. Introduction

In 2015, the United Nations, committed to end "World Hunger" by 2030, as one of its Sustainable Development Goals. However, two converging phenomena are driving the likelihood of major implications for urban planners in terms of achieving such a goal [1]. The first is the fact that concentration of people in the world's urban centers is witnessing a dramatic rise. According to recent estimates by the United Nations Fund for Population Action, by the year 2050 over 9 billion people are forecasted to be residing in urban centers [2]. It is estimated the rise in urban population will dramatically increase the demand for food, and considering the impact of climate change and reduction in arable land for cultivation, there is likelihood of food shortages [3]. Furthermore, the economic disparity between rural and urban dwellers is also expected to drive younger people from rural farming communities, to seek better lifestyles in large cities, rather than continue on the footsteps of their predecessors [4]. This trend is already having an impact on availability of farm workers in rural communities in countries such as China, Thailand, Vietnam and India [5].

The second phenomenon is a more recent manifestation that is the global pandemic in 2020 attributed to the nouvelle coronavirus (Covid-19) that has brought about unprecedented changes in socioeconomic order of human society, with greater impact on people residing in crowded urban centers [1]. The pandemic severely impacted distribution of fresh products from farms to centers of consumption. Additionally, in many countries such as USA, the lockdown prevented farm workers to work in the fields, which led farmers to destroy large portion of their crops [6].

A recently published study in The Lancet indicates that future occurrences of virus-borne diseases will evolve and continue to emerge in rapid succession [7], while the movement of people looking for better economic opportunities will increase pressure on large cities to accommodate more influx of such people, thus driving them into urban concrete jungles [8].

One of the major fallouts of above two converging trends will show up in the disruption of food supply chains, thus impacting food security [9]. Particularly, demand for fresh perishable products (e.g., vegetables and certain types of fruits) will be difficult to cope with [10] . The economic prosperity that are expected to drive growth of urban jungles will also increase demand for transporting people and goods, thus creating severe traffic congestions making the situation more dire [8]. The time taken to transport fresh food items and the corresponding cost of transportation from far away farms will render the supply of such products from distant locations less feasible.

One sustainable solution to ensuring reliable fresh products supply within urban jungles could be through vertical farming in unutilized urban spaces using some of the technologies that have been developed for urban centers [11]. Some of the latest advances in vertical farming technology are driven by advanced hyper-connected systems aligned with technologies that drive Industry 4.0 (such as AI and IoT) [12]. These emerging technology applications in agriculture are also driving down capital cost of in-door farms that can be set up in small spaces.

The large concentration of people in major metropolises is likely to create pressure on availability of horizontal space, making them prohibitively expensive to use for agriculture [13]. Ironically, however it appears that one of the scarcest resources in large cities, idle space, is also widely available in the form of vertical space in most large cities, but out of the view of most people [14]. For instance, there are many abandoned warehouses, underground structures underneath tall skyscrapers, rooftops, underground shelters beneath railway stations, unutilized factory spaces, unused space at stadiums and government buildings, parking lots, etc. These spaces may be used for installing self-contained vertical farms in controlled environments [11].

The goal of this chapter is to present emerging entrepreneurship opportunities through vertical farming in unutilized spaces in crowded cities around the world (interchangeably referred to as urban jungles in this study). The chapter starts by presenting a description of vertical farming along with an overview of technologies that are presently driving them, followed by discourse on advantages and disadvantages of vertical farming based on economic, social and environmental impact. The following section presents some of the challenges faced by entrepreneurs that have ventured into the business of vertical farming in urban spaces. Finally, the chapter discusses several cases related to the different models of vertical farming being implemented around the world. These models are expected to serve as potential roadmaps for tech-savvy youth that will be entering the job market over the next few decades. Such educated workforce may be incentivized to consider entrepreneurial forays into the field of high-tech vertical urban farming.

2. Vertical farming

The concept of vertical farming on a domestic scale has been around for quite some time; however, the modern concept of vertical farming on a commercial scale using advanced technologies is relatively recent. It represents the application of technology in controlled environments to grow agricultural plants such as vegetables, fruits and flowers [11]. Such farming techniques have been applied using abandoned ocean shipping containers where empty space is available, and also inside buildings such as abandoned warehouses, environmentally damaged land space, underground or rooftops of structures of existing buildings, in dilapidated buildings and even under railway stations [15]. In general, such farming can be done in any unutilized space whether the space is in a closed or open environment [16].

2.1 Classification based on technology

Although the approach to vertical farming comes in different sizes and shapes, one common factor is that they all grow plants without soil and use the height of a structure effectively in growing such plants. The plants are supplied with nutrients mainly through three systems: hydroponics, aeroponics and aquaponics [13]. Each system is contained inside an environment where the amount of light, temperature and supply of nutrients is controlled based on the type of plant that is being grown. Multiple layers of plant-beds are stacked parallelly above each bed, thus making best use of vertical rather than horizontal space [17]. Such environments are usually free of insects, weeds and pests thus allowing the plants to grow without any damage [18].

2.1.1 Hydroponics

The application of modern hydroponics is credited to a California based scientist, Willaim F. Gerrick about 100 years ago [19]. The system utilizes water as a base for the roots of the plants where the fluid is filled with the optimum balance of nutrients required for the plants to grow. The present-day application of hydroponics uses computerized systems to control the nutrient solution in which the base of each plant is submerged. The plants do not require any inert media to support them such as sand or gravel (see **Figure 1**).

The hydroponics method has relatively low maintenance cost as it does not require tilling, soil removal, fertilizers, etc. The water is recycled, and the composition of the nutrients including oxygen is controlled by automatic feedback loops. Depending on which vegetable or fruit is to be grown, the nutrient solution is controlled by computer software with customized settings for each type of crop [12].

2.1.2 Aeroponics

In 1990, NASA worked to develop a system to substitute soil for a spray of nutrient rich mixture of air and mist so that astronauts on missions to space stations can grow their own food [12]. Aeroponics is considered a technological leap forward in high-tech farming [20]. In fact, while hydroponics uses water solution as a growing medium, aeroponics does not require a growing medium. The mist that is sprayed over the roots is sufficient to enable the plant to grow in a healthy manner (See **Figure 2**) [11].

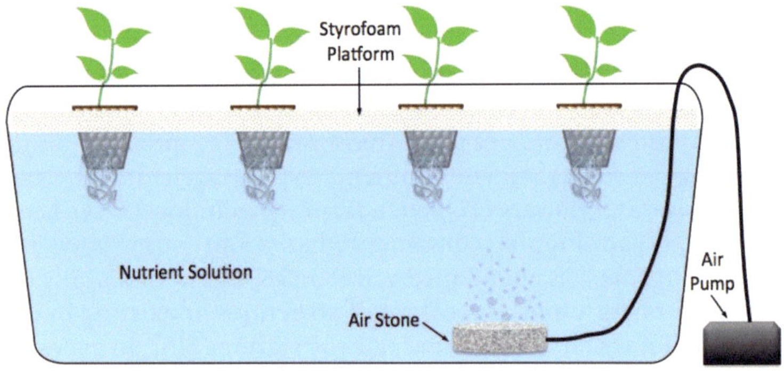

Figure 1.
Illustration of a basic hydroponic system. Source: [20].

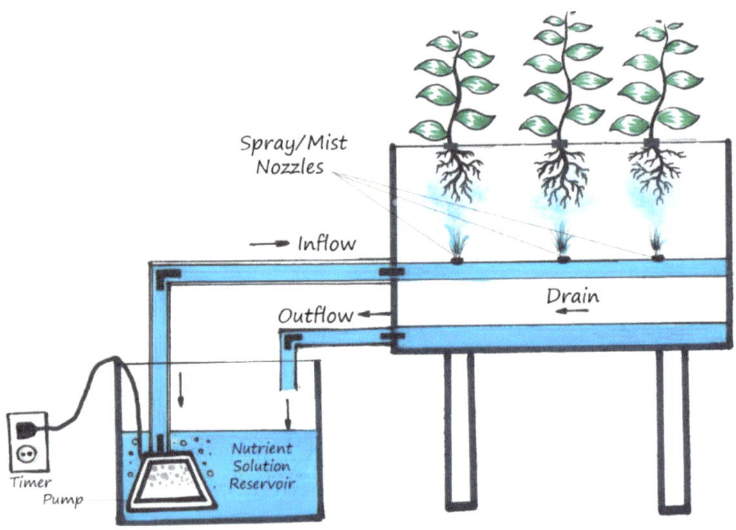

Figure 2.
Illustration of a basic aeroponic system. Source: [12].

The technology has now been commercialized and is used by pioneering companies such as Aero-Farms in USA. The system is revolutionary because it uses 90% less water than hydroponics. Plants grown with aeroponics technology have shown to have higher uptake of vitamins and other essential minerals such as potassium and magnesium required for healthy human bodies. This technology is now widely applied in arid regions of the world where water is scarce and costly to provide such as hot places in the Middle East and extremely cold places such as Antarctica [21] .

2.1.3 Aquaponics

This system differs from hydroponics because, the water solution where the plants are submerged, are also used to grow certain variety of fish (such as tilapia and perch) that thrive in such an environment [22]. In fact, the fish and the plants have a symbiotic relationship, where the waste produced by the fish serve as a natural source of organic fertilizer for plants, and in return the plants purify the water from the waste. Typically, aquaponics requires substantially more water supply than hydroponics. However, the additional cost of supplying water to aquaponic systems is made up through the availability of two kinds of cash crops, vegetables and fish [6]. The diagram in **Figure 3** shows a basic aquaponic system.

2.2 Classification based on structure

Vertical farming can also be classified based on the type of structure they are housed in. Two of the most popular structures are: (i) building-based vertical farms and (ii) shipping-container vertical farms [23] .

2.2.1 Building-based vertical farms

Such farms are situated inside abandoned warehouses and buildings, new buildings in the basement or rooftops, unused basement parking space, abandoned subway stations, etc. The spaces occupied for the farming projects are closed and controlled through special HVAC systems and LED lighting [24]. Once the environment is built and vegetables are planted, the system requires minimum human involvement during the growth stage of the vegetables. Human labor is involved only during picking the vegetables and packing, and for re-plantation [25].

A new trend in such farming has also been initiated where such farms are set up close to large hypermarkets, restaurants and hotels that have a daily requirement for large amounts of fresh products such as leafy green vegetables, tomatoes, cucumbers, etc. For the customers, the proximity of the farms to the customers reduces transport cost, inventory cost and also ensures that extremely fresh products that are available 24/7 (see **Figure 4**). For the farmers, they have ready customers close by that will buy their daily production.

2.2.2 Shipping-container vertical farms

This type of structure has become quite popular mainly due to the mobility offered by such a system. Basically, 40-feet ocean shipping containers are refurbished with drip irrigation, lighting and HVAC systems controlled by computers. These containers can be moved into any space where the containers can fit into

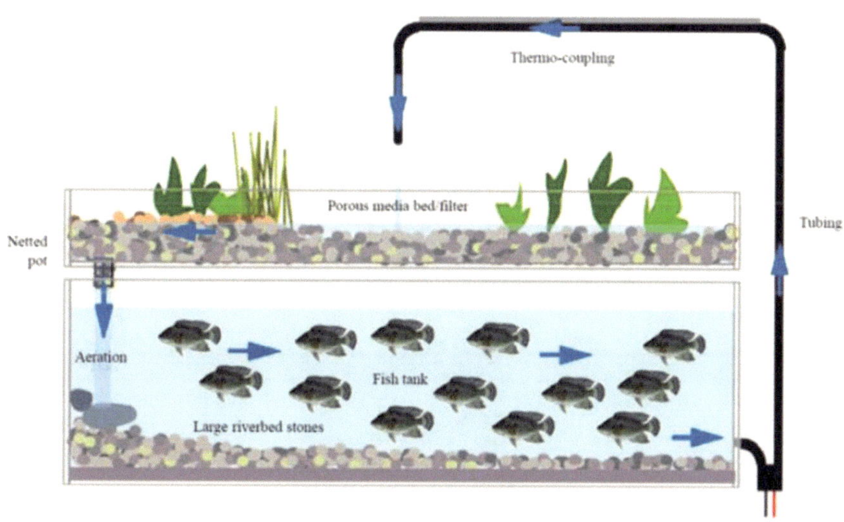

Figure 3.
Illustration of a basic aquaponic system. Source: [6].

smaller spaces such as empty car parking lots, environmentally damaged land spaces, or even in places where the weather is harsh such as deserts or extremely cold places. Such structures can also be moved to places where there are military bases on large groups of people residing temporarily (see **Figure 5**).

2.3 Advantages and disadvantages of vertical farming

2.3.1 Advantages

Vertical high-tech in-door farming has numerous advantages over traditional open field horizontal cultivation. Traditional cultivation requires vast amount of arable space where large equipment such as tractors that run on fossil fuel are required, along with large quantity of farm workers. Furthermore, the open-field cultivation requires synthetically produced chemicals such as urea-based and phosphate-based fertilizers that over a period of time diminish the land's ability to

Figure 4.
Vertical farm housed inside a commercial building. Source: [26].

Figure 5.
A vertical farm inside a shipping container. Source: [27].

sustain crops. Most agricultural lands are developed by destroying forests, such as in Brazil where the Amazon rain forests are reduced each year to create for space for planting agricultural products. This not only contributes to displacements of indigenous flora and fauna, but also contributes to global warming [28] .

Additionally, the yield per meter-square from open field cultivation is much lower than that of vertical farming [29]. Open field crops are susceptible to weeds, pests and adverse weather conditions. Finally, products such as vegetables need to be transported a long distance from the fields to urban centers thus increasing fuel consumption and other related costs factors.

In contrast, high-tech vertical farming has several advantages as noted below:

i. The most obvious advantage of vertical farming is the relatively small amount of horizontal space required to produce multiple varieties of fresh crops (e.g., vegetables, flowers and certain variety of fruits) in the same space. Vertical farming on the other hand enables utilization of unused vertical space in urban centers where typically horizontal space is an expensive resource.

ii. The system ensures that crop production can be done round the year even in harsh weather conditions. In fact, in dry arid places with plenty of sunshine, the energy needed to operate the equipment inside the system can be run on solar power, thus reducing dependence on electricity from the power grid.

iii. This type of farming does not require use of pesticides and herbicides as they are in closed environments. As a result, the products are free of toxins.

iv. Unlike open-field cultivation, vertical farming does not require too many farm workers to be present all the time. Finally, the environment within vertical farming enclosures, are typically safer for people compared to open field cultivation.

v. Entrepreneurs can conduct market feasibility and locate their farms close to the market centers where the products can be sold quickly after plucking them without having to preserve them. This is a great value proposition for both the buyer and seller, as buyers do not need to maintain large inventories, and the time and cost of transporting the products to the retailers is much lower.

vi. Finally, application of advanced technologies, enable people to get real-time feedback on the plants in terms of their stage of growth, health and available finished goods inventory.

2.3.2 Disadvantages

The vertical in-door farms nevertheless have some disadvantages also:

i. The first disadvantage of vertical farming in urban metropolises is the availability of space. Horizontal space in crowded cities, are typically a costly resource. Nevertheless, due to closure of manufacturing industries in places like United States and Western Europe, substantial amount of space is becoming available for alternative uses such as indoor farming. However, in cities that are on a high economic growth trajectory such as cities in Asia: Shanghai, Shenzhen, Singapore, Taipei, Tokyo, etc., it would be very difficult to find sufficient horizontal space to establish such farming projects (except for vertical and roof-top farming).

ii. Second, the consumption of energy and water are quite high, and can prove to be prohibitive in certain cities unless the government subsidizes the electricity tariff for such projects, or there is access to renewable energy sources such as solar power.

iii. In order to compete with traditional farm cultivated products, the present vertical farms are promoting their products as organic, as they do not use pesticides and herbicides. However, in some countries they face obstacles due to government regulations to promote their products as organic. For instance, the USDA (US Department of Agriculture) is very stringent in certifying such products as organic because the nutrients used are not completely organic. The present definition of organic products according to agencies such as the USDA is much wider, that includes systems that promote biodiversity and biological cycles.

iv. Another limitation of vertical farming is that they can offer a limited range of products that have quick turnover cycles such as leafy greens, cauliflower, tomatoes, bell pepper, eggplants, strawberry, etc., while producing grains is not feasible.

v. Finally, since insects are excluded from the environment, there is no natural pollination. Hence, pollination has to be done by human hands, thus requiring workers for this purpose. Although, new technology is being developed to use insect drones to do the pollination.

3. High-tech vertical farming projects

The following are three large scale high-tech vertical farming projects depict how these farms are being managed for producing high-yield fresh products:

3.1 Green spirit farms

The Green Spirit Farms (GSF) first project was established in 2011 in an abandoned plastic factory in Buffalo, New York. The project has been set on a 44,000 square-feet built-up space. Currently, GSF's business model is to locate abandoned commercial and industrial buildings and set up their vertical farming projects through long-term lease agreements with the building owners. The company enters into these spaces and sets up their farming project through agreements with equipment suppliers on the basis of pay-as-your-earn. Therefore, GSF sets up vertical farms without much initial capital investments in structures and equipment, which allows them to focus on their core competency, that is to be a provider of fresh non-GMO (genetically modified) high-value products such as kale, basil, peppers, stevia, spinach, brussels sprouts, tomatoes, strawberries, etc. They select locations that are close to large-scale customers such as hotels, fresh products wholesale markets and major urban centers. Besides, selling farm products inside the United States, due to the proximity of their farm sites to the Canadian border, they are also able to service customers in Ontario, Canada [26].

GSF mostly utilizes hydroponics technology such as Rotary Vertical Growing Stations (RVGS) that has a high level of efficiency in terms of use of water and energy. In fact, GSF claims to use 90% less land, 80% less water and 40% electricity compared to conventional hydroponics farms [11]. The company has received strong support from state and federal agencies through public-private partnerships in the United States for having high social and environmental impact. The company has not only created employment in the local communities, but it has also fostered development of small entrepreneurs who are service providers in terms of food delivery, supply of chemical nutrients, maintenance of facilities, etc. Among the most lasting social impacts is the availability of fresh products throughout the year within a range of 75 km form any of their facilities [11].

3.2 Plenty farms

The company was set up in 2015 in Seattle, Washington with investment from Jeff Bezos of Amazon [30]. Plenty is one of the few companies in this business that has received a USDA certification as an organic food supplier. The company sells large quantity of its products to retail chains such as Whole Foods and Good Food. In fact, the company claims to be providing 6% of all the fresh products in the greater Seattle area [31] . The technology adopted by the company uses hybridized technology combining aeroponics and aquaponics. The project is housed on a space of 100,000 square-feet. Therefore, the company produces fresh organic products and also fish. The company uses sophisticated technology to produce large quantities of multiple varieties of fresh vegetables and fruits in the same site. The farm grows algae, which serve as feedstock for the fish, while the waste produced by the fish serves as organic fertilizer for the plants [31].

The company has recently raised additional capital for expansion from new investors such as Google's Eric Schmidt. The farm has proven to be instrumental in ensuring regular supply of fresh products and sweet water fish to supermarkets especially during the Covid-19 pandemic that hit Seattle area quite hard. Had the city relied on supplies from conventional sources such as farms in California, there would have been massive food shortages [31].

3.3 Aero-farms

This company was established in 2004 in the New Jersey area through joint collaboration between IKEA, David Chang, SoftBank and the Ruler of Dubai [32]. The $100 Million project is the largest aeroponic farms in the world that uses state-of-the-art agricultural technologies such as AI, aerial drones, IoT and climate control technology [33]. The farm has reported yields that are 390% higher than conventional open cultivation fields. The farm has also enabled agricultural researchers to team up with engineers and scientists to experiment with some of the most sophisticated technologies in the world. The technology is now being replicated in arid regions of the world such as UAE, Qatar and Saudi Arabia in collaboration with MIT and King Abdullah University of Science and Technology by using seawater (instead of fresh water), which is abundantly available in those regions [34].

4. Challenges for entrepreneurs without access to substantial capital

The vertical farm projects described in the previous section are all fairly large-sized investments that make them highly capital intensive. Despite the fact the output of such projects has readily available markets there are numerous challenges for entrepreneurs to get into this business without having substantially deep pockets. Some of these challenges are:

4.1 High initial capital requirements

Even when space is available on lease, the initial investments in preparing the space to make it suitable for installing equipment along with arrangements for water and electricity involves substantial capital. Furthermore, the equipment used in building a controlled environment requires large investments in systems that are made by a limited number of vendors. The other initial investments are in deposits required for leasing space, deposits for obtaining commercial utility connections, permits, etc.

4.2 Reluctance of banks to fund vertical farming projects

Most commercial banks and financial institutions are typically reluctant to provide capital to small entrepreneurs entering into a new field. Banks usually look at the worst-case scenario in assessing loan applications for such projects. For example, if the business fails to meet its goals, then for the bank to recuperate their investments it would be difficult to liquidate the assets of the company.

4.3 Lack of training facilities for entrepreneurs

The operation of high-tech vertical farms requires knowledge and experience with insights into the critical aspects of managing such a business. For new entrepreneurs without exposure to such businesses it will be difficult to develop and sustain such as venture. Without availability of training facilities to prepare them it may turn out to be a risky venture for new entrepreneurs without substantially deep pockets.

4.4 High operational expenses due to cost of energy

These projects consume substantial amount of electricity due to lighting and temperature control. Current developments in renewable energy technologies are trying to bring down operational costs of such projects through recycling biomass gas produced by the plants. Nevertheless, the operating costs related to energy, water supply, equipment maintenance and chemical composition of the plant-bed (fluid base) require sufficient working capital.

4.5 Creating opportunities for entrepreneurs: less capital

Emerging smart technologies are creating opportunities for entrepreneurs who desire to venture into vertical farming with lower levels of investments. Such technologies are enabling indoor farming projects to be set up in relatively small spaces using energy efficient processes that recycle and reuse the resources deployed in the system. For instance, the new generation of LED lights is replicating the same intensity of light with significantly lower energy requirements [13]. Similarly cloud computing, SAAS (Software as a Subscription Service) and Internet of Things are enabling automation without investing heavily into computer systems [24].

Increasing demand for fresh products in urban centers and advances in innovation related to farming technology alone may not be sufficient to create viable opportunities for new individuals with limited capital who wish to commit to entrepreneurship in high-tech indoor farming. The above developments must parallelly be followed up with support from policymakers and urban planners. For instance, government-initiated programs should be channelized to such entrepreneurs through training and start-up funding. The training programs can be implemented through business incubation initiatives managed by agencies of the government, universities and other technical instructions. Training need assessment will reveal the type of technical and management training that needs to be imparted including internship programs with established vertical farming companies.

In addition to capacity building through training, such entrepreneurial ventures should be supported with seed funding for startups followed up by financial assistance for growth. Financing for such projects will initially require subsidized soft-term lending initiatives by the government implemented through financial institutions. Once the projects gather traction and start generating revenues, they will be able to attract venture capital for further growth.

5. Conclusion

Overpopulation of urban centers around the globe calls for long-term strategies for policymakers and urban planners. In absence of measures to bolster food production close to the consumption-base there are likely to be food-shortages caused by the fallout of overcrowded cities and occasional environmental shocks due to climate change, infectious diseases, and other natural calamities. Simply relying on traditional cultivation and transporting agricultural products from distant farms to urban centers may turn out to be a recipe for disaster. The United Nations' forecast of over 9 billion people concentrated in large cities by 2050 is a matter of concern that needs proactive solutions based on innovative methods of food production and supply.

The long-term prognosis for resilience of food supply chains that depend on traditional farm cultivation also faces threats from reduction in soil fertility caused by excessive use of synthetic fertilizers. After several cycles of cultivation, the land requires time to recover as it loses its ability to support growth of plants. In this way the available land for cultivation is also getting smaller. In many countries, rain forests are being cut down to make space for crop cultivation. This practice will have an adverse impact on the environment thus further exacerbating the negative fallouts of climate change. Traditional open-field cultivation is also exposed to attacks by insects, pests and weeds where the crop needs to be protected from such attacks with the use of pesticides, herbicides and other chemicals. The toxic elements in such chemicals can seep into the underground water system with consequences for human health.

The concept of utilizing vertical space to cultivate cash crops in controlled environments, offer a viable alternative to challenges that lay ahead for traditional farming. Emerging technologies that were originally developed to support manufacturing industries (e.g., to drive Industry 4.0) are now being leveraged to drive innovations in vertical indoor farming. Such agricultural projects not only increase the yield of crops per acre, but also grow the products in close proximity to the centers of consumption, thus reducing the cost of fresh food. Furthermore, these crops are produced in environments where they are free from pests and weeds, which means they are free of harmful pesticides, making the products healthy for human consumption.

Majority of the vertical in-door farming projects around the world, were initially driven by large investors with access to substantial capital. Entrepreneurs without access to such capital find it difficult to venture into vertical farming. However, with the advent of new technological breakthroughs, it is now becoming feasible for entrepreneurs to set up such projects in smaller spaces with significantly less start-up capital. Nevertheless, several obstacles still remain that need to be addressed by public policymakers and city planners. These obstacles are mainly related to access to finance and lack of opportunities for technology transfer.

Besides the entrepreneurs being familiar with the technology and the intricacies of the business, there also needs to be availability of a large pool of human resource that are capable of working in such high-tech vertical farming projects. Therefore, programs led by public-private partnerships, government backed-support, etc. are needed to get the momentum going. The efforts from urban planners and think tanks connected to food supply resilience, need to focus on training and development of potential entrepreneurs and technical staff that can manage high-tech vertical farming, and also providing seed- and growth-funding for such entrepreneurial ventures. The future of urban jungles becoming manageable from the perspective of reliable and resilient food supply chains may depend on how entrepreneurial initiatives in vertical high-tech farming are being planned and developed by policymakers and urban planners.

Author details

Suaad Jassem[1] and Mohammad Rezaur Razzak[2]*

1 Al-Zahra College for Women, Muscat, Oman

2 Sultan Qaboos University, Muscat, Oman

*Address all correspondence to: rezaur25@gmail.comm

References

[1] United Nations. Everyone Included: Social Impact of Covid-19. United Nations Department of Economic and Social Affairs [Internet]. 2020. Available from: https://www.un.org/development/desa/dspd/everyone-included-covid-19.html

[2] UNFPA Annual Report. Global Highlights: United Nations Population Fund [Internet]. 2019. Available from: https://www.unfpa.org/annual-report-2019

[3] Szabo S. Urbanisation and food insecurity risks: Assessing the role of human development. Oxford Development Studies. 2016;**44**(1):28-48. DOI: 10.1080/13600818.2015.1067292

[4] Egidi G, Salvati L, Vinci S. The long way to Tipperary: City size and worldwide urban population trends, 1950-2030. Sustainable Cities and Society. 2020;**60**:102148. DOI: 10.1016/j.scs.2020.102148

[5] Kuang B, Lu X, Han J, Fan X, Zuo J. How urbanization influence urban land consumption intensity: Evidence from China. Habitat International. 2020;**100**:102103. DOI: 10.1016/j.habitatint.2019.102103

[6] Martin P. COVID-19 and California farm labor. California Agriculture. 2020;**74**(2):67-68. DOI: 10.3733/ca.2020a0017

[7] Ruan S. Likelihood of survival of coronavirus disease 2019. The Lancet: Infectious Diseases. 2020;**20**(6):630-631. DOI: 10.1016/S1473-3099(20)30257-7

[8] Guillen P, Komac U. Cities are more important than ever. In: City Form, Economics and Culture. Springer Briefs in Architectural Design and Technology. Singapore: Springer; 2020. DOI: 10.1007/978-981-15-5741-5_3

[9] Pashchapur A, Bhat C. Urban Agriculture: The Saviour of Rapid Urbanization. KRISHI [Internet]. 2020. Available from: https://krishi.icar.gov.in/jspui/handle/123456789/34552

[10] Kwil I, Piwowar-Sulej K, Krzywonos M. Local entrepreneurship in the context of food production: A review. Sustainability. 2020 Jan;**12**(1):424. DOI: 10.3390/su12010424

[11] Al-Kodmany K. The vertical farm: Exploring applications for peri-urban areas. In: Smart Village Technology. Cham: Springer; 2020. pp. 203-232. DOI: 10.3390/buildings8020024

[12] De Clerq M, Vats A, Biel A. Agriculture 4.0: The Future of Farming Technology. Report at World Government Summit [Internet]. 2018. Available from: https://www.oliverwyman.com/ourexpertise/insights/2018/feb/agriculture-4-0--the-future-of-farming-technology.html

[13] Kalantari F, Mohd Tahir O, Mahmoudi Lahijani A, Kalantari S. A review of vertical farming technology: A guide for implementation of building integrated agriculture in cities. In: Advanced Engineering Forum. Vol. 24. Switzerland: Trans Tech Publications Ltd; 2017. pp. 76-91. DOI: 10.4028/www.scientific.net/AEF.24.76

[14] Spencer G. Indoor Vertical Farming in Asia and Beyond: Digging DEEP in Data. Microsoft Asia Stories [Internet]. 2018. Available from: https://news.microsoft.com/apac/features/indoor-vertical-farming-digging-deep-data/

[15] Muller A, Ferré M, Engel S, Gattinger A, Holzkämper A, Huber R, et al. Can soil-less crop production be a sustainable option for soil conservation and future agriculture? Land Use Policy. 2017;**69**:102-105. DOI: 10.1016/j.landusepol.2017.09.014

[16] Astee LY, Kishnani NT. Building integrated agriculture: Utilising rooftops for sustainable food crop cultivation in Singapore. Journal of Green Building. 2010;**5**(2):105-113. DOI: 10.3992/jgb.5.2.105

[17] Munoz H, Joseph J. Hydroponics: Home-Based Vegetable Production System. Inter-American Institute for Cooperation on Agriculture (IICA) [Internet]. 2017. Available from: http://legacy.iica.int/Eng/regiones/caribe/guyana/IICA%20Office%20Documents/Hydroponics%20Manual/Hydroponics%20Manual.pdf

[18] Pullano G. Indoor Vertical Grower Touts concept's Benefits. VGN, Vegetable Grower News [Internet]. 2017. Available from: http://vegetablegrowersnews.com/index.php/magazine/article/indoor-vertical-grower-touts-concepts-benefits

[19] Evett SR, Colaizzi PD, Lamm FR, O'Shaughnessy SA, Heeren DM, Trotut TJ, et al. Past, Present and Future of Irrigation on the U.S. Great Plains. American Society of Agricultural and Biological Engineers [Internet]. 2020. Available from: https://elibrary.asabe.org/abstract.asp?aid=51079&t=2&redir=&redirType=

[20] Birkby J. Vertical Farming. ATTRA Sustainable Agriculture. National Centre for Appropriate Technology (NCAT) [Internet]. 2016. Available from: https://www.scribd.com/document/342934556/Vertical-Farming

[21] Ackermann O, Zhevelev HM, Svoray T. Agricultural systems and terrace pattern distribution and preservation along climatic gradient: From sub-humid Mediterranean to arid conditions. Quaternary International. 2019;**502**:319-326. DOI: 10.1016/j.quaint.2018.09.032

[22] Cıceklı M, Barlas NT. Transformation of today greenhouses into high technology vertical farming systems for metropolitan regions. Journal of Environmental Protection and Ecology. 2014;**15**(4):1779-1785. Available from: https://docs.google.com/a/jepe-journal.info/viewer?a=v&pid=sites&srcid=amVwZS1qb3VybmFsLmluZm98amVwZS1qb3VybmFsfGd4OjQ1MzQ3ZTRhYzI2YTRlNjk

[23] Al-Chalabi M. Vertical farming: Skyscraper sustainability? Sustainable Cities and Society. 2015;**18**:74-77. DOI: 10.1016/j.scs.2015.06.003

[24] Benke K, Tomkins B. Future food-production systems: Vertical farming and controlled-environment agriculture. Sustainability: Science, Practice and Policy. 2017;**13**(1):13-26. DOI: 10.1080/15487733.2017.1394054

[25] Thomaier S, Specht K, Henckel D, Dierich A, Siebert R, Freisinger UB, et al. Farming in and on urban buildings: Present practice and specific novelties of zero-acreage farming (ZFarming). Renewable Agriculture and Food Systems. 2015;**30**(1):43-54. DOI: 10.1017/S1742170514000143

[26] Smiechowski J. Vertical Farming Venture Achieves Sustainability and Success in New Buffalo, Michigan, Seedstock [Internet]. 2017. Available from: http://seedstock.com/2013/06/10/vertical-farming-venture-achieves-sustainability-and-success-in-new-buffalo-michigan/

[27] Trotter G. Farmed Here, Indoor Farm in Bedford Park, Turning off the Lights for Good, Chicago Tribune [Internet]. 2017. Available from: http://www.chicagotribune.com/business/ct-farmedhere-closing-0117-biz-20170116-story.html

[28] Nobre CA, Sampaio G, Borma LS, Castilla-Rubio JC, Silva JS, Cardoso M. Land-use and climate change risks in the Amazon and the need of a novel

sustainable development paradigm. Proceedings of the National Academy of Sciences. 2016;**113**(39):10759-10768. DOI: 10.1073/pnas.1605516113

[29] Touliatos D, Dodd IC, McAinsh M. Vertical farming increases lettuce yield per unit area compared to conventional horizontal hydroponics. Food and Energy Security. 2016;**5**(3):184-191. DOI: 10.1002/fes3.83

[30] Peter A. Robots Are Already Farming Crops Inside This Silicon Valley Warehouse. Fast Company World Changing Ides [Internet]. 2019. Available from: https://www.fastcompany.com/90365627/robots-are-already-farming-crops-inside-this-silicon-valley-warehouse

[31] Tan G, Roof K. SoftBank-Backed Farming Startup Plenty Is in Talks to Raise Cash. Bloomberg News [Internet]. 2020. Available from: https://www.bloomberg.com/news/articles/2020-03-29/softbank-backed-farming-startup-plenty-is-in-talks-to-raise-cash

[32] Clark B, Schneider L. Vertical Farming Company AeroFarms is Making Vegetables Tastier and FEEDING Communities in Need. ABC News [Internet]. 2019. Available from: https://abcnews.go.com/Business/vertical-farming-company-aerofarms-making-vegetables-tastier-feeding/story?id=67147957

[33] Fortado L, Trazono E. AeroFarms Raises $100m as Investors Rush to Indoor Farms. Financial Times [Internet]. 2019. Available from: https://www.ft.com/content/cac48190-9d8a-11e9-9c06-a4640c9feebb

[34] Newton L. The farm in the sky. In: Urban Agriculture and Community Values. Cham: Springer; 2020. pp. 105-118. DOI: 10.1007/978-3-030-39244-4_7